Failure and Hope

In 2015, 60 million people were displaced by violent conflict – the highest since World War II. National and international policy prevents the displaced from working or moving freely outside the camps set up to "temporarily" house them. This policy has left the displaced with no right to work and move while they remain displaced for years, if not decades. Based on data on all 61 protracted displacement crises worldwide, fieldwork in seven conflict zones around the world, in-depth interviews with more than 170 humanitarian aid workers, government officials and refugees, this book systematically details the barriers to effective advocacy at every level of governance and shows that failure is the norm. Unlike many academic monographs, it goes further and proposes an alternative way forward that capitalizes on advances on social entrepreneurship, crowd-funding and micro-finance to improve the lives of those that have been forced to flee their homes to find safety.

Christine Mahoney is an Associate Professor of Public Policy and Politics at the Frank Batten School of Leadership and Public Policy and Director of Social Entrepreneurship at the University of Virginia. She studies social justice advocacy and social innovation. Her book *Brussels vs. the Beltway: Advocacy in the United States and the European Union* was the first large-scale comparative study of lobbying in the United States and the EU.

Failure and Hope

Fighting for the Rights of the Forcibly Displaced

CHRISTINE MAHONEY
University of Virginia

CAMBRIDGE
UNIVERSITY PRESS

University Printing House, Cambridge CB2 8BS, United Kingdom

One Liberty Plaza, 20th Floor, New York, NY 10006, USA

477 Williamstown Road, Port Melbourne, VIC 3207, Australia

4843/24, 2nd Floor, Ansari Road, Daryaganj, Delhi - 110002, India

79 Anson Road, #06-04/06, Singapore 079906

Cambridge University Press is part of the University of Cambridge.

It furthers the University's mission by disseminating knowledge in the pursuit of education, learning and research at the highest international levels of excellence.

www.cambridge.org
Information on this title: www.cambridge.org/9781316614983

© Christine Mahoney 2016

This publication is in copyright. Subject to statutory exception and to the provisions of relevant collective licensing agreements, no reproduction of any part may take place without the written permission of Cambridge University Press.

First published 2016
First paperback edition 2017

A catalogue record for this publication is available from the British Library

Library of Congress Cataloging in Publication data
Names: Mahoney, Christine, author.
Title: Failure & hope : fighting for the rights of the forcibly displaced / Christine Mahoney, University of Virginia.
Other titles: Failure and hope
Description: Cambridge, United Kingdom: Cambridge University Press, 2016. | Includes bibliographical references and index.
Identifiers: LCCN 2016018481| ISBN 9781107162815 (hardback) | ISBN 9781316614983 (pbk.)
Subjects: LCSH: Refugees–Government policy. | Refugees–Civil rights. | Refugees–International cooperation. | Forced migration–Government policy. | Emigration and immigration–Government policy.
Classification: LCC HV640.M326 2016 | DDC 323.3–dc23
LC record available at https://lccn.loc.gov/2016018481

ISBN 978-1-107-16281-5 Hardback
ISBN 978-1-316-61498-3 Paperback

Cambridge University Press has no responsibility for the persistence or accuracy of URLs for external or third-party internet websites referred to in this publication, and does not guarantee that any content on such websites is, or will remain, accurate or appropriate.

Contents

List of figures		*page* vi
List of tables		vii
Acknowledgments		ix
1	Failure is the norm	1
2	Global attention to displacement crises	21
3	Explaining global attention: Geopolitics vs. advocacy	38
4	Frontline advocacy: Lobbying for refugee rights at the national level	66
5	Frontline advocacy: Lobbying for IDP rights at the national level	81
6	Frontline mobilization: Advocating for rights in displacement camps	101
7	An innovative global campaign for action	124
8	Conclusion	136
References		141
Index		149

Figures

2.1	EU and US role in displacement aid – NGOs	page 22
2.2	EU and US role in displacement aid – contributions to UNHCR	22
2.3	Displacement cases that received coverage by more than one news story in 2010	30
2.4	Displacement crises with at least five news stories in the Global North	31
2.5	US coverage – *Washington Post* vs. *New York Times*	32
2.6	EU coverage – the *Guardian*, *Le Monde* and *Suddeutsche Zeitung*	33
2.7	Comparison of share of the global agenda attention to the proportion of the global displaced population	33
2.8	Global attention by region vs. scope of displacement by region	35
3.1	Overall attention to displacement issues in the *New York Times* (2001–2010)	39
3.2	Attention to displacement in Iraq and Afghanistan (2001–2010)	41
3.3	Attention to displaced Palestinians	41
3.4	Attention to displacement in Sudan (Darfur) (2001–2010)	43
3.5	Attention to displacement from Tibet (2001–2010)	44
3.6	Attention to displacement from Bosnia and Croatia (2001–2010)	47
3.7	Attention to displacement from Somalia (2001–2010)	49
3.8	Attention to displacement from Bhutan (2001–2010)	51
3.9	Attention to displacement from Burma/Myanmar (2001–2010)	54
3.10	Attention to displacement in Uganda (2001–2010)	59
3.11	Attention to displacement in Sri Lanka (2001–2010)	60
3.12	Attention to displacement in Colombia (2001–2010)	64
7.1	Proposed structure of fund flows depending on context	131

Tables

1.1	Sixty-five global displacement crises with more than 10,000 displaced (as of 2015)	*page* 6
1.2	Major refugee situations with UNHCR-aided camps more than 2,500 (as of 2008, during case selection)	14
1.3	Major IDP situations where the UNHCR is assisting (as of 2008 during case selection)	15
2.1	Major displacement situations (more than 10,000 displaced) year-end 2009 and whether there was any media coverage in any of the analyzed US or EU papers in 2010	28
3.1	Displacement cases with more than 20 news stories over the decade	40
6.1	Level of collective action among the displaced	110

Acknowledgments

I would like to first thank all the staff of the international NGOs and the UN agencies that so graciously granted me interviews; taking time from their life-saving work to talk with me about their advocacy on behalf of the displaced was critical to my understanding of the activities they engage in and the obstacles they face. Seeing what these aid workers deal with on a daily basis, in effort to relieve suffering and find solutions, was awe-inspiring. The endless hours I spent on planes, buses, rickshaws, tuk tuks, boda bodas and bicycles to conduct interviews was well worth the effort, it gave me insight into their struggles on the frontlines that would not have been possible from afar.

This project would also not have been possible without out the financial support of the Moynihan Institute of Global Affairs at Syracuse University, the Maxwell Dean's office at Syracuse University, and the Batten School of Leadership and Public Policy at the University of Virginia. Thank you for helpful recommendations on early drafts of the manuscript by participants at meetings of the European Consortium for Political Research, to colleagues Beth Leech, Herman Mark Schwartz and Craig Volden, and to the anonymous reviewers.

Thank you to a number of students at Syracuse University, whose interest in the project kept me moving forward, including: Mark Hibben and Angélica Suárez for research assistance, to Felipe Estefan for translation in Colombia, to Anirban Archana for fieldwork in Sri Lanka, and Beau Miller and Emily Rose for fieldwork in Nepal. Thank you also to Caitlin Carr, Sean Callahan and Genevieve Heckel at the University of Virginia for their meticulous research assistance collecting data on attention to these issues by the international community. Thank you to Anna Sofia Yurtaslan and Emily Laser for help with the content analysis of the new stories.

Thank you also to all the Karen, Karenni and Bhutanese children that I tutored in Syracuse, New York – they were a weekly reminder of the millions of displaced citizens around the world that still have not found durable solutions and a constant motivator that we can and must speak out on their behalf.

Finally to my family, especially Ann Mahoney, Karen Mahoney and Karen Homer for being supportive when I continued to do fieldwork in places that were not the safest. To truly hear the voices of the vulnerable living on the frontlines, it is sometimes necessary to go to dangerous places.

1

Failure is the norm

A failed international policy

Throughout 2014 and 2015, the headlines continued to report the expanding reach of the Islamic State of Iraq and Syria (ISIS) across Syria, Iraq, Lebanon and into Turkey. Fighting between the extremist terrorist group, state forces and other rebel groups have left citizens fleeing in every direction: more than a million Iraqi internally displaced persons (IDPs), more than three million Syrian refugees in Turkey, Lebanon, Jordan and Europe, and more than 7.5 million Syrians internally displaced inside Syria.

By 2015, the conflict in Syria had been ongoing for four years, since the 2011 Arab Spring sparked democracy protests against the regime of President Bashar al-Assad. A violent crackdown on demonstrators and arrests and torture of activists, spurred larger and larger protests across the country. The Syrian people were calling for democracy, government reforms and an end to al-Assad's regime. As demonstrations grew, government crackdowns intensified, leading to an armed rebellion and civil war. Barrel bombing and indiscriminate attacks on civilians, as well as fighting by a number of rebel groups, led to massive displacement. The conflict dragged on, destruction inside Syria continued, and more and more territory came in under the control of a range of rebel groups including ISIS – peace and return home appeared further and further out of reach. Hundreds of thousands of the more than three million refugees have rationally responded by migrating to the gateways of Europe with the hopes of resettlement and starting a new life. Conditions inside Syria and in the refugee camps had become so dire that many risked working through human smugglers to attempt a dangerous crossing of the Mediterranean Sea on rafts and lifeboats.

With more than 715,000 asylum-seeking applications to the European Union in 2015, bodies of refugee families and children washing up on the shores of Greece, and easy access for journalists to tell the story of their ordeal – Western media outlets began paying attention to the issue of forced displacement for the first time in decades (BBC 2015, *Guardian* 2015). The links between the terrorists that carried out the Paris attacks in November 2015 and ISIS led to even greater coverage and scrutiny of the massive migration of refugees into Europe (*The Atlantic* 2015). While the Syrian displacement case is unique – it is currently the largest in the world with 11 million people displaced and it is receiving regular news coverage – it is not the only displacement crisis, there are 65 other major displacement crises. In fact, 2015 marked a new record: 60 million people displaced by violent conflict globally – the highest since World War II.

The current refugee regime fails them all. *The UN Convention on the Status of Refugees*, written to aid the refugees from World War II, only mandates the office of the United Nations High Commissioner for Refugees (UNHCR) to help those who have crossed international borders, not IDPs trapped inside their own borders. Refugees and IDPs have suffered the same types of violence, require the same types of aid and are currently being denied the same rights by the international response to displacement crises.

Host governments almost always prohibit the displaced from working or moving freely outside the camps set up to "temporarily" house them. The fundamental problem with this policy is that the displaced often remain displaced for years, or decades, trapped in limbo with no right to work and no right to move – a situation the US Committee for Refugees and Immigrants refers to as "warehousing." Whether Somali refugees in Kenya or Tamil IDPs in Sri Lanka, the displaced are interned in camps, unable to provide for themselves or their families.

This policy of warehousing leads to countless bad outcomes from aid dependence, to drug addiction, to sexual exploitation and militia recruitment, further fueling violence, devastating lives and leading to conflicts between the host communities and the displaced. There is a pattern to their suffering. In country after country, the displaced endure similar conditions and face similar barriers to escaping their destructive situation. The question is: Why does this failed warehousing policy endure and why has advocacy to end this situation failed so miserably?

Based on data on all 61 protracted displacement crises worldwide, fieldwork in seven conflict zones in Africa, Asia, Eastern Europe and Latin America, in-depth interviews with more than 70 humanitarian aid workers and government officials and interviews with nearly 100 refugees, the book systematically details the barriers to effective advocacy at every level of governance and shows that failure is the norm. Unlike many academic monographs, it goes further and proposes an alternative way forward that capitalizes on advances in social entrepreneurship, crowd-funding and micro-finance to improve the lives of those that have been forced to flee their homes to find safety.

Focus on the problems, not the action

Advocacy is inherently infused with agency. Activists act. They mobilize supporters and engender change – in policy, government and society. Scholarship on advocacy has tended to study the advocates, what they do and how that impacts outcomes. The literature has argued policy entrepreneurs are critical to getting attention for a cause – an issue without an advocate is not an issue (Baumgartner and Jones 1993, Kingdon 1995, Jones and Baumgartner 2005). We see evidence of the power of transnational advocacy in a number of case studies that explore advocacy across borders with books and articles being written about the anti-apartheid movement (Klotz 1995), anti-slavery movement (Hochschild 2005), anti-nuclear movement (Kitschelt 1986), the fight against gender-based violence (Joachim 2007), the Kimberley Process to end the trade in "blood diamonds" (Bieri 2010), climate change negotiations, and numerous environmental and human rights movements (Kriesi 1996, Keck and Sikkink 1998, Tarrow 2006). In each of these cases, advocacy movements have successfully placed issues on the agenda of the global power players (primarily the nations of the Global North and the international institutions they have created) and successfully changed public policies. This research is important, it shows us that transnational advocacy on global issues can succeed and inspires us to continue to work across borders to change policies and improve conditions for the world's citizens.

Much of the research on global advocacy focuses on campaigns and due to the case-study dominant approach to studying global advocacy, researchers often choose a single or a few successful campaigns. The tendency to focus on successful cases, however, has led us to believe that success is the norm. We have missed the fact that failure is the norm when it comes to advocacy, and this goes not only for scholars but also for practitioners, policymakers, advocates, constituents and funders.

This is particularly evident in the growing debate about non-governmental organization (NGO) accountability over the past decade. As the philanthropic community demanded more and more in the way of accountability, deliverables and "quantifiables" from service provisions organizations, those same demands were quickly made of advocacy organizations as well. If the Red Cross needs to show the effectiveness of its programs, so too does Human Rights Watch. With the rise of Charity Navigator, Guidestar and other NGO-rating schemes, advocacy organizations have been expected to show levels of success that are improbable.

The tendency to study campaigns, and successful ones at that, can lead us to overestimate the power of advocacy; and underestimate the significant hurdles facing advocates. It is equally important to have an empirically accurate picture of what global advocacy entails, and what global advocates are up against so that they can best prepare for the fight and have the tools they need to succeed.

I take a different approach – instead of selecting on the dependent variable (successful global advocacy campaigns) I select instead a sample of "policy problems" (major displacement crises) for in-depth fieldwork, and study all 61 major protracted displacement cases at the global level. I study a fixed set of problems and ask: "Did transnational advocacy occur? How was it carried out? And to what effect?" Shifting to this research approach reveals a much more complete picture of reality than if we select only the exceptional cases. We begin to understand why the problem of massive forced displacement, like many other wicked problems of global inequality, continues. The powerless are powerless in the arenas of global politics. They and their potential advocates lack the resources and political and economic leverage to change the status quo. Until we begin to tip the scale on these fundamental resource imbalances, nothing will change.

While global advocacy initiatives are interesting and inspiring, it is important to begin with problems rather than campaigns. First, when we begin with problems and ask if there was advocacy or not, it provides us a lens to more clearly view the role of advocates in getting an issue on the agenda. This is one of the most important stages of the advocacy process. Advocates and scholars have a difficult time evaluating whether their advocacy was successful in shaping policy once the issue is on the agenda, but the role of advocates in getting an issue on the agenda has been even more difficult. With a universe of policy problems that seems infinite, how do we determine what got on the agenda and what did not? How do we study issues that aren't there? These questions have proven difficult for scholars to answer, and resulted in researchers focusing only on those cases that make it to the agenda and not explaining the issues that stay off the agenda.

Second, since getting an issue on the global agenda is so difficult, advocacy on behalf of the world's marginalized and oppressed often has to be carried out at lower levels of governance, with national and local level officials. However, much of the research on global advocacy remains confined to the capitals of the "Global North." Few studies systematically research advocacy on the same topic at local, national and global levels. When we do collect data at all of these levels, it becomes even more evident that failure is the norm.

I study the global advocacy (or lack thereof) around the 61 protracted displacement crises that were ongoing in 2011, with a focus on seven of the world's worst displacement crises – accounting for millions of people forced to live in camps and slums for years on end – in Africa, Asia, Europe and South America. Studying global advocacy around displacement situations provides unique analytical leverage when it comes to advocacy at the global level. Since the "problems" – major displacement crises – are somewhat static at any given point in time, it provides a fixed universe of issues to which the international community may pay more or less attention. From a research standpoint, this allows us to parse out the factors that play a role on getting issues on the global public agenda.

Studying advocacy on-the-ground in seven of the largest displacement crises provides another point of leverage. Researching the advocacy being carried out by the displaced and on behalf of the displaced in multiple countries allows us to understand under what conditions displaced community-based organizations (CBOs), NGOs, and international organizations (IOs) like the UN and its agencies (such as UNHCR, UNICEF – United Nations Children Fund and WFP – the World Food Program) can have an impact on improved access to rights for the displaced. This research aimed to identify *who* is advocating for the displaced at each level of governance, *how* they are going about it (the types of tactics and arguments they are using, the types of coordinating, networking and coalition building they are engaging in), and to *what* effect.

This chapter first introduces the problem of displacement as a major transnational issue of our time as well as the primary international actors involved in advocating on behalf of the displaced. Second, I review the research on global advocacy and argue that to truly understand the global fight for social justice (and ultimately make it more effective), we need to study advocacy on cases that are not successful as well as those that are, and we need to study what is happening "on the ground" as well as in the halls of global governance in Washington, Brussels and Geneva. Finally, I present the data collection process, which is a significantly different approach to previous research.

It is important to note what this book is not: it is not a comprehensive history of the conflicts that led to these displacements, it is not a handbook on the humanitarian situation in each case, it is not an international law book about human rights and it is not a book about geopolitics. It is a book that seeks to more completely understand the failure, and rare successes, of transnational advocacy generally, through the specific study of the international policy area of forced displacement.

Displacement is not living

Worldwide, 60 million people have been displaced by violent conflict. The vast majority are trapped in protracted displacement crises; languishing for decades as endless cycles of violence prohibit them from returning home and resuming normal lives (Loescher *et al.* 2007). The perpetuation of refugee and internal displacement camps further fuels the violence as humanitarian aid is misappropriated to perpetrators of violence, armed elements take refuge among the displaced and displaced populations are marginalized (Terry 2002). As of 2015, there were 65 identifiable major protracted displacement crises, defined as more than 10,000 people displaced for more than five years. Table 1.1 reports the most recent data on the total number of displaced citizens "of concern" (refugees, IDPs, asylum seekers and returnees) to the UNHCR.

Confined to camps or urban slums, the displaced are denied the right to work, to move freely, to adequate standards of living, to education, and the

TABLE 1.1. *Sixty-five global displacement crises with more than 10,000 displaced (as of 2015)*

Country of origin	Displaced	Country of origin	Displaced
Togo	11,018	Rwanda	100,081
Kenya	11,535	Western Sahara	117,662
Venezuela	12,831	Iran	118,066
Cambodia	13,334	Côte d'Ivoire	121,858
Honduras	14,307	Ethiopia	149,191
Tibetan	15,085	**Bosnia and Herzegovina**	**165,787**
Nepal	15,280	Sri Lanka	170,993
Gambia	15,772	**Uganda**	**191,987**
Liberia	15,963	China	258,562
Indonesia	16,183	Georgia	277,717
Cameroon	16,292	**Serbia and Kosovo**	**316,611**
Congo, Republic of	18,076	Viet Nam	316,635
Armenia	18,809	Philippines	322,991
Guatemala	23,290	Burundi	335,068
Bhutan	**23,834**	Libya	371,241
Albania	25,370	Eritrea	416,996
Egypt	27,002	Yemen	425,304
India	28,093	Mali	427,336
El Salvador	29,006	Azerbaijan	637,992
Ghana	29,850	**Myanmar (Burma)**	**907,264**
Senegal	31,918	Ukraine	1,076,165
Bangladesh	32,977	Nigeria	1,380,219
Guinea	33,194	Central African Rep.	1,490,913
Mexico	40,020	Pakistan	1,832,858
Mauritania	41,142	**Somalia**	**2,306,072**
Croatia	**56,316**	South Sudan	2,465,460
Zimbabwe	65,097	Sudan	2,909,808
Haiti	73,129	Afghanistan	3,713,242
Turkey	75,462	Dem. Rep. of the Congo	4,039,313
Chad	86,935	Iraq	4,105,397
Angola	89,743	Palestine*	5,000,000
Russian Federation	98,371	**Colombia**	**6,409,190**
		Syrian Arab Rep.	11,606,526

* UNRWA (the United Nations Relief and Works Agency for Palestine Refugees in the Near East) provides assistance, protection and advocacy for some five million registered Palestinian refugees in Jordan, Lebanon, Syria and the occupied Palestinian territory, pending a solution to their plight. The number UNHCR was aiding in 2015 was 104,049, however I don't use this figure as it is not representative of the number of displaced Palestinians. See: www.unrwa.org.

right to political participation – to have a say in their own self-determination. The forcibly displaced are denied nearly every right that is laid out in the 1948 *Universal Declaration of Human Rights*.

Observers and practitioners familiar with the issue of displacement immediately draw distinctions between refugees and IDPs. Rightfully so, whether one has crossed an international border has significant implications in the realm of law and policy. We have written definitions and laws, and structured state behavior in a way that there is a difference if one crosses an invisible line in the sand. However, in terms of pain and suffering, trauma and loss, hardship and duration, there are few differences between the forcibly displaced that have crossed a boundary and those that have not. IDPs have not crossed an international border but they often face similar encampment situations and are unable to work or move freely – because security does not allow it, government forces do not allow it and access to humanitarian aid is predicated on residing in a camp.

What is life like in one of the hundreds of refugee and IDP camps worldwide? Take an 18-year-old in the Dadaab Refugee Camp Complex in Kenya, 100 kilometers from the Somali border, which has been there since the early 1990s. It is arid, hot, and a 10-hour drive over dusty roads before one reaches any sizable town. He has never seen his home country; he was born in the camp; he has lived in the camp and will likely die in the camp – with no hope, no options. He has likely seen siblings die of cholera outbreaks, perhaps had a sister raped at the edges of camp collecting what sparse firewood can be found. He suffers from skin afflictions, worms and a myriad of other ailments. Home is a white, UNHCR-issued tent, blazing hot in the heat, no comforts, no bed, no privacy. Meals are the same mix of corn meal and lentils every day, day-in and day-out for 18 years. Life consists of waking, doing basic chores of standing in line to get water, standing in line to get food rations, and sitting around – waiting, waiting for an end that will likely never come. If he is lucky enough to be one of those that gains access to schooling in the camp, and smart enough to be one of the very few that gets secondary schooling, he will graduate and find he is still not able to move out of the camp, still not able to work. The only result is despair and depression; a generation lost.

The office of the UNHCR has been tasked with protecting the rights and wellbeing of refugees since 1950 but at the time of the signing of the 1951 *UN Convention Related to the Status of Refugees* its mandate was constrained to refugees displaced by fighting in Europe during World War II. With the 1967 Protocol, the office's mandate was extended to all refugees worldwide, that is:

Any person who, owing to a well-founded fear of being persecuted for reasons of race, religion, nationality, membership of a particular social group or political opinion, is outside the country of his nationality and is unable, or owing to such a fear, is unwilling to avail himself of the protection of that country; or who, not having a nationality (*stateless*) and being outside of the country of his former habitual residence as a result of such events, is unable, or owing to such fear, is unwilling to return to it.

The *UN Convention Related to the Status of Refugees* lays out basic minimum standards for the treatment of refugees and makes provisions for providing them with documentation (Hollenbach 2008). States signatory to the convention commit to working with the UNHCR to protect refugees and to never forcibly expel refugees that cross their borders for protection (the principle of *non-refoulement*). However, since the terrorist attacks in the United States on September 11, 2001 and the global war on terror, states have increasingly worked to close their borders leading to ever-higher numbers of IDPs. In addition, while there has been a steady decrease in intra-state warfare, there has been an increase in inter-state conflicts also contributing to the rise in the numbers of IDPs.

The UNHCR does not officially have a mandate to protect IDPs, but has increasingly been doing so over the past 60 years. The UN, along with the NGOs and other agencies that aid the displaced, came together to formulate a Best Practices in IDP response in 2008. The logic of protection is similar to that found in the international norm of "Responsibility to Protect," namely that it is the responsibility of governments to protect their people but when that does not occur, the responsibility falls on the international community:

> The prevention of displacement and the protection of IDPs and other affected populations within their own country are the responsibility of national authorities. Particularly in situations of armed conflict, IDPs may find themselves in territories over which State authority is absent or difficult to enforce. In such situations, the prevention of displacement and the protection of IDPs are also the responsibility of non-State actors. In those situations where States require support or where national protection is not ensured, a critical protection role falls to the international community. It has been difficult to address this "protection gap" not only because of the sensitivity of the subject within the country concerned, but also because of various gaps within the international framework. (UNHCR 2009b)

The UNHCR carries out its mandate to protect and advocate for the displaced with the help of an army of Implementing Partners (IPs) and Operating Partners (OPs). This includes the large international NGOs primarily based in the United States and Europe that specialize in refugee affairs and humanitarian aid such as: the American Refugee Committee (ARC), the Norwegian Refugee Committee (NRC), the Danish Refugee Council (DRC), the International Rescue Committee (IRC), the Jesuit Refugee Service (JRS) and Catholic Relief Services (CRS). Many national and local NGOs also partner with the UNHCR to aid the displaced, including local bar associations to aid with legal representation of the displaced, local health workers and national human rights groups.

Failure is the norm, successes are rare, but they exist

In the chapters that follow, I show that, again and again, advocacy on behalf of the displaced fails at the global, national and local levels. But it is important to define what a "success" would look like, so we know it when we see it. Essentially, a "success" would be a policy change that would allow the young man in the Dadaab refugee camp described above to escape that camp and live a normal life. A second best outcome would be improved access to rights, especially to not be imprisoned or barred from providing for himself as he waits for a solution.

The UNHCR is mandated to not only protect refugees and IDPs but also find resolution to displacement problems; the organization pursues three different "durable solutions":

1. *Repatriation* – returning the displaced home to their homeland.
2. *Resettlement* – settling the displaced in a new, third country often in the Global North.
3. *Local integration* – naturalization and integration into the country of first asylum.

Through each of these solutions, the displaced are reinstated as citizens of a country and granted access to the rights that come with that distinction. While the displaced wait for these solutions, however, they lack access to most rights and lack access to any policymaking processes through which they might advocate for their rights.

These categories were clearly devised for refugees, who have crossed a border into "the country of first asylum." For example, a Somali that flees to Kenya can be *re*-settled in a *third* country, like the United States; he can return home to Somalia and be repatriated once peace comes to that nation; or he can locally integrate in Kenya. Realistically, however, two of these durable solutions are out of the question for most of the world's refugees (repatriation and resettlement) and the third (local integration) is a long shot as well.

Somalia is a failed state, it has been in constant war for more than two decades and the violence there is indescribable. For repatriation to be possible there often needs to be some type of humanitarian or military intervention to bring about peace or begin a peace-building process, a burden which normally falls on coalitions of the US and European countries. Many in Washington remember *Black Hawk Down* – the book and film by the same name depicting the failed 1993 UN peacekeeping military intervention in Mogadishu. The West has little appetite for intervention after such a traumatic failure in Somalia as well as failures in Iraq and Afghanistan. In short, *Repatriation* is not going to be an option any time soon.

The United States has a relatively generous resettlement policy compared to the rest of the world, receiving between 20,000 and 90,000 refugees per year. These refugees naturalize and become citizens of the United States. The EU takes a much smaller number but plans to take more in the future. Canada and Australia are other major recipient countries. It would take nine years of the US government taking only Somali refugees every year to achieve a durable solution for the Somali refugees in Kenya. And, that solution would still not address the 300,000 Somali refugees in Ethiopia, the one million Somalis displaced inside Somalia, or the tens of millions of other displaced citizens around the world. And those numbers keep growing, as the refugees have children, and as more refugees continue to flow over borders, as they do from Somali, Burma, Sudan and Syria, among countless other countries. *Resettlement* will not be an option for most refugees, and it is never an option for IDPs.

That leaves *Local Integration*, and the odds are not in their favor here either. Most of the countries that host the displaced are extremely poor, they do not have the capacity to provide infrastructure and services for their own citizens, let alone manage the burden of hundreds of thousands of newly arriving refugees. In addition, unemployment is often high and they can't afford additional competition in the labor market squeezing out their own citizens. Finally, if they are democracies, however weak, there would be vociferous protest against integration by their own citizens. Tensions between refugee and host communities are already often quite high.

While there are many structural barriers to each of these durable solutions, we do see instances of them occurring. Durable solutions often take decades to materialize, however. It took 16 years for the international community to realize Bhutan would never take back the citizens it expelled from its southern regions. In year 5 of the crisis, the international community had hope, in year 9 they were getting pessimistic, in year 14 they were more and more convinced that government of Bhutan was not going to give in, and in year 16 they began talks to negotiate a resettlement operation. Burundian refugees had to wait in camps from 1976 until 2004, before the Tanzanian government agreed to finally allow them to locally integrate. Tamil IDPs and Ugandan IDPs had to wait two decades for each of their respective civil wars to burn themselves out before the displaced could begin to trickle home to their places of habitual residence. There are still hundreds of thousands in IDP camps or "transit centers" – which have the horrible conditions of the camps, but are geographically closer to their original homes, and they have the added advantage of making the IDP numbers look like they are decreasing, a public relations win for governments with internal displacement problems.

Realizing that durable solutions occur, but are rare, and often take over a decade to materialize, leaves us with a need to define a lower level of "success" – that is improved access to rights while the displacement persists. Considering the long duration of displacement, I argue that it is useful to consider the distinction between short-term and long-term rights. *Short-term rights* include access to those rights that would improve the quality of life of refugees and IDPs during the long displacement. This primarily means the right to work and move freely during the displacement. By *long-term rights*, I mean the right to live with dignity, as a full citizen, in a safe environment – that is access to one of the three durable solutions outlined above.

The interventions required to bring about durable solutions – brokering talks to bring about peace at home; putting pressure on host governments to allow refugees to naturalize and become citizens and finally the decision to allow thousands of refugees to resettle, often in the United States or Europe – all require decisions and actions by the governments of the Global North, actions they have largely failed to take for 60 years. It is possible to imagine global advocacy campaigns pushing for each of these durable solutions, but in Chapters 2–6 I document the numerous barriers standing in the way.

Global or transnational advocacy

There is guarded optimism among academics and observers that the emergence of a global civil society could usher in new civility in global affairs. In this new world order, Transnational Actors (or TNAs) are significant players, challenging the traditional power of the nation state and influencing national and supranational structures (Risse 2001). Some argue that transnational civil society organizations could fill the democratic deficit that has been created by the re-regulation of activity at regional and international levels (Scholte 2002).

There are a number of relatively recent studies highlighting the success of global activist campaigns in advancing human rights, environmental protection and other aspects of the social justice movement. As mentioned, Keck and Sikkink (1998) wrote the seminal work on this topic reviewing a wide range of successful global advocacy campaigns from the human rights, environmental and women's rights sectors (as well as one less successful campaign – that to end female genital mutilation in Kenya). From these cases, the authors see two common characteristics: if they can establish a short causal chain (it is clear who is to blame for a social problem) and if they can convey that the situation is leading to bodily harm, activists are more likely to see success. When these two conditions hold, local activists are better able to "boomerang" – get their plight picked up by better-connected and better-resourced activists in the developed world, who can in turn bring pressure to bear back on the local level.

We can distill a number of lessons from past successful transnational activist networks. In a study of activists working to get gender-based violence and reproductive rights on the international agenda, Joachim finds that: frames are the weapons of the weak, that changes in the broader institutional and international context create opportunities for advocacy NGOs, that changes in political alignments can be an opportunity to get something on the agenda, policy entrepreneurs are the most essential resource, and, like many studies of advocacy find, advocacy influence is also a matter of luck and serendipity (2007, 178–82).

There are two ways that local movements can improve their chances of linking up with more powerful actors in the developed world: raise awareness and frame the movement in a way that aligns with the powerful gatekeeping NGOs in the Global North. A local campaign is more likely to be able to do this if it has a charismatic leader (preferably who speaks English), who has contacts and some access to resources (Bob 2005, 44). The presence of a "matchmaker" – someone who promotes a cause to powerful global NGOs – can also significantly improve a local movement's chances of plugging into a transnational advocacy network and all the resources and contacts that affords.

These "connectors" (to use Malcolm Gladwell's term) are critical to the success of a transnational activism movement. Tarrow refers to these key players as "rooted cosmopolitans" in *The New Transnational Activism* – "individuals and groups who mobilize domestic and international resources and opportunities to advance claims on behalf of external actors, against external opponents, or in favor of goals they hold in common with transnational allies" (2006, 29). Tarrow's goal, however, is not to determine which strategies, tactics or conditions lead to successful global activism, but to identify and describe the types of transnational activism:

1. The Global in the Local – in this case global issue framing is used in domestic conflicts or grievances with foreign bodies are voiced in the domestic realm.
2. Transitional Processes – where strategies diffuse across countries or activism shifts up to another level of governance.
3. The Local in the Global – when domestic grievances are projected into the global arena or transnational coalitions are formed to work toward a common goal.

Much of the research on transnational or global activism has focused on this third process, where we see coalitions of activists working across borders for a common goal.

Through these studies we have come to understand key elements that are important for the success of transnational activism and how movements in the developing world have induced power players in the developed world to get involved on their issue. Most studies of transnational activism have understandably studied cases where there was a certain degree of success – where a local movement successfully courted the attention of an organization in the developed world or where a transnational advocacy coalition was formed.

We know less about the cases when global activism hasn't been successful (Bob's 2005 comparative case study is an exception), when a transnational coalition hasn't been formed, when advocates are trying to advocate in the field, but haven't been able to boomerang their message out, scale shift it up, or project it out into the global arena. Thousands of communities around the globe are in crisis; many of them are fighting for their rights on the frontlines. To gain a better understanding of the ways global advocacy can succeed, we need to begin with the crises, and go to the field, asking who is giving these grievances voice, how are they trying to do it, and what is standing in their way.

We need a different research approach – one that studies problems and searches for activism rather than studying successful activism and searching for marginal variation.

New data on global advocacy

The data presented in this book stem from a multi-year, multi-country, pan-regional study of global advocacy fighting for the rights of the displaced. It is based on fieldwork in seven countries suffering from major protracted displacement crises: Colombia, Croatia, Kenya, Nepal, Sri Lanka, Thailand and Uganda. Seventy-six in-depth interviews with aid workers, many more informal discussions and participant observation, and nearly 100 structured interview surveys with refugees, are combined with data on health, sanitation and security indicators as well as in-depth reports collected in the field from UNHCR and NGO staff. In addition, data on agenda attention to all 61 global protracted displacement crises is collected from five European and American news outlets for all of 2011 and a decade of coverage data of these issues (2000–2010) in the *New York Times*. This data and content analysis of the media coverage is presented in more detail in Chapters 2 and 3.

For the national and local levels, the first critical step in collecting data that can lead to generalizable conclusions is selecting a representative sample of displacement crises. In order to study the impact of the most important factors affecting advocacy on behalf of the displaced (Chapters 4 and 5) and variation in levels of community building and political mobilization among the displaced (Chapter 6), I worked to control for other variables by selecting only displacement situations that are conflict induced, so I do not investigate displacement due to natural or man-made disasters which likely have very different dynamics. Second, I constrain my study to only those displacement crises that are protracted, defined as situations where the displaced have been so for at least five years. Finally, security must be taken into consideration and, for practicality, active war zones are not included, such that the displacement situations in the Middle East and the most violent conflicts in Africa are excluded.[1] I acquired the list of countries in which the UNHCR was aiding refugees and where it is aiding internally displaced populations as of 2008 from UNHCR headquarters in Geneva (see Tables 1.2 and 1.3).

I also sought to maximize geographic variation and to include the largest displacement crises. For the selection of the refugee country cases with major protracted displacement crises, I acquired the database of countries and camps housing more than 2,500 residents from the UNHCR. Major displacement crises were defined as any country with more than five refugee camps with more than 2,500 residents. This criteria, requiring a country to have at least five sizable refugee camps, is for the sake of feasibility, since conducting fieldwork in one country with multiple camps is more efficient than conducting fieldwork in many more countries which have only one or two camps. Following these criteria, while seeking to maximize geographic variation, led

---

[1] This excludes: Afghanistan, Iraq, Congo, DRC, Sudan, Somalia, Central African Republic, Chad and Côte d'Ivoire.

TABLE 1.2. *Major refugee situations with UNHCR-aided camps more than 2,500 (as of 2008, during case selection)*

Country of displacement	# of camps	# of UNHCR-assisted refugees	Selected for study
Africa			
Algeria	5	89,260	
Angola	1	6,232	
Benin	1	5,303	
Botswana	1	3,179	
Burundi	1	7,318	
Chad	16	265,110	
Central African Rep.	1	6,657	
Congo	1	2,811	
Côte d'Ivoire	1	3,963	
Djibouti	1	6,739	
Eritrea	1	3,838	
Ethiopia	6	94,557	
Ghana	1	36,159	
Guinea	3	21,678	
Kenya	6	256,039	**
Malawi	2	7,750	
Mozambique	1	5,019	
Namibia	1	6,486	
Nigeria	1	5,044	
Rwanda	4	43,750	
Sierra Leone	5	15,703	
Sudan	9	102,865	
Tanzania	12	287,078	
Zambia	4	64,690	
Uganda	11	223,493	
Asia			
Nepal	7	107,803	**
Papua New Guinea	1	2,677	
Thailand	9	145,096	**
Middle East			
Iraq	1	11,900	
Islamic Rep. of Iran	4	24,321	
Pakistan	20	424,620	
Yemen	1	9,298	
South Asia			
Bangladesh	1	10,144	
India	1	69,609	

New data on global advocacy 15

TABLE 1.3. *Major IDP situations where the UNHCR is assisting (as of 2008 during case selection)*

Country	# of UNHCR-assisted IDPs	Selected for study
Latin America		
Colombia	3,000,000	**
Africa		
Congo	1,400,000	
Côte d'Ivoire	709,200	
Uganda	1,586,200	**
Dem. Rep. of the Congo	1,075,300	
Somalia	400,000	
Sudan	1,325,200	
Burundi	13,900	
Central African Rep.	147,000	
Chad	112,700	
Asia		
Myanmar	58,500	
Nepal	100,000	
Timor-Leste	155,200	
Middle East		
Iraq	1,834,400	
Lebanon	200,000	
Afghanistan	129,300	
South Asia		
Sri Lanka	469,200	**
Europe		
Croatia	4,000	**
Bosnia and Herzegovina	135,500	
Montenegro	16,200	
Serbia	227,600	
Central Eurasia		
Azerbaijan	686,600	
Georgia	246,000	
Russian Federation	158,900	

to the selection of: Kenya (Somali refugees), Nepal (Bhutanese refugees) and Thailand (Burmese refugees).

For the selection of the IDP country cases, major displacement crises were defined as any country with more than 300,000 IDPs. Again, following this criteria, and those discussed above, led to the selection of Colombia, Sri Lanka and Uganda. For geographic variation, Croatia was selected in Europe, which has more than five camps and which host both IDPs and refugees (though absolute numbers are much lower). The resulting sample of cases is representative of the most significant displacement crises globally (as noted in Tables 1.1 and 1.2).

Africa
- Uganda (IDPs)
- Kenya (Somali refugees)

Asia
- Thailand (Burmese refugees)
- Sri Lanka (IDPs)
- Nepal (Bhutanese refugees)

Americas
- Colombia (IDPs)

Europe
- Croatia (Bosnian refugees and Croatian IDPs)

For each case, I spent 2–3 weeks in the field conducting semi-structured, in-depth interviews with UN agency staff and NGO staff in field outposts.[2] Interviewing NGO staff in field office outposts made the scale of the project feasible since I could collect data on their activities and the conditions in many camps all at once. In addition, this strategy ensured I could gather information even in the event the camps could not be accessed. This follows from the reality that camp and settlement access is sometimes quite difficult to attain (Vogler 2007), and in the case of northern Sri Lanka, impossible. Field outposts are the small town base of operations that exist in most displacement crises. In most camp-based displacement situations, NGO staff are spending significant time each day in camps or are visiting regularly and have a solid understanding of the activities being carried out in the camps. Interviewing NGO staff both international and national also avoided the cost and difficulty of translation since most NGO staff are fluent in English, though the fieldwork in Colombia required a translator for NGO staff interviews and the interviews with refugees in the Bhutanese camps in Nepal required translators.

The UNHCR NGO Liaison office provided lists of Implementing Partners in each of the case study countries. I attempted to interview representatives of every NGO implementing partner as well as other NGOs working in the area but that are not funded by the UNHCR, which I identified through online searches, coalition reports and meeting minutes. The interview protocols were designed to gather information on indicators of collective action, advocacy and contextual conditions as detailed in Chapter 6. In addition

---

[2] I conducted all fieldwork and interviews except for the case of Sri Lanka, which was done by my research assistant Anirban Archayana. Over all, this research is based on 20 weeks, or five months, of fieldwork carried out from 2008 to 2010, and publicly available data collection gathered from 2010 to 2013.

to the in-depth interviews, I requested data collected by the NGOs and IOs on camp condition indicators, NGO reports, surveys and questionnaires, maps and any other material available which provides information on the displacement context.

In-depth field interviews are the only reliable method to collect information on community building within these displaced populations and in-country national-level advocacy efforts. Interviews with NGO staff in headquarters in Washington, DC, Brussels, and even Bangkok and Kampala displayed a lack of knowledge of the situation "on the ground." For many areas of inquiry, headquarter staff responded that the staff in the field would be the ones that would know about camp conditions, community building activities, and advocacy targeted at local authorities. I conducted a preliminary online study of the 786 NGO implementing partners of the UNHCR and found extremely limited publicly available information on their activities with displaced populations: First, only 42 percent (234/566) maintained a web presence. Of those that did, only 5 percent (41) had detailed information about their operations broken down by country and describing their community building initiatives, while still having no information on local advocacy efforts. For many of the NGOs, work with refugees and IDPs is only one aspect of their broader programming and thus it receives limited coverage in their publications. Moreover, NGOs are generally quite vague in their online publications and annual reports, focusing on success stories and not reporting on failed community building or advocacy initiatives. To accurately collect information on which collective action initiatives are being carried out in the camps and in which types of advocacy groups are engaging, in-depth interviews in the field are the only reliable method.

Interviewees were promised full anonymity to ensure the most open discussion, such that they are not directly quoted in the analysis and their names, and the names of their organizations are not disclosed. If interviewees were comfortable with taping, the interviews were digitally recorded, while if they were not, detailed notes were taken.

To get a better understanding of the individual-level factors that influence community engagement and participation in CBOs in camps, I, along with a research team of graduate students,[3] conducted 98 structured interview surveys with displaced citizens in the Bhutanese refugee camps in Nepal. While in the Beldangi I refugee camp to conduct a Geographic Information System (GIS) mapping and GIS staff training for the UNHCR and Implementing Partners, we worked with six translators to conduct interviews with a clustered random sample of huts from a random sample of camp blocks. Participants were promised full anonymity, their names were not taken, and they are not directly quoted.

---

[3] Thank you to Beau Miller and Emily Rose for helping carry out the survey, as well as to Michael Zanchelli, Gina Barbone and Clint Misamore for preparation of the survey.

This data at the individual level, camp level, country level and global level is woven together to produce one of the most expansive and comprehensive pictures to date of advocacy on behalf of the forcibly displaced.

Layout of the book

This triangulation of data collection reveals that, unfortunately, successful cases of advocacy on behalf of the displaced are the exception. More often than not, the plight of the displaced is silenced, and advancement of their rights blocked, at every level of government. I describe how this is so at the global, national and local levels in each of the subsequent chapters. The first two empirical chapters explore the relative attention by the international community to different displacement crises. At the global level the number of massive forced displacement crises in 2011 was 61, advocates for these communities not only need to compete with each other for attention to their cause but also vie for agenda space with the many other crises burning worldwide – natural disasters, human rights violations and environmental devastation, to name just a few. If it seems like there are an infinite number of possible problems it is because there are, and the displaced – who have been marginalized, demoralized and demobilized – have fallen through the cracks. Furthermore, in the majority of the cases there are no advocates working on behalf of specific displaced populations. However, where there are organized advocates running public education campaigns, those cases do see more attention to their cause. Chapter 3 studies how attention to various crises has waxed and waned over the past decade and presents the findings of a content analysis to uncover the factors that drive attention. This chapter highlights a number of exceptional cases, like Darfur, and introduces the seven conflicts that are the subject of the rest of the book.

The following three chapters present the findings of fieldwork in seven protracted displacement crises. Chapter 4 explores the types of advocacy international NGOs engage in on behalf of the refugees at the local and national level, the effectiveness of that advocacy and the barriers they face. This chapter considers the difficulty of advocating for unwanted citizens with limited resources, no leverage and lobbying hostile or indifferent authorities. National governments hosting refugee populations see them at best as a nuisance and a drain on resources, and at worst a security threat with embedded armed elements. Host governments don't want them there, they don't want them to stay and they don't want more to come so they have no incentive to improve their conditions.

Chapter 5 turns to exploring who is advocating, how and to what effect in the cases of internal displacement. While some of the humanitarian aid organizations working with the displaced attempt to plead their case to national authorities, their advocacy often falls on deaf ears. Internally displaced groups are often marginalized, or actively oppressed, segments of society – the Tamils

Layout of the book

in Sri Lanka, the Acholi in Uganda and Durfuri in Sudan. In many of these cases, the governments also have little incentive to improve the conditions of the displaced. In both refugee and IDP situations, the humanitarian organizations aiding the displaced are in a very difficult advocacy position, and if they push too hard or act too politically, they can be expelled by the hosting government, keeping them from fulfilling their primary mission to provide life-saving food and medicine. In certain cases though, advocates for the displaced have collaborated with governments of the Global North to bring about limited improvements in a few of these cases.

Chapter 6 explores when the displaced mobilize to advocate on their own behalf and what factors explain that variation. Drawing on social movement literature, I take a political opportunity structure approach to systematically evaluate which factors promote and which inhibit mobilization of the displaced. In most cases, there is very little mobilization of any kind other than some economic activity, and almost no political mobilization. Interviews with nearly 100 refugees in the Bhutanese camps provide insight into why.

Chapter 7 weaves together the findings from the data collection at the global, national and local levels, and argues that the international community is failing the forcibly displaced. Outcomes are a far cry from the rhetoric of international conventions and doctrines. Advocacy on their behalf is uncoordinated and often ineffective. This chapter lays out a number of alternative strategies that, based on the fieldwork and *realpolitik*, will not work. Then, it proposes a new strategy based on ideas from the burgeoning field of social entrepreneurship that could work: mobilizing new funds to use as economic and thus political leverage. I propose a global advocacy campaign that highlights the crisis of displacement but directs concerned citizens toward a clear ask: to give small donations. These donations can be used in two different ways:

1. as person-to-person micro-finance grants to support new small businesses run by the displaced to facilitate direct economic empowerment and improve living conditions; and
2. those small donations can be aggregated into large micro-finance pools of funding that will be released for a given crisis if, and only if, the host government changes its policies to allow freedom of movement and freedom to work.

With direct economic empowerment will come a pathway to a life of dignity as the displaced await a durable solution. The conditional pools of investment will act as a carrot to incentivize host governments to begin seeing the displaced as an asset rather than a burden. Finally, Chapter 8 provides a summary of the major findings and proposals.

While there are billions of people in the world that still do not have access to their rights, I argue that we owe a special responsibility to the forcibly displaced to improve their access to rights. First, these are arguably some of the most vulnerable people in the world – they enjoy no citizenship (*de jure* for refugees and stateless persons, *de facto* for IDPs) and thus the protection of no government. They have run for their lives, fleeing genocide, ethnic cleansing and war. Second, these individuals are denied the right to rely on themselves, as one would theoretically be able to do even in an impoverished country. The rules we have created as an international society have been to restrict the movement of the displaced and limit their opportunities to engage in income-generating activities.

Following the Rwandan genocide, an international expert group was set up to consider how the international community should respond when communities around the world find themselves in grave danger. The resulting document, *The Responsibility to Protect*, commits the international community to a new norm: "sovereign states have a responsibility to protect their own citizens from avoidable catastrophe – from mass murder and rape, from starvation – but that when they are unwilling or unable to do so, that responsibility must be borne by the broader community of states" (ICISS 2001, VIII). It is this new framework along with the Universal Declaration of Human Rights (UDHR) that should be the benchmark to which we compare the reality of forced displacement.

The international refugee regime and the UNHCR are tasked with the protection of the displaced, but protection has been narrowly defined to mean life-sustaining aid and protection from violence and *refoulement*. The UN is not funded at a level to engage in true humanitarian intervention and the UNHCR and its Implementing Partners are not funded at a level to ensure individuals access their rights.

Since the international community has established the international norms of universal human rights, has accepted the responsibility to provide asylum for those fleeing for their lives and has declared the Responsibility to Protect, we have the responsibility to see these norms, codified in international policy, through to changes in outcomes. It is in the final step that we are falling tragically short. This book systematically documents the status quo and proposes a new way forward to enable the displaced to live lives of dignity and realize their dreams.

2

Global attention to displacement crises

Getting it on the agenda

If an advocacy group hadn't been present in a particular displacement crisis, would there be any attention paid to the crisis? Systematically investigating why some issues get on the political agenda and others receive little attention has been a traditionally difficult endeavor – how do we study the issue that wasn't there? We could propose to look at all the possible policy issues and then see which make it onto the official agenda – but the list of potential policy problems is virtually endless. When we move from national agendas to talking about the "global agenda" this becomes even more pronounced.

Agenda-setting research has shown how critical policy entrepreneurs are to getting issues on the crowded political agenda – an issue without an advocate is not an issue (Kingdon 1995). Baumgartner and Jones show the critical role of anti-nuclear advocates in getting nuclear power on the agenda and the influence of consumer protection advocates in changing the debate around tobacco policy (1993; 2005). Joachim documents the role of women's right advocates in getting gender-based violence on the UN agenda (2007). Agenda-setting is recognized as a key step in a policy change process – there must be attention before there can be action.

Previous research would suggest then that advocacy on behalf of the displaced – by advocacy organizations, international organizations and third country governments – should be a key explanatory factor in understanding which displacement crises get attention and thus see improved access to rights and which do not. I test this by collecting data on the attention to, and advocacy on, these issues.

Understanding why some crises receive international attention and others go forgotten requires collecting systematic data on the level of attention to each displacement situation on the "global agenda." I will focus on the US and EU public agendas (or the Global North's agenda) due to the powerful role

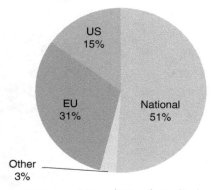

FIGURE 2.1. EU and US role in displacement aid – NGOs

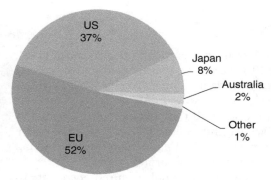

FIGURE 2.2. EU and US role in displacement aid – contributions to UNHCR

they play in this issue area as funders of displacement camps, as mediators in conflicts and as recipients of refugees. Figures 2.1 and 2.2 show that the large majority of NGOs aiding the displaced are headquartered in and are funded by the United States and the EU and that the largest proportion of the UNHCR's budget is contributed by the United States and the EU, comprising 89 percent of the overall budget. In addition, the United States received 60 percent of the world's resettled refugees in 2007 (26,532 individuals) and the EU collectively received 10 percent (the rest being received by Australia, Canada and New Zealand). The United States and the EU dominate the "Global North," and they are *the* major actors in the realm of global displacement policy. As discussed in Chapter 1, the pathway to policy change begins with attention to a policy problem; only once there is a recognition of a policy problem do policymakers begin considering alternative policies to address the problem, mobilizing support for specific alternatives, and finally passing new policy to institute a particular solution and implement that solution.

Setting the "global agenda"

While collecting data on the dependent variable of attention to displacement issues in the Global North is relatively straightforward through news archives, collecting independent measures of interest group activity is somewhat more complicated. I rely on two independent registries of organized interest: the Lobby Disclosure report database in the United States and the European Commission's voluntary register of advocacy organizations in the EU. In addition, the articles gathered in the media search were coded for mentions of advocacy groups, human rights organizations and statements by American and European government officials. Finally, an iterative search process was conducted to identify groups working in this space that are not registered in the registries. If an organization was mentioned, their website was searched to find related coalitions or other partner organizations. As we see with other powerless groups worldwide, the forcibly displaced, who lack resources and leverage, have few people advocating on their behalf.

This chapter first further discusses the theoretical literature on powerless groups and the under-represented. Second, it reviews the literature on agenda-setting and extends it to thinking about a "global agenda." Third, the data collection strategy to study the relationship between advocacy and agenda attention in the case of forced displacement is described, followed by the analysis and conclusions.

Setting the "global agenda": global issues, global actors and global agendas

To which instances of violent conflict and massive forced displacement does the international community pay attention? And can advocacy by international NGOs on the topic help explain what issues get on the agenda of the Global North and which do not? Anecdotal evidence would suggest the answer is yes. The violence and related massive displacements in Darfur and Tibet are two examples of displacement issues the public and policymakers in the Global North have heard about and for which two very active global campaigns – the Save Darfur Campaign and the International Campaign for Tibet – can be pointed to as potential drivers for public attention.

Kingdon defined the agenda as "the list of subjects or problems to which governmental officials, and people outside of government closely associated with those officials, are paying some serious attention at any given time" (1995, 3). Cobb and Elder (1983) distinguish between the systemic or public agenda and the institutional agenda, which describes the list of problems and potential solutions policymakers are giving active attention. Issues often need to first make it to the public agenda, before they move on to the institutional agenda. "Agenda setting is central to the policymaking process: if an issue does not attract the appropriate attention, chances are it will languish without government response" (Kraft and Furlong 2010).

Kingdon highlights the importance of a policy entrepreneur to facilitate the movement of an issue onto the agenda when a window of opportunity opens related to the political environment, the understanding of the problem and the available policy options. Policy entrepreneurs can be policymakers or non-governmental advocates that invest much of their time and resources in the issue. Often, in the area of human rights generally and displaced rights specifically, it is the advocates of human rights organizations that fulfill this role. Sometimes they are known international figures like the Dalai Lama, while others are the lesser-known advocates tirelessly working day-in and day-out for small and large human rights groups and country/conflict specific advocacy groups. Bob shows that insurgent/freedom fighter groups are most successful at gaining the attention of the international community when they have a charismatic leader coupled with organizational and material resources (Bob 2005). Keck and Sikkink (1998) similarly show that activists in the Global South often need partners in the Global North to mobilize pressure on their governments to ultimately put pressure on governments in the South to affect change. Joachim's (2007) recounting of the women's suffragist movement and the movement to get gender-based violence on the UN agenda both demonstrate the powerful role unrelenting advocates play in getting the international community to pay attention to an issue.

This is not to say that if there is no advocacy and attention there is no governmental or international governance attention or action on an issue. Governments can attend to social problems before there is a major advocacy campaign drawing their attention to it. However, decades of political science research and hundreds of years of observation show that it often takes the campaigning of advocates to draw attention to a problem and pressure policymakers and policy actors to behave differently. While it is possible for the governments of the Global North, international institutions and implementing partners to change their behavior and better respond to the problem of massive protracted displacement, they are not doing so. Chapter 1 established that there is a failure of global policy and action when it comes to forced displacement. There are 60 million people forcibly displaced, living in terrible conditions, with no access to basic rights and the three "durable solutions" ostensibly available to them are not actually available to them. There is a major social problem and advocacy is needed to draw attention to that social problem (or set of social problems), as with most social problems.

Based on previous research and observation, we would expect then, across all global displacement crises, to see more attention to cases or populations that have an advocate in the Global North, all else being equal. Before we can begin to explore the factors that drive international attention to massive forced displacement issues, we need to begin with systematically collecting baseline data on what is on the American and European agendas when it comes to massive forced displacement; it is this I turn to next.

Data collection

In order to understand which displacement crises the international community pays attention to and which it does not requires systematic data on the global public agenda. But what constitutes the global agenda? The global justice movement often makes a distinction between the Global North and the Global South; the Global North is dominated by Europe, the United States, Australia and Japan. These are the countries that are the heavy hitters when it comes to the global trade regime, global development initiatives, humanitarian interventions and conflict resolution initiatives. In short, they are the wealthy countries of the world – those with the resources to have an impact on global problems if they choose to act.

Following on from the agenda-setting literature that has used media attention to study agendas at the national level in the United States and Europe, I rely on systematic coding of major papers to develop a measure of attention to each of the global refugee cases. Keyword searches of "refugee" or "internally displaced persons" or "internally displaced" were conducted on the archives of the *New York Times*, the *Washington Post*, the *Guardian*, *Le Monde* and *Suddeutsche Zeitung* to gather quantitative and content measures of media attention to each of the protracted displacement crises during 2010.[1] Articles were reviewed for relevance, and those that actually focused on a current displacement crisis were included in the database and coded. For the French and German papers, research assistants first pasted the article texts into Google Translate[2] and then read the translation to determine relevance. Every relevant article in both the cross-sectional and time-series database was coded for:

1. what country the displaced originated from (i.e. Afghanistan);
2. what country the displaced were currently located in (i.e. Pakistan);
3. if the article focused on the displacement situation or if it was a secondary mention;
4. if conflict or violence was mentioned;
5. if there was a mention of a US government position or statement related to the situation;
6. if there was a mention of a European government or EU position or statement related to the situation; and
7. whether an advocacy organization, international organization or other group is mentioned in the article.

---

[1] The following search terms were used: for the *New York Times*, the *Washington Post* and the *Guardian*: (refugee) OR (internally displaced) OR (internal displacement) OR (IDP); for *Le Monde*: (réfugié) OR (personne intérieurement déplacée); for *Suddeutsche Zeitung*: (Flüchtlinge) OR (Flüchtling) OR (Intern Vertriebene).
[2] http://translate.google.com/.

The cross-sectional database of coverage in 2010 includes 642 articles on displacement issues in Europe and the United States. Chapter 3 analyzes a second, time-series database of displacement coverage in the *New York Times* from 2001 to 2010, including 2,439 articles.

In addition to the data on the dependent variable of agenda attention, it was necessary to collect independent data on advocacy organizations potentially lobbying on behalf of the displaced in the Global North. To gather this data, searches were conducted of the US Lobby Disclosure Act (LDA) Report Database to find international or national organizations that were advocating on behalf of the displaced. Searches of the "Issue Data" field of the LDA on the terms "refugee" and "displaced" resulted in the small database of the 25 organizations that reported lobbying on issues that had to do with refugees or the internally displaced. Only five of these organizations were focusing on a specific displacement crisis, while the rest focused largely on S.3113 – the 2010 Refugee Protection Act. A similar search was conducted of the Europa Transparency Registry,[3] searching for those entities whose declaration included the term "refugee"; this resulted in a small database of 16 organizations, all of whom were advocating on general displacement topics save for two organizations – one focusing on the specific topic of refugees from Bosnia-Herzegovina and one on Iranian refugees. A third database of organizations working on displacement issues was constructed from mentions in the news articles; this database includes 164 local, national and international organizations that were mentioned in the media coverage but not necessarily actively advocating for the displaced or seeking to increase attention to the issue. Analysis of this data collection is presented next, coupled with data on the scale of displacement crises from the UNHCR. Finally, an iterative process was used to identify all advocacy groups advocating on displacement issues based on their linkages to other groups through coalitions or joint advocacy actions.

The data on the size of the displaced population in each case comes from the UNHCR annual compendium of asylum-seekers, IDPs, returnees (refugees and IDPs), stateless persons, and others of concern to UNHCR by origin, at year-end 2009. These figures are the numbers of people aided by the UNHCR. These are the most complete figures that can be found but experts in any given case may take issue with the number since there may be many more displaced that the UNHCR is not aiding, or not aware of or had no way to count. For example, the figure in the table for Tibetan refugees is 20,840; this number is much smaller than the estimated 127,935 Tibetans living in exile, but many of those Tibetans have naturalized, for example in the United States, so are no longer being aided by the UNHCR.[4] In other cases, such as refugees from Myanmar and Somalia, the

---

[3] Europa Transparency Registry: http://europa.eu/transparency-register/.
[4] www.hindustantimes.com/India-news/NorthIndia/127935-Tibetans-living-outside-Tibet-Tibetan-survey/Article1-634405.aspx.

Analysis

host governments of Thailand and Kenya both officially closed their borders in 2007, leaving new arrivals unregistered and uncounted. While there are likely omissions in these data, they are the best figures out there, and can be taken to be accurate especially as a relative measure of the scale of displacement compared to the other cases – as it is used here. The only figure that is changed from the UNHCR figures is that of the Palestinian refugees. The figure from the UNHCR is 97,702 Palestinian refugees aided by the UNHCR, but the UN has a special agency to aid Palestinian refugees – the United Nations Relief and Works Agency (the UNRWA). The UNRWA's official figure is five million people, which is used in the analysis that follows.[5]

Analysis

The first clear finding is that there is a great deal of variation in attention across displacement issues. Table 2.1 reports which of the 61 major displacement crises received any attention and which did not; the majority of massive displacement crises (62 percent) received absolutely no coverage in the media markets of the Global North. Sixteen of these 38 unreported cases each involves hundreds of thousands of people that are living with little to no access to their most basic rights.

Out of all 642 articles on the topic of refugees or IDPs published in the five American and European papers in the year of 2010, 180 of them were on general discussions of refugees often within the country of the national paper (i.e. domestic refugee laws in France, problems with resettled refugees in Germany, improving services to resettle refugees in the United States, etc.). Turning to the 462 articles that discussed specific displacement crises and refugee camps, the situation of Palestinian refugees received by far the greatest amount of agenda space with more than a third of all articles on this topic (160). This may seem proportional since the Palestinian refugee crisis is an extremely protracted one and large, with estimates of the number of refugees since 1948 and their descendants registering at around five million people, however, Colombia also has a displaced population of four million people, but did not see a *single* article published on their plight across all five papers.

Figure 2.3 presents data on the attention paid to each displacement case that received more than one news story across the five papers in 2010. Therefore, not appearing on this graph are the stories of the displaced citizens of Colombia, Burundi, Ethiopia, Uganda, Central African Republic, Yemen, Chad, among countless others. What is important to note is that there were many stories mentioning displacement that are *not* one of the 61 cases of massive displacement studied in this book. For example, South Korea is not a country that has produced more than 10,000 displaced (the definition of a major displacement crisis used in this book), however in November 2010, North Korea

---

[5] www.unrwa.org/etemplate.php?id=47.

TABLE 2.1. *Major displacement situations (more than 10,000 displaced) year-end 2009 and whether there was any media coverage in any of the analyzed US or EU papers in 2010*

Origin	Number displaced	Coverage
Peru	12,088	NO COVERAGE
Bangladesh	12,258	NO COVERAGE
Guinea	13,749	
El Salvador	14,802	NO COVERAGE
Guatemala	14,881	NO COVERAGE
Ghana	16,241	NO COVERAGE
Senegal	16,938	NO COVERAGE
Cameroon	17,024	NO COVERAGE
Cambodia	17,248	NO COVERAGE
Albania	17,303	
Lebanon	18,032	NO COVERAGE
Sierra Leone	18,593	NO COVERAGE
Togo	19,632	NO COVERAGE
Tibetan	20,084	
Indonesia	20,534	NO COVERAGE
Syrian Arab Rep.	23,484	
Congo, Rep. of	23,826	NO COVERAGE
Zimbabwe	23,872	NO COVERAGE
India	24,236	NO COVERAGE
Nigeria	25,272	
Ukraine	26,066	NO COVERAGE
Mexico	26,848	NO COVERAGE
Haiti	36,015	NO COVERAGE
Mauritania	52,067	NO COVERAGE
Malaysia	62,010	NO COVERAGE
Liberia	77,710	NO COVERAGE
Iran	86,526	
Bhutan	**90,078**	**NO COVERAGE**
Croatia	**103,409**	**NO COVERAGE**
Armenia	104,312	NO COVERAGE
Ethiopia	111,645	
Western Sahara	116,495	
Rwanda	154,517	
Turkey	156,012	NO COVERAGE
Tanzania	156,458	NO COVERAGE
Angola	158,648	NO COVERAGE
China	198,899	
Russian Federation	203,605	
Eritrea	223,570	NO COVERAGE
Burundi	231,465	
Bosnia and Herzegovina	**236,863**	**NO COVERAGE**
Chad	250,439	NO COVERAGE

Analysis

Origin	Number displaced	Coverage
Yemen	252,554	NO COVERAGE
Viet Nam	340,610	NO COVERAGE
Central African Rep.	357,477	NO COVERAGE
Georgia	377,692	
Kenya	417,052	NO COVERAGE
Serbia	436,775	NO COVERAGE
Burma (Myanmar)	**496,542**	
Azerbaijan	605,933	NO COVERAGE
Sri Lanka	**684,276**	
Côte d'Ivoire	714,476	
Uganda	**862,551**	NO COVERAGE
Sudan	1,619,296	
Somalia	**2,249,454**	
Dem. Rep. of the Congo	2,662,821	
Pakistan	3,040,845	
Afghanistan	3,279,471	
Iraq	3,565,375	
Colombia	**3,758,127**	NO COVERAGE
Occupied Palestinian Territory*	5,000,000	

From UNHCR, year-end 2009 – figure represents "Total population of concern" which includes refugees, asylum-seekers, internally displaced persons (IDPs), returnees (refugees and IDPs), stateless persons and others of concern to the UNHCR by origin.
* Figure for number of Palestinian refugees comes from the UNRWA.

shelled the South Korean island of Yeonpyeong resulting in the displacement of island residents (Fackler 2010). This is not a major case of massive protracted displacement, but it is a case that received attention in 2010. Similarly there were 12 stories covering the displacement of Roma from Romania, attempts by France to kick out Roma, efforts by Germany to care for Roma refugee children, and general discussions of Roma being unwelcome everywhere in Europe. Again, this is not a major displacement crisis of more than 10,000 forcibly displaced and being cared for by the UNHCR, but nonetheless the plight of displaced Roma received coverage. Therefore, many of the 61 cases of massive displacement received no coverage, while other cases that are not among the 61 did receive coverage.

After the Palestinian refugee crisis, other cases that receive the bulk of attention on the global agenda include Kyrgyzstan, refugees resulting from the conflicts in Iraq and Afghanistan, those fleeing the repressive military junta in Burma, and two of the largest displacement crises in Africa: Sudan and Somalia. Most of the conflicts causing these massive displacements are fairly well-known save for perhaps that of the June 2010 Kyrgyzstan crisis which involved ethnic conflict between the majority ethnic Kyrgyz and the minority ethnic Uzbeks in southern Kyrgyzstan. Some reports blame the conflict on the

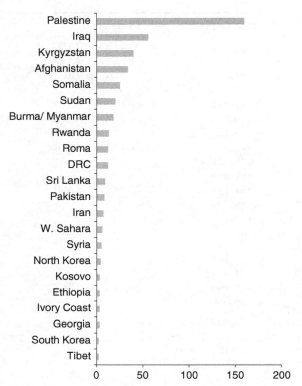

FIGURE 2.3. Displacement cases that received coverage by more than one news story in 2010
* Number of news stories across all five papers

Kyrgyzstan government, suggesting government security forces were complicit in or perpetrated the violence, while others suggest Islamic extremist groups – specifically Islamic radicals from the Islamic Movement of Uzbekistan – were brought in to incite violence in Uzbek neighborhoods (Kramer, *New York Times*, June 27, 2010).

So how do the papers differ? Are there distinctive patterns of coverage for each? Figure 2.4 displays the levels of coverage attributed to the displacement crisis for the *New York Times*, *Le Monde*, *Suddeutsche Zeitung* and the *Guardian* (for those cases that received at least five news stories of coverage). The US paper has a much heavier focus on the Palestinian case, while the British paper focused on the case of the Democratic Republic of the Congo – an issue under-covered by the American and French media. The German paper spent more time highlighting the situations of refugees in Iraq in 2010 in comparison to the other media markets.

Analysis

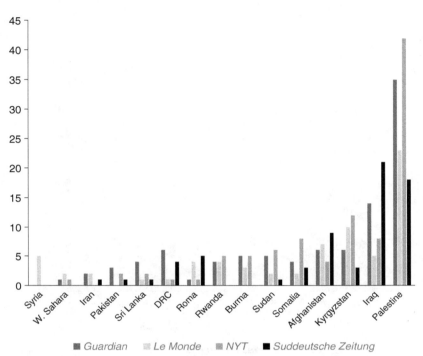

FIGURE 2.4. Displacement crises with at least five news stories in the Global North

Figure 2.5 shows that the US papers are fairly similar in their coverage with the *Post* focusing a bit more on Afghani refugees. As might be expected, the French, German and British agendas exhibit more differences, as seen in Figure 2.6. *Le Monde* published more articles on Syria and Kyrgyzstan, and the *Guardian* published more on Sudan, the DRC, Pakistan and Burma. But again, generally their overall attention patterns are similar.

How can we explain the variation in attention? Does the variation in global agenda space reflect the scale of the displacement? The correlation between the scale of displacement and the level of coverage has a Pearson's r of 0.73. Figure 2.7 presents a scatterplot of the percentage of the global agenda allocated to each of the major displacement crises to the percentage of world's displaced that that crisis constitutes and shows that those cases that receive the most coverage are large displacement situations. The unit of analysis here is the 61 cases of massive displacement. As mentioned 38 of those cases received no coverage, of those 23 that did receive some attention there were 389 articles on those cases across the five newspapers in 2010. Therefore, Palestinian refugees, discussed in 160 articles, constitute 41 percent of the global agenda space discussing major protracted displacement. Iraq and Afghanistan also register large numbers of displaced as well as high levels of media coverage. But, there

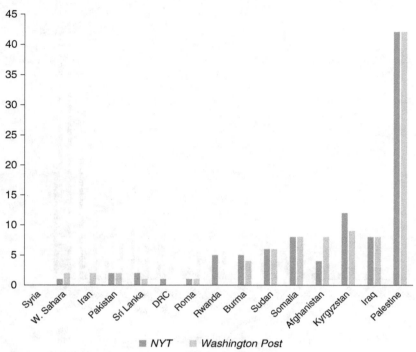

FIGURE 2.5. US coverage – *Washington Post* vs. *New York Times*

are exceptions as well, like Colombia, DRC and Uganda with high levels of displacement and low levels of coverage.

The scale of the problem may be part of the explanation for what receives attention and what does not, but it is not the entire story.

Advocacy does not seem to be a major explanatory factor in understanding what the Western media covers. The Palestinians do not have a famously well-organized Palestinian lobby in Washington, DC, Brussels or the capitals of the EU member states, there are not hip magazine ads by the International Campaign to Save Somalia. Of the 25 organizations that reported lobbying in the United States on issues that had to do with refugees or the internally displaced, only five were focusing on a specific displacement crises: Tibet, Iran, Iraq (2) and Sudan. Of the 16 organizations that reported lobbying on refugee or displacement issues in the EU, all were advocating on general displacement topics save for two organizations: one focusing on Bosnia-Herzegovinian refugees and the other on Iranian refugees.

Of the top 10 crises receiving attention, only one, Sudan, can be said to have had a concerted advocacy campaign mobilized around it – the Save Darfur Coalition. Yet this case is also the only crisis that has been officially declared a genocide by the US Congress and the European Parliament – so it is possible,

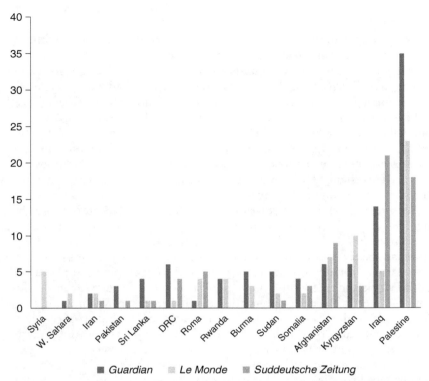

FIGURE 2.6. EU coverage – the *Guardian*, *Le Monde* and *Suddeutsche Zeitung*

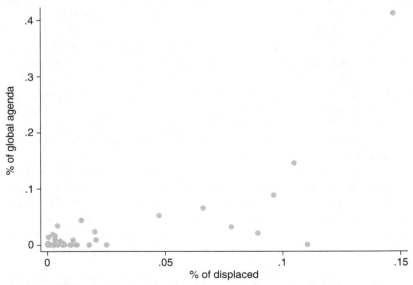

FIGURE 2.7. Comparison of share of the global agenda attention to the proportion of the global displaced population

though not guaranteed, that we would see attention to this case, even without vocal activists raising our awareness about the case.

Across the 642 articles, 164 organizations are mentioned as being involved in the issue or were directly quoted. The most commonly cited advocacy organizations are Human Rights Watch (18 times), the Bavarian Refugee Council (14 times), the International Committee of the Red Cross (ICRC) (14 times), Amnesty International (14 times), the Refugee Council (8 times), International Crisis Group (7 times), Refugee and Migrant Justice (4 times) and Pro Asyl (4 times), while all other groups are mentioned only once or twice. None of these organizations are Palestinian, Kyrgyzstani, Somali, Afghani or Iraqi-focused groups. They may give a comment if a journalist calls requesting one, but it is not clear that they are pushing for attention on these five cases any more than they advocate for the right of Congolese refugees or IDPs suffering from the unending conflict in Colombia.

There are a handful of refugee-specific organizations doing incredibly important advocacy work on behalf of the displaced, but necessarily this advocacy largely focuses on increasing aid and just keeping people alive; freedom to work and freedom to move don't make it to the agenda given the crush of other needs. Refugees International, with offices in Washington, DC, New York and London, was started in 1979 to advocate on behalf of refugees from Indochina. Since then it has "expanded to become the leading advocacy organization that provokes action from global leaders to resolve refugee crises ... Each year, Refugees International conducts 15 to 20 field missions to identify displaced people's needs for basic services such as food, water, health care, housing, access to education and protection from harm" (RI 2013). It also works to "challenge policy makers and aid agencies to improve the lives of displaced people around the world" (RI 2013). Refugees International carries out work in 23 countries.

Another major US-based advocacy organization, US Committee for Refugees and Immigrants, also states its mission is primarily advocacy: "To protect the rights and address the needs of persons in forced or voluntary migration worldwide by advancing fair and humane public policy, facilitating and providing direct professional services, and promoting the full participation of migrants in community life" (USCRI 2013). It partners with civil society groups to advocate for the displaced in 19 countries as well as representing refugees and immigrants arriving in the United States.

The ARC does some advocacy but focuses on providing humanitarian aid. It describes in its mission: "ARC works with its partners and constituencies to provide opportunities and expertise to refugees, displaced people and host communities. We help people survive conflict and crisis and rebuild lives of dignity, health, security and self-sufficiency. ARC is committed to the delivery of programs that ensure measurable quality and lasting impact for the people we serve" (ARC 2013).

Other refugee-focused organizations such as the Jesuit Refugee Service (JRS), International Rescue Committee (IRC), Danish Refugee Council (DRC)

Analysis

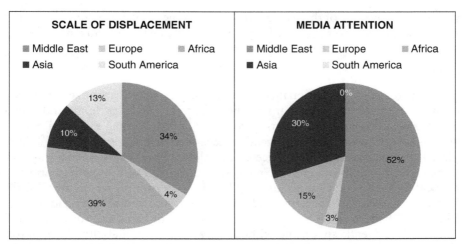

FIGURE 2.8. Global attention by region vs. scope of displacement by region

and the Norwegian Refugee Council (NRC) all primarily focus on providing life-saving humanitarian assistance, coupled with advocacy for resources needed to continue their work. If they engage in case-specific advocacy, it tends to be for increased funds for that crisis.

The cross-sectional data suggests there is little evidence that advocacy drives attention. Reading all the articles makes clear that geopolitics and violence are stronger explanatory factors. Figure 2.8 shows comparatively the level of media attention by region and the scale of displacement by region; immediately apparent is the over-coverage of the Middle East – ground zero for the global war on terror. Conflicts in the Middle East received a great deal more attention than conflicts burning elsewhere. When these conflicts are covered, the displaced are often mentioned as part of the story. Therefore, as we've seen, the cases of displacement of Palestinians, Iraqis, Pakistanis and Afghanis are much higher on the global agenda than those forced from their homelands in Africa, Asia or South America. Research assistants coded whether the article focused on the displaced or if the focus was on violence, with the plight of the displaced as a secondary topic: nearly half the articles (49 percent) focused on the violence.

The seven cases that are the subject of more in-depth analysis and fieldwork in the rest of this book are bolded in Table 2.1 – as is clear there is a mix of both those that received no coverage, as well as those with some degree of coverage such as Somalia and Bhutan. Here in the sub-sample, we see the same variation that we find in the universe of cases: though each of the seven cases involves hundreds of thousands of displaced persons, four cases (Uganda, Colombia, Croatia/Bosnia-Herzegovina and Bhutan) received no attention at all across the American and European media markets. Chapter 3 explores the variation in coverage of these cases, and presents the results of a content analysis of a decade of coverage in order to untangle the factors driving attention.

Conclusion

It is clear that the international community differentially grants agenda space to the various communities that have been forced to flee their homelands due to violence. The evidence suggests advocacy is not the leading explanation for what is on and what is off the agenda since, overwhelmingly, the world's displaced do not have a strong voice at the global level. The vast majority of displaced communities do not have well-resourced and well-organized groups advocating for an end to their suffering before the power players in the Global North. So here we see the first set of data supporting the argument laid out in Chapter 1: Failure is the norm. The vast majority of cases are not granted a single inch of agenda space, and without *attention*, the probability of *action* to change their circumstances is nearly zero.

Perhaps this should not be surprising, as Kingdon argues, a policy entrepreneur is an important player in getting an issue on the agenda, but he or she is most effective when a window of opportunity occurs with the coupling of the problem, politics and policy streams. Focusing events can help that coupling come about, and an effective policy entrepreneur can help guide an issue onto the agenda at the moment a focusing event occurs. Unfortunately for the world's displaced, not only do they lack policy entrepreneurs to call attention to their plight but seemingly one of the only events that focuses the attention of the international community is particular spikes in violence, violence of a scale or intensity that is out of the ordinary from the continual violence that led to the displacement in the first place.

What may also have been missing is what Kingdon calls the "policy stream" – that policy alternatives exist to solve the problem; or what Clay Shirky (2008) refers to as a "plausible promise." We need a plausible policy alternative to the current refugee regime that could actually bring about change on the ground for the millions of people suffering in displacement.

More and more, it is clear that this policy change needs to be immediate freedom of movement and freedom to work, coupled with an incentive of investment to encourage that policy change. This is the call of the one strong voice for the displaced in Washington: the US Committee on Refugees and Immigrants in their "End Warehousing" campaign. Facilitating freedom of movement and freedom to work is feasible: today, when a person is displaced over borders they receive an identity card they use to access aid – food and shelter materials. This ID card could serve as a temporary international work and movement permit in the location of refuge. The same type of ID card could be issued for both refugees and IDPs, giving them equal access to rights and aid, regardless of if they have crossed man-made borders. This proposal is a simple policy shift, but one that would have massive positive implications for

Conclusion

the displaced. The state of the world's languishing refugees – dependent on aid, unable to work and imprisoned in camps – is a situation enforced by the international community. To change it requires a change in political will: an agreement among governments of the Global North and the Global South, the UN and international NGOs that these individuals have rights and that they should be allowed to access them. It also requires a change in strategy, one that raises new investment funds and begins to change the fundamental power balance. This possibility is discussed in more detail in Chapter 7.

3

Explaining global attention
Geopolitics vs. advocacy

Most cases of massive displacement see no attention whatsoever by the international community, those that do have no identifiable advocates and tend to only make it onto the public agenda when there are particular spikes in violence or are related to conflicts where the US or European powers have troops deployed.

To better understand what factors explain increases in global attention, this chapter studies attention to all 61 protracted issues for an entire decade (2,439 articles in all). The same search terms described in Chapter 2 were used to build a second database of relative media attention to all displacement crises over the last decade (2001–2010) in the *New York Times* (see Figure 3.1). If we look at the overall number of articles on refugee and IDP issues over the decade it is important to note that there is a downturn in 2008, the year of the global economic downturn, presumably as the media turned its attention to economic news and spent fewer inches on the world's conflicts and the displaced communities that resulted.

The few advocacy organizations that are trying to get attention for their specific displacement crisis are in an incredibly difficult position. They are up against a packed agenda and a saturated media landscape. Only 17 cases out of 61 had more than 20 stories across the decade, or an average of two stories per year. I discuss these higher-profile cases and why they even made a blip on the international community's radar.

The findings presented in this chapter confirm what the cross-sectional analysis suggested – that spikes in violence and US/NATO military action are stronger drivers of attention than advocacy. However, there are exceptions. Advocacy by international NGOs based in the Global North highlighting grassroots mobilization on the ground – like the case of Tibetan activists during the Chinese Olympics, or Buddhist activists during the Saffron Rebellion in Burma – does get attention for the related displaced populations.

Explaining global attention 39

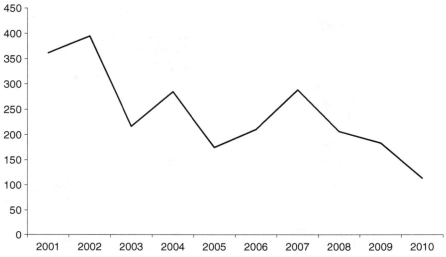

FIGURE 3.1. Overall attention to displacement issues in the *New York Times* (2001–2010)

After discussing what the international community does pay attention to, I turn to the seven representative cases studied in the rest of this book. I present brief overviews of the nature of the conflict that led to these massive displacements, brief histories of their prolonged displacement, and a content analysis of the news coverage in each case to uncover the drivers behind the international attention to their plight over the past decade. In most cases, strategic global advocacy campaigns are just not being organized to draw attention to these cases, rather it is happenstance and particular spikes in violence that explain the attention.

While failure is the norm in gaining *attention* to an issue and encouraging *action* to bring about improved access to rights, there are exceptions that can give us hope and offer a model of change: in two of the seven cases we saw global level advocacy going on – but taking two different routes to policy change. The first campaign was an internal and external advocacy initiative led by First Lady Laura Bush to raise awareness about the situation in Burma/Myanmar and the related refugee crisis in Thailand. This campaign succeeded in getting the issue on the global agenda, and coincided with a major policy change – the US government's agreement to resettle 60,000 Karen and Karenni (from Burma) refugees in 2006. The second was a more behind-the-scenes global-level advocacy approach where officials from Norway brokered an international agreement between the United States and Nepal, paving the way for the resettlement of another 60,000 Bhutanese refugees in 2007.

TABLE 3.1 *Displacement cases with more than 20 news stories over the decade*

Country of origin	Total # of stories across the decade (2001–2010)
Palestine	869
Sudan	278
Afghanistan	257
Iraq	200
Chechnya	52
Somalia	54
Liberia	48
DRC	47
Georgia	43
Pakistan	41
North Korea	35
Sri Lanka	36
Myanmar	31
Lebanon	29
Colombia	26
Bosnia/Croatia	24
Uganda	20

Violence sells

The time-series data along with content analysis of the articles supports what the cross-sectional data showed: that geopolitics and violence, especially new types or higher levels of violence, drive attention more than advocacy. Table 3.1 presents the top 17 cases that received more than 20 articles over the decade. The four cases with the most attention, and significantly more attention than any of the other cases, are about the forcibly displaced in Afghanistan (257 articles), Iraq (200 articles), Palestinian camps (869 articles) and Sudan (278 articles).

Taking geopolitics and the War on Terror first, as seen in Figure 3.2, the US invasion of Afghanistan in 2001, and the US invasion of Iraq in 2003 and then the troop buildup in Iraq in 2007, known as the "surge," all led to increased violence, increased displacement, and consequently increased media coverage of the related refugee and IDP situations.

By far the greatest amount of attention is paid to the case of Palestinian refugees, as seen in Table 3.1. Figure 3.3 shows there was a spike in attention in 2002 with more than 250 articles being published that year in the *New York Times* on the violence in and around Israel and related mentions of Palestinian refugees. The Palestinian case is a unique one indeed, as while it is one of the largest displacement crises worldwide, the level of coverage is out of step with the scale of displacement. With roughly five million people displaced including the children

Violence sells

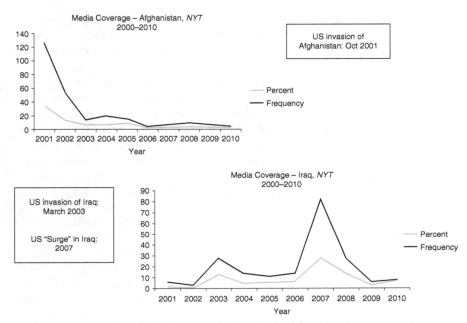

FIGURE 3.2. Attention to displacement in Iraq and Afghanistan (2001–2010)

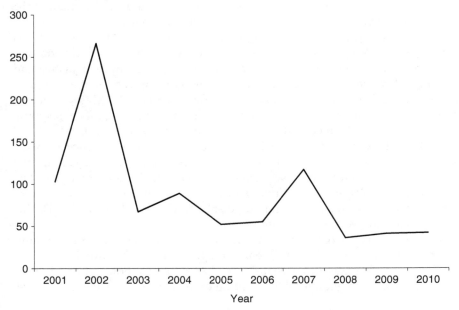

FIGURE 3.3. Attention to displaced Palestinians

born in exile, the nearly 900 articles across the decade is many times higher than the second largest displacement crisis worldwide – Colombia with an estimated four million people displaced including the children born during the displacement, which only saw 26 articles on their plight over the entire decade.

The cases of Chechnya, Lebanon, Georgia and Pakistan also suggest that it is violence that gets an issue on the agenda, with each case showing a large number of articles in a single year when there were particular escalations in the conflict and little attention across the rest of the decade otherwise. In these cases, we see spikes in attention in Chechnya with 20 articles in 2002 when that conflict came to a head with Chechen rebels taking hostages in a theater in Moscow, and the Russian government forcibly closing Chechen refugee camps on the border. We see attention turn to refugees in Lebanon with 30 articles 2006 during the "July War" or the 2006 Israel–Hezbollah War began by Hezbollah rocket attacks on southern Israeli towns. The UN Security Council, through Resolution 1701, expressed "its utmost concern at the continuing escalation of hostilities in Lebanon and Israel since Hizbollah's attack on Israel on 12 July 2006, which has already cause hundreds of deaths and injuries on both sides, extensive damage to civilian infrastructure and hundreds of thousands of internally displaced persons" and called for an end to the violence (UNSC 2006, 1). Similarly, we see attention to the forcibly displaced in Georgia with 38 articles in 2008 when conflict flared between Georgia and Russia in the "5 day war" in South Ossetia. Finally, we see the international media shine some attention on the forcibly displaced in Pakistan with 31 articles in 2009 when the Pakistani army launched a major offensive against the Taliban in the Swat Valley, which displaced more than 1.5 million people.

The violence and ethnic cleansing that begin in Darfur, Sudan in 2003, is the only case among the 61 that has been declared a genocide by the international community. That year the Sudan Liberation Army and the Justice and Equality Movement took up arms against the government for their oppression of the agricultural communities in Darfur – the Fur, the Masalit and the Zaghawa. Government forces responded with a disproportionate response and supported the Arab nomadic Janjaweed militia to systematically attack villages. Secretary of State Colin Powell declared the systematic violence genocide in testimony before the Senate Foreign Relations Committee in 2004 and the European Union described it as "tantamount to genocide" that same year. The level of violence was extreme with more than 300,000 people dead, many from starvation and disease, and 2.7 million displaced either as IDPs within Darfur or as refugees across the border into Chad.[1]

The Save Darfur Coalition formed in 2004 at a Darfur emergency summit organized by the US Holocaust Memorial Museum and the American Jewish World Service. It grew into a coalition of 180 religious, political and human rights groups. The highest level of attention to the issue was during 2004–2005

---

[1] BBC: http://news.bbc.co.uk/2/hi/africa/3496731.stm.

Violence sells 43

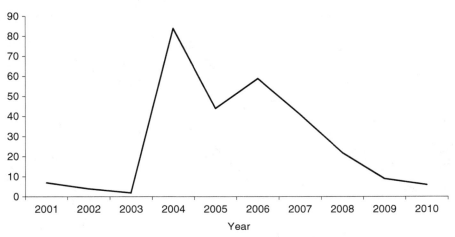

FIGURE 3.4. Attention to displacement in Sudan (Darfur) (2001–2010)

with a peak of 80 articles in 2004 – at the start of the genocide. This fits with the pattern of media coverage which focuses on the sensational and then loses interest as the violence becomes "normal." The Save Darfur Coalition and related advocacy groups continued to work to keep the issue on the agenda throughout the rest of the decade. This case shows the most sustained coverage with more than 20 articles per year for more than five years (see Figure 3.4).

The UN Security Council passed United Nations Security Council Resolution 1564 in 2004 determining "that the situation in Sudan constitutes a threat to international peace and security and to the stability in the region," the resolution called "upon the Government of Sudan and the rebel groups, particularly the Justice and Equality Movement and the Sudanese Liberation Army to work together under the auspices of the African Union to reach a political solution" and urged member states of the UN to "support the AU in these efforts including providing all equipment, logistical, financial, material and other resources necessary to support the rapid expansion of the African Union Mission" (UNSC 2004, 3). The United States and the EU provided support to the United Nations Mission in Sudan (UNMIS) and the African Union Mission in Sudan (AMIS). AMIS and UNMIS observers were sent to engage in proactive monitoring and later to ensure the implementation of the 2005 ceasefire agreement. Continued international pressure for a peace agreement led to the 2006 agreement with the Sudanese People's Liberation Army (SPLA) and the 2011 agreement with the Liberation and Justice Movement.

This is a case that it is difficult to parse out how much the level of violence was driving attention and how much advocacy by concerned groups was driving advocacy. The level of violence was extreme, 90 percent of the 257 articles on the topic discussed the level of violence. However, 77 percent of the articles mentioned a statement by the US government, the EU or/and EU member state

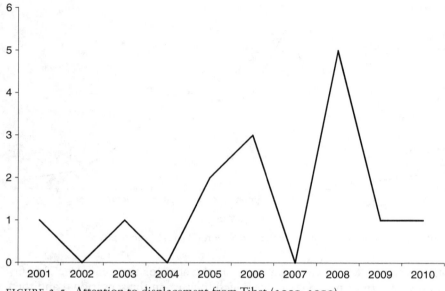
FIGURE 3.5. Attention to displacement from Tibet (2001–2010)

government, a UN official or an international NGO. UN policymakers or its agencies were mentioned 125 times across all the articles on Darfur across the decade, as little leverage as the UN may have, the organization does succeed in giving a voice to those that do not have one. Many of the large human rights and humanitarian aid organization commented in the news throughout the decade, describing the severity of the situation and stressing the need for action, including Human Rights Watch (quoted 8 times), Doctors Without Borders (10 times), the International Crisis Group (10), the Save Darfur Coalition (6) and the IRC (5). In the case of Darfur, steady attention by the international community, and international pressure and intervention in the form of African Union (AU) monitors helped pave the way for a peace agreement and a cessation of hostilities.

A second case that shows some evidence of the role of advocacy in getting an issue on the agenda is the case of Tibet (see Figure 3.5). The Tibetan community is one of the few with a strong and visible set of advocacy organizations speaking out on their behalf, including the International Campaign for Tibet and Students for a Free Tibet – regarding the human rights violations in China that have led to more than 150,000 refugees to flee across the Himalayas. We see spikes in coverage in 2006 (13 articles) – when a Romanian filmmaker captured a Chinese border patrol shooting two Tibetan refugees attempting to flee over the Himalayas. Chinese authorities claimed the refugees attacked the authorities and they shot in self-defense, but the video that captured the incident was picked up by human rights organizations and disseminated: showing a 25-year-old Buddhist nun being shot in the back as she walked slowly over a mountain ridge (Kahn, *New York Times*, 2006). In 2008, leading up to the Chinese-hosted Olympics there was a harsh crackdown by Chinese authorities on Tibetan activists and much attention to the proposed refugee march from Dharamsala, India (the largest community of Tibetan refugees) back to Lhasa (the capital of Tibet). However, while we see advocacy and protest as the reason for granting some international agenda space to Tibetan refugees, the level of attention is still quite low, with a total of only 10 stories on the human rights violations in Tibet and the related refugee crisis across the decade, with a maximum of five during the year of the Olympic protests.

Next I turn to the seven cases that are the focus of the rest of the book, five made it to the list of cases with more than 20 articles across the decade: Somalia (54 articles), Sri Lanka (36 articles), Burma/Myanmar (31 articles), Colombia (26 articles) and Uganda (20 articles). In each of these cases hundreds of thousands of people are displaced, in two (Colombia and Uganda) millions are displaced; the average of 2–3 stories per year of suffering on this scale is just one indication that the international community is largely unaware of their plight. In the case of refugees and IDPs from Bhutan and Bosnia/Croatia, the level of awareness was even lower.

Seven specific cases of violent conflict and varying attention

It is difficult to grasp a problem affecting 60 million people. Hard to imagine what that means, how a problem on that scale can be addressed. Sixty-one massive protracted displacement crises are similarly daunting – how can we comprehend them all simultaneously, on every continent, understand their histories and the current context?

The UNHCR notes: "Globally, one in every 122 humans is now either a refugee, internally displaced, or seeking asylum. If this were the population of a country, it would be the world's 24th biggest" (UNHCR 2015).

The UN High Commissioner for Refugees, António Guterres, argues:

We are witnessing a paradigm change, an unchecked slide into an era in which the scale of global forced displacement as well as the response required is now clearly dwarfing anything seen before … It is terrifying that on the one hand there is more and more impunity for those starting conflicts, and on the other there is seeming utter inability of the international community to work together to stop wars and build and preserve peace. (UNHCR 2015)

To understand international advocacy, national advocacy and local advocacy more deeply on all of these cases, I focus on seven specific cases in Europe, Asia, Africa and Latin America as a representative sample of the bigger problem. I present them each briefly here. These are cases that scholars, historians, activists and displaced representatives have described in much more detail elsewhere. These seven cases collectively involve millions of displaced persons, decades of conflict and hundreds of aid organizations. My purpose here is not a comprehensive history on each case, but rather a brief introduction so the reader knows the contours of the conflict and the conditions of the displaced so that they have some context when we turn to trying to understand advocacy on behalf of these specific displaced populations. No doubt readers will be familiar with some of these conflicts and crises, and unfamiliar with others. I also present data on the attention to each of these displacement crises over the past decade to give a sense of when these cases appear on the international agenda.

Bosnia-Herzegovina/Croatia

Croatian IDPs and refugees from Kosovo and Bosnia-Herzegovina still remained in camps in Croatia in 2008, unsolved cases left over from the wars of the breakup of former Yugoslavia in the 1990s. In *A Problem from Hell*, Samantha Power details the series of conflicts that unfolded beginning in 1991 as Serbia began an offensive to create an ethnically homogenous state. Ethnic cleansing and genocide happened in waves in Bosnia, with 200,000 Bosnians killed and more than two million displaced over the ensuing three-and-a-half years. In the UN "safe area" of Srebrenica in 1995, 8,000 Bosnian Muslims were killed in a systematic mass murder. The violence continued, flaring again in Kosovo in 1998 when the Kosovo Liberation Army attacked Serbian police and "Serbian forces swept into the region of Drenica and ... torched whole villages suspected of housing KLA loyalists. In the following year, some 3,000 Albanians were killed and some 300,000 others were expelled from their homes, their property burned and their livelihoods extinguished" (Powers 2002, 445). Many of the displaced fled or were flown north, to camps in Croatia.

This case is included for geographic variation but it is the smallest of the seven cases in numbers – with "only" a few thousand left as of 2008 when I was conducting fieldwork. A UN official described the status of the camps in 2008:

There are 8 collective centers in Croatia, one is specializing on returns. 1,600 BiH refugees and 309 from Kosovo. Fifty percent of refugees are still living in collective centers, others have found other places to live but remain with refugee status. The government plans to close them all – that is way Cepin was just closed, they are closing them and moving the cases to other collective centers. (Interview March 10, 2008)

Nearly all international NGOs and UN agencies have pulled out since this was no longer a conflict zone. Croatian Ministry of Interior officials described the situation as people waiting to die; elderly and disabled displaced persons had no options of returning home and little hope of resettlement in a third country.

It is perhaps not surprising then that there was very little coverage for most of the decade. In the case of Croatian IDPs, there was no coverage at all, in the case of refugees from Bosnia there was a high of seven stories at the beginning

Somalia/Kenya

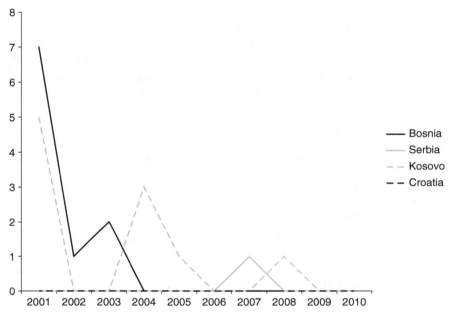

FIGURE 3.6. Attention to displacement from Bosnia and Croatia (2001–2010)

of the decade in 2001, but then no coverage, and for Kosovar refugees similarly a high of five news stories discussing their plight in 2001 but then that falls off with only one story in 2008 (see Figure 3.6). Most of the articles in the early part of the decade focused on stabilizing the region and on ensuring cooperation between ethnic and political groups and mention refugees as an afterthought. The articles that did focus on refugees were about their return home and the tension created between refugees and their neighbors. The articles that appear in 2003–2007 paint the situation as a lost cause. One journalist stated that millions remain displaced and "will probably never return" and another wrote that refugees in Kosovo were "no closer to going home" five years after fleeing Kosovo. These refugees and IDPs left in limbo a decade after the Yugoslav wars finally burned themselves out, were not on anyone's radar as a problem that needed solving.

Somalia/Kenya

Somalia has been described as a failed state by many international observers; after decades of civil war, more than two million have been internally and externally displaced, with more than 400,000 refugees in the Dadaab refugee camp complex 100 kilometers from the Somali border in Kenya. This number was up from the population of 270,000 that were housed in the camps during my fieldwork there in 2009. While Kenyan authorities officially closed the border in 2007, refugees continue to come. The drought in the Horn of Africa led to an increase in numbers through 2011 and 2012. Hundreds of new arrivals were coming each day, but the camps were too full to receive them so refugees that had walked for days set up makeshift tents. InterAction's 2007 annual report concisely reviews the long history of the conflict that led to the current displacement crisis:

Somalia has effectively remained a failed state since early 1991, persistently characterized by violence, famine, and chaos. In 2004, the Transitional Federal Government was established after a two-year reconciliation process, but it was replaced when the Union of Islamic Courts gained control of the capital. At the end of 2006 Ethiopia invaded Somalia, ousting the Union of Islamic Courts. Renewed heavy fighting involving the Ethiopians and opponents backed by Eritrea has caused a new flow of refugees and IDPs to flee, especially from Mogadishu and surrounding areas. (Ressler 2007, 5)

The primary insurgency group – Al Shabaab ("The Youth") has attacked refugees during their escape and has abducted aid workers in the area. It is reported to have ties to Al Qaeda and piracy in the Gulf of Aden. The International Crisis Group notes that the 2008 Djibouti peace talks accomplished little:

not least because the parts of the Islamist insurgency that have the most guns and territory are not participants. The key aim of its architects was to create a powerful political alliance, capable of stabilising the country, marginalising the radicals and stemming the tide of Islamist militancy. This was quickly made un-achievable by splits within the insurgent Alliance for the Re-liberation of Somalia (ARS) as well as the Transitional Federal Government, and the rapid advance by the parts of the opposition, in particular radical militias like Al-Shabaab, that reject the process. (ICG 2008a, *i*)

Somalia is unstable and the border regions are unstable. Aid workers serving the Dadaab camp complex live in a barbwire secured compound.

According to the UN's security system, the entire North East province of Kenya is classified a security level four – indicating a level of substantial threat. Trips to the various camps that make up the Dadaab complex need to be taken under a security escort to mitigate the risks, some of which include raids by bandits and attacks by forces loyal to al-Shabab. (Essa 2011).

The Dadaab camp complex was set up in 1991, originally to house 90,000 refugees, the camps are long past capacity, and conditions are terrible. Rations and materials are in under-supply; refugees sit in white tents in the blazing hot sun, in an arid desert, with nothing to do and no hope of returning home. The story of one refugee recounted by a *Telegraph* reporter is similar to the hundreds of thousands of others:

"We had no choice but to leave our homes. The journey has been too tiring, we were chased by wild animals. It was terrifying." Aden Issack Ibrahim was one of 30 people who had all decided to leave Sakow, their village in Somalia. The children were

Somalia/Kenya

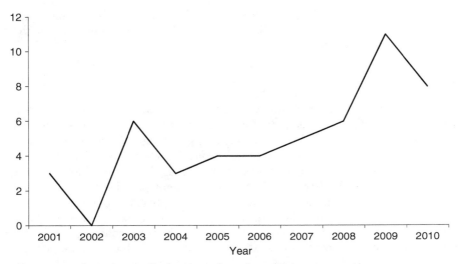

FIGURE 3.7. Attention to displacement from Somalia (2001–2010)

barefoot, clutching empty water canisters. Between them, the villagers only had a handful of possessions, including a single live chicken. "Our children haven't eaten for days and we are tired and hungry. We are begging for help from the UN, from anyone in a position of power." He said his village had no future. It had become an arid wasteland like so much of Somalia, where the rains have failed two years running and famine may not be far away. The twin curses of drought and endless civil war had convinced them they had no choice but to leave. (Brown 2011)

Refugees are not allowed to move freely or to work. Violence within the camps and around the camps is a major concern. As an analysis of the psychosocial needs of refugees in the camps reports: "Violence directed especially at women and children are common occurrences and with far reaching psychological consequences in the three refugee camps. Common in the camps are sexual and gender based violence (SGBV) basically involving physical and psychological abuse of women. In 2005 there were 656 reported cases of SGBV" (Papadopoulos and Ljubinkovic 2007, 17).

Considering the scale of displacement, which got progressively worse at the end of the decade as a famine spread out across the Horn of Africa, ballooning the already over-stretched camps to a population of 400,000, it should be quite shocking that the issue only received a maximum of 11 news stories in 2009 (see Figure 3.7). For most of the decade, while thousands upon thousands continued to flee every year, we never see more than six news articles per year until 2009 when there was a sharp up-tick in violence, as the *Times* reported:

Fighting in Somalia has forced more than 100,000 people to flee their homes since May 8, the United Nations refugee agency said Tuesday. The agency said Somalis were experiencing atrocities nearly every day, including rape and the shelling of civilian areas.

"It's a critical humanitarian situation, with regular atrocities being committed," said William Spindler, spokesman for the United Nations High Commissioner for Refugees in Geneva. (*New York Times* 2009)

Bhutan/Nepal

For most people the remote mountain kingdom of Bhutan is not on their radar. If they have heard of it, it is likely for the concept of GNH – Gross National Happiness – a term coined by Bhutan's King Jigme Singye Wangchuck in 1972 as a counter concept to Gross National Product (GNH 2012). The idea has received increased attention in the past decade as Westerners have become more concerned with "happiness" and development practitioners have been frustrated by the domination of GDP as a measure of development. But while the Government of Bhutan likes to advertise that its citizens are among the happiest in the world, it is much more reserved about discussing the forced expulsion of nearly 100,000 of its citizens (about one-sixth of its total population). Amnesty International calls it "one of the most protracted and neglected refugee crises in the world" (AI 2012).

The Bhutanese government, very concerned about protecting its unique Buddhist national identity, passed a series of measures in the mid-1980s to strip ethnic Nepalese (or Lhotshampas) of their citizenship rights. The Lhotshampas had been residents for generations but were majority Hindu and spoke a different language. What began as discriminatory measures ended with revocation of citizenship and the mass expulsion of 90,000 Lhotshampas, who fled across northern India into Nepal; as of 2010, there were an estimated 103,000 refugees in the camps in southeastern Nepal.

Conditions in the camps are harsh, since refugees are not allowed to work they are dependent on the international aid community; food rations are insufficient and health outcomes are poor, as an indicator: 28 infants die per 1,000 live births in the camps (substantially higher than the four deaths per 1,000 births in Europe or six per 1,000 births in the United States). Families live in mud and thatched-roof huts, which collapse during the monsoons and catch fire at regular intervals due to open cooking methods and the incredible population density of the camps. During the monsoon season parts of the camp flood regularly with 2–3 feet of standing water since they are located on unwanted land in a river valley, the huts are wet, the clothes are wet, the blankets are wet, and the children get skin infections. The pit latrines fill up. One raised slatted wood platform per hut serves as the family's bed. An entire generation has been raised in the camps, never having known the outside world, never having had a proper bath, never experiencing privacy, eating the same food rations for a lifetime.

Figure 3.8 gives an indication of how off-the-radar this case is, with only two stories about these refugees in 2001 and one in 2007 and 2008 each. The two extremely brief articles in 2001 mention the foreign secretaries of

Bhutan/Nepal

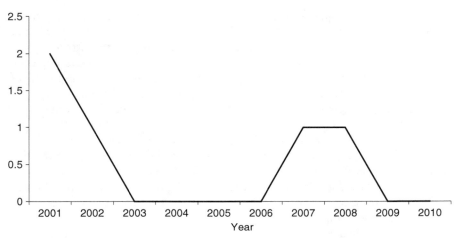

FIGURE 3.8. Attention to displacement from Bhutan (2001–2010)

Nepal and Bhutan meeting for talks about the refugees. In 2002 part of an article devoted to the UNGA's Special Assembly on Children mentions a 16-year-old Bhutanese refugee who has brought a 50,000-signature petition to several prominent international leaders, but the cause is not taken up. And in 2007–2008, there are one-line mentions of the refugees as the group excluded from the elections in Bhutan. There is no mention of advocacy on behalf of this exiled community.

While this is a case that has been off the global agenda, there was ultimately high-level negotiations behind the scenes, aimed at changing the minds of Nepali and American officials on the question of resettlement in a third country. Aid workers on the ground attributed the negotiated agreement to an unwillingness by the Europeans and the Americans to continue to fund the camps in a situation that seemed to have no solution – as it became clear Bhutan would not allow repatriation and Nepal would not allow integration.

In 2007, there was finally a breakthrough when a third country resettlement plan was drawn up. In 2008:

For the first time in 17 years there was progress towards durable solutions for refugees in Nepal. The Core Working Group – an informal group of resettlement countries – called for the urgent implementation of comprehensive solutions, offering third-country resettlement as a solution independent of the outcome of the bilateral process between Nepal and Bhutan. The Government has agreed to large-scale resettlement within the framework of a comprehensive approach. The United States has announced its readiness to receive 60,000 refugees for resettlement and has begun preparations for large-scale resettlement processing. Canada has offered 5,000 places over the next five years, and other countries including Australia and New Zealand have indicated their commitment to provide resettlement places. (UNHCR Global Appeal 2008–2009, 232)

The Core Working Group consisted of the governments of Australia, Canada, Denmark, the Netherlands, New Zealand, Norway and the United States. A communiqué released on May 16, 2012 stated their "strong desire to see a comprehensive and sustainable resolution for the protracted refugee situation of Bhutanese refugees in Nepal. Indeed, the refugees living in Nepal cannot wait indefinitely. The physical, social, and emotional costs of living in the camps with uncertain futures are too high. In addition, the international community cannot be expected to continue to assist the Bhutanese refugee camps indefinitely" (Core Working Group 2007). Here we see one of the major drivers behind the seemingly sudden action – that the international community did not want to endlessly fund the refugee aid, when it finally became clear to them after 15 years that Nepal would not allow them to naturalize and Bhutan would under no circumstances let them back in their country, it was either funding endless encampment or resettlement.

The Core Countries had leverage – in that they provided a solution to the government of Nepal and had the power to implement it – that is, taking the refugees in, primarily to the United States. However, even the powerful Core Countries had little leverage over the government of Bhutan, and no matter how much they advocated, they were unable to persuade the Bhutanese government to budge on its position. Though the communiqué was essentially the result of giving up on repatriation, the Core Countries still included a last plea to Bhutan, the weakness of the plea reminiscent of Human Rights Watch's call to the Somali parties to the conflict:

We welcome the stated commitment of the Royal Government of Bhutan to find a just and durable solution to the situation of the refugees in the camps. We encourage the Royal Government of Bhutan to work with the UNHCR and the Government of Nepal to provide written terms and conditions of return, including on property rights, and a clear timeline for implementation of agreed commitments for those who have already been identified for return and for those who may wish to return in the future. We also call on the government of Bhutan to ensure conditions within Bhutan that will not cause further refugee outflows in the future.

Sadly, no matter how much the international community "welcomes," "encourages" or "calls on" the government of Bhutan to grant its expelled citizens their human rights – it fails to do so.

While the announcement of massive resettlement was celebrated by many, it was not by all and the process did not go smoothly, an aid worker I interviewed discussed the attacks on refugee leaders, the International Organization for Migration (IOM) compound, and buses transporting refugees to the airport to be resettled (UNHCR May 6, 2008). Many of the refugee leaders feared that massive resettlement would release the pressure on the Bhutanese government to allow the refugees to return home, destroying their chances of ever repatriating to their homeland. To try to stop the process rogue refugee activists, some suspected to have been trained by Nepali Maoists (that in turn are suspected of being trained by Chinese Maoists) threw improvised explosive devices into the IOM staff compound in Damak – the main town which serves as the base of operations of the aid organizations, and threatened refugee leaders that were supportive of resettlement. A writer for *Refugee Watch* describes the rationale:

Despite the incessant concern of the refugees on all options of durable solutions, the core group has so far given importance only on resettlement when repatriation should have been the priority and thus the apathetic stand on repatriation. Giving respite on the perpetrator, the Bhutan regime, has angered most of the Bhutanese refugees, especially the youths. The youths who belong to revolutionary organizations have been vehemently opposing the resettlement process, which preceded the repatriation, the first option of the refugees. (Subba 2008)

The refugees had little leverage to get the Core Countries to prioritize a durable solution they themselves did not have the leverage to implement.

Burma/Thailand

When Aung San Suu Kyi won the Nobel Peace Prize in 1991, it put the Burma/Myanmar conflict on the international agenda for a time. Under house arrest for the better part of 21 years since 1989, Aung San Suu Kyi was a democratic activist in a country run by a military junta.

Less known is the fact that the Burmese junta has been continually fighting with more than 30 different ethnic groups since its violent takeover of the country in 1984; one of the most intense areas of fighting has been in the traditional semi-autonomous states of Karen and Karenni. One hundred and ninety thousand refugees have been forced across the border into Thailand where they have been languishing for 20 years in refugee camps. Conditions in the camps are harsh. Similar to Bhutan it is a tropical area, so rains cause constant damage to the mud huts. Like Dadaab, the overcrowding is oppressive. Tham Hin refugee camp housed 46,000 refugees in just a few square kilometers in 2008.

As Figure 3.9 shows, international attention to the massive displacement crises from violence in Burma/Myanmar is quite low with just a handful of stories over the decade, with a slight up-tick in 2007 and again in 2009 with a high of 10 stories in 2009.

Content analysis of the media coverage shows some evidence of advocacy playing a role in getting these issues on the agenda of the international community – advocacy by both the US government and human rights groups. The US Campaign for Burma is the main NGO that is referenced in the articles, indicating some level of successful activism by them. There is also repeated mention of the Thai-based Burmese magazine called *Irrawaddy*, whose staff is composed of exiled Burmese journalists, led by Director Aung Zaw. They have contacts inside Burma so have access to information that other news sources do not.

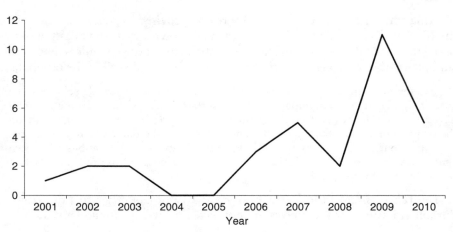

FIGURE 3.9. Attention to displacement from Burma/Myanmar (2001–2010)

In 2002–2003, there was media coverage due to allegations of rape being used as a weapon of war against civilians. The media coverage seems to be, in part, caused by the US State Department, which twice conducted investigations into the rape charges and issued a report by the State Department's Bureau of Democracy, Human Rights and Labor.

In 2006 the narrative regarding the Bush administration's involvement with the issue begins when thousands of Burmese refugees are resettled in the United States. In September 2007 there is the first mention of the US First Lady Laura Bush's engagement with the campaign for Burma and a brief description of her activism in the past year. In 2006 there is also a burst of media attention regarding the US success in putting Burma on the United Nations Security Council (UNSC) agenda.

Similar to the case of Bhutanese refugees in Nepal, and just a year earlier – in 2006 – we finally saw a breakthrough and a durable solution for a large portion of the refugees from Burma. In 2006, the Bush administration announced it would begin the processing of 9,300 refugees in Thailand (Swarns 2006). The decision took almost immediate effect:

> The number of Burmese refugees coming to the US shot up eight-fold in the past fiscal year. About 14,000 Burmese refugees were resettled in the US in 2007. The year before, only 1,612 refugees came from Burma. The dramatic spike is the result of a pledge by the US government to resettle tens of thousands of Burmese refugees because of the protracted nature of their plight, and "due to the lack of any other durable solution," according to the State Department. (Burma to New York 2007)

Why after decades did the United States finally decide to make this dramatic and generous policy change is a point of speculation. Some aid workers I spoke with attribute it to Laura Bush's personal involvement with the case. As mentioned earlier, Buddhist monks took to the streets in political protest, igniting the "Saffron Rebellion." The junta responded with a violent crackdown, which was captured on video by Burmese undercover reporters secretly filming the protests and shared with the world through the 2008 documentary *Burma VJ*. During the crackdown, Laura Bush began speaking out even more on the issue. *Time* magazine interviewed her on the topic:

US First Lady Laura Bush rarely speaks out strongly on foreign affairs. One exception: Burma. She has been a consistent critic of the military junta and a supporter of jailed opposition leader Aung San Suu Kyi ... The First Lady spoke to TIME's Hannah Beech about the latest anti-regime protests in Burma. Excerpts:
"I've been interested in Burma for a long time. I hosted a roundtable during the UNGA [United Nations General Assembly] last year. I've been briefed by Ibrahim Gambari [the UN Secretary General's special advisor on Burma]. Like many people, especially women, I got interested because of Aung San Suu Kyi, and I learned about Burma and how she represents the hopes of the people of Burma, and how those hopes were being dashed by her house arrest and the fact that her party won the elections and never had the opportunity to have power at all. I did work with women Senators to make sure we sent out a letter to Ban Ki-Moon. I've also met with ethnic minorities and talked with them.
It's important for governments to put as much pressure [as possible] on the military regime to listen to the people. That's all these protesters are asking to do. That's what national reconciliation is about. [The people of Burma] don't want violence or civil war.
What can we really do, what can we do for national reconciliation? Certainly, one thing we can do to work toward national reconciliation in Burma is for the Security Council to speak out formally. Will that work? I don't know. But it's the least we can do. That's what Aung San Suu Kyi wants, she wants a diplomatic reconciliation. Those are the first things we can do and then move from there". (Beech 2007)

While it is difficult to say how much First Lady Bush's public advocacy and behind-the-scenes advocacy with her husband played a role, one thing is for certain, the announcement to accept just fewer than 10,000 refugees in 2006 quickly expanded to become a success story. This was one of her first public political statements, and she became an active advocate on the issue, keeping the topic in the press through 2008 and joining the long-time campaign calling for the release of the Burmese pro-democracy activist, Aung San Suu Kyi, from house arrest, which finally happened after 15 years in captivity in 2010.

While resettlement was picking up pace, violence continued and advocacy groups kept a spotlight on it. In 2007, there was media coverage of the release of satellite photos of rural Burma that confirmed reports of human rights abuses. The US Campaign for Burma was integral in getting the photos released. In 2008, the US Campaign for Burma launched a campaign that used celebrities to gain attention for the issue.

Details about violent crackdowns by the Burmese government against a range of opposition groups surfaced in 2009. The government wanted to quell opposition before the adoption of a disputed constitution. There were reports of violence and renewed displacement of thousands as the government tried to deal a final blow to rebel groups. One article mentioned that the June offensive was potentially inspired by the Sri Lankan government's successful crackdown on its own insurgents in May – President Rajapakse of Sri Lanka even visited Yangon to share his experiences. In 2010, as results of the first election appeared, there were more allegations of violence.

On July 1, 2009, the UNHCR announced "that it had resettled the 50,000th Burmese refugee from Thailand's nine border refugee camps as part of the world's largest refugee resettlement programme" (Wade 2009). As of that date, there were around 140,000 refugees still in the camps. The Democratic Voice of Burma noted in 2009 that:

> The ongoing conflict in Burma's western Karen state, which borders Thailand, has forced another 4000 refugees into Thailand in the last month, although few of these have ended up in camps. The UN High Commissioner for Refugees (UNHCR) has been operating the programme since 2004, with the number of resettlements rising dramatically in 2005 when the US opened its doors to refugees from the camps. UNHCR spokesperson William Spindler said that resettlement in a third country had become the only viable option for Burmese refugees in Thailand's camps, given problems settling permanently in Thailand and the dangers of returning to Burma. (Wade 2009)

As discussed in Chapter 1, return and local integration often remain elusive solutions to many displaced populations.

Uganda

The insurgency of Joseph Kony's Lord's Resistance Army terrorized the people of northern Uganda for two decades, with more than 1.5 million people internally displaced and more than 30,000 children abducted and forced to be child soldiers. This conflict may be the most well known to readers due to the successful advocacy campaign that reached more than 100 million viewers: KONY 2012 by the advocacy group Invisible Children. While it rocketed on to the global agenda in March 2012, this conflict had been burning since 1986 when Kony began his armed insurgency against the government of Uganda in an attempt to establish a theocratic government based on the Bible and the Ten Commandments.

This was the same year that President Yoweri Museveni became president but Uganda had already had a long history of violence. Following independence from the United Kingdom in 1962, two dictators came to power in succession that made use of extreme violence to suppress opposition and dissent: Idi Amin (1971–1979, more than 300,000 killed) and Milton Obote (1980–1985, another 100,000 killed) (CIA Factbook 2012). Museveni is credited with bringing peace to the south of Uganda, but despite many military operations aimed at hunting down Kony and his men, the LRA continued to operate in northern Uganda, moving back and forth across the porous borders with South Sudan, Democratic Republic of the Congo (DRC) and the Central African Republic, evading capture by government forces for the next quarter of a century. The KONY 2012 campaign documented the nature of the violence: children were abducted from their homes at night. Boys were forced to be child soldiers; usually being forced first to murder their own parents and siblings so that they have nowhere and no one to return to. Girls forced to be "bush wives" – sex slaves to Kony's militants. Kony's forces would often capture citizens and cut off their lips, noses and ears and send them back to their villages – spreading the sense of terror. As fewer and fewer forces volunteered to fight for Kony, more and more children were abducted, the estimate stands at 30,000 children abducted and forced to endure a nightmare of trauma until they were killed, died in the bush or escaped.

In the mid-1990s, Kony launched a wave of brutal attacks that led the government of Uganda to institute a new policy of "protected villages" – these were essentially forced encampment in an effort to consolidate the rural population of the north into areas that were easier for government forces to protect. However, Acholi (the ethnic majority in the north) found little protection there and many criticized the government's actions as another indication of the south's approach to the population in the north as second-class citizens. Citizens had little choice about their displacement, and many aid workers I spoke within the field said IDPs were warned that if they tried to leave the camps they would be shot by the guards supposedly protecting the camps. As Patrick argues:

> Early on, the protected villages policy could have been considered in keeping with the UN's Guiding Principles on Internal Displacement (1998). Principles 6 and 7, for example, allow for displacement when the security of the civilians or imperative military reasons so demand. These same principles, however, also clearly specify that displacement should last no longer than required, and that authorities should ensure that the movement of civilian populations is conducted in satisfactory conditions of safety, with adverse effects minimized, and with free and informed consent of those displaced. Nearly a decade after their establishment, it is difficult to reconcile the continued existence of the villages with the requirement that displacement last "no longer than required." Continued looting and atrocities against civilians in the villages are a clear indication that they are not "protected." Nor has a military victory over the LRA been achieved. (2005)

The internment continued however for another decade, and at the height of the conflict 1.6 million people, or almost 90 percent of the population of the north, were living in internal displacement camps. A generation of children was born in the camps, with no memory of their villages, no idea how to till the land, or their traditional way of life, and constantly at risk of attack.

Each time the government launched operations aimed at finding and capturing Kony, his forces would retreat across the border into Sudan. Many observers suspected al-Bashir's administration of supporting the LRA, since the border insecurity provided additional support for the need for military rule in South Sudan.

The LRA's only known backer during its two decades of existence has been the Sudanese government, which provided arms as well as shelter for LRA combatants in parts of southern Sudan. At least officially, however, Sudan ended its support for Kony and his rebels as a result of pressure by the Ugandan and US governments, and allowed a major Ugandan military offensive, Operation Iron Fist, inside southern Sudan beginning in March 2002. (Patrick 2005)

During my fieldwork in Gulu and the surrounding district in 2008 there were unconfirmed reports of an LRA attack on an SPLA camp just over the border into Sudan, and similar reports the summer before when I first traveled to the country for preliminary research.

Some learned of these horrors in part through a multi-country advocacy campaign called Gulu Walk, started in 2005. Gulu is the largest town in northern Uganda. Tens of thousands of children would walk each night to sleep on the streets in Gulu in effort to protect themselves from murder and abduction from the camps. This was a clear signal of the insecurity of the "protected villages." The Walk began as a 30-day attention-raising campaign in one town, and spread to more than 100 cities, in 16 countries (GuluWalk 2012). In 2005, Dateline highlighted the issue in an interview with a top UN official:

Around northern Uganda, little children who don't find a safe place at night are in danger. And so are adults. People who are found by the rebels can be burnt to death, or beyond recognition. Body parts are cut off – noses, lips, ears, fingers. Jan Egeland is the United Nation's head of disaster relief. He's seen it all. But nothing like this. "His is terror like no other terror," he says. "I've been in a hundred countries. I've been working with human rights, peace, and humanitarian problems for 25 years. I was shocked to my bones, seeing what happened in Uganda. For me, this is one of the biggest scandals of our time and generation." The root of this trauma is a civil war that has raged for 19 years in northern Uganda, almost unnoticed by the rest of the world. (Morrison and Sandler 2005)

The squalor and deprivation in the camps is difficult to convey. Morrison and Sandler capture the scene to some degree:

On the scale of sheer misery, there's little that can top Pabbo. About 63,000 souls are jammed into a vast sea of tiny, round mud-huts, ten to a room or more. There is one water well for every five thousand people. There's malnutrition, malaria, cholera, HIV. People here have grown accustomed to tragedy upon tragedy. In the past year alone, Pabbo has been burned out, flooded out, and attacked constantly. But if life in the camp is dreadful, outside it is a catalog of horrors. Children are taught early that to stray to the edges of Pabbo, for fun or firewood, is to risk being abducted, or raped or hacked to death by the rebels. (2005)

In 2005 a series of failed peace agreements began, each time with Kony agreeing to ceasefires or peace talks and then reneging. That same year the International Criminal Court announced an international arrest warrant for Kony and four of his deputies. In 2006, a Cessation of Hostilities agreement was signed, and then again he reneged. Then Kony began using the International Criminal Court (ICC) warrant as a bargaining chip – arguing that he would not come out of the bush unless the warrant was lifted. In October 2011,

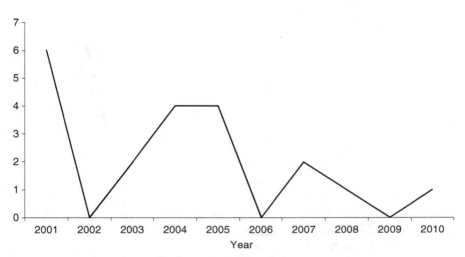

FIGURE 3.10. Attention to displacement in Uganda (2001–2010)

the US government sent in military advisors to aid government troops to find and arrest Kony. Reports in 2012 placed him and his army somewhere in the Central African Republic.

Despite the level of violence and the scale of displacement resulting from this conflict this issue was largely off the international agenda, with only six stories in 2001 and four stories in 2004–2005 (see Figure 3.10). The majority of articles in which Uganda is mentioned are about refugees from other nations entering Uganda. The few articles that focus on northern Uganda are, without exception, one paragraph long and give no background information or description of the conflict. The most important news of 2001, an article that stated that the ICC had issued arrest warrants for members of the LRA, was brief and did not even mention the name "Lord's Resistance Army." Even in the only full article written about refugee camps, the conflict is vague and only mentioned in passing: "Fighting in northern Uganda, where rebels who purport to fight for the Ten Commandments abduct children to reinforce their ranks and chop off the lips and ears of those who dare resist, has taken an estimated 100,000 lives." It is even more surprising since there was some organized advocacy around this issue including Gulu Walk starting in 2005 and the Invisible Children documentary and ensuing public education campaign that began in 2006.

Sri Lanka

The 25-year-long civil war in Sri Lanka between the LTTE (Liberation Tigers of Tamil Eelam) rebel movement, representing the Tamil Hindu minority fighting for an autonomous Tamil homeland in northeast Sri Lanka, and the government of Sri Lanka, representing the Sinhala Buddhist majority, ended in

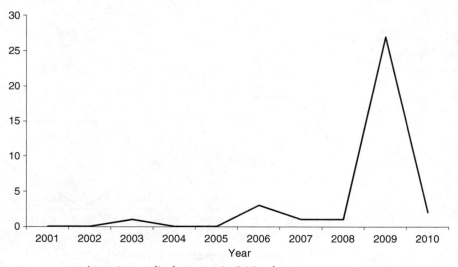

FIGURE 3.11. Attention to displacement in Sri Lanka (2001–2010)

2009. During the course of the conflict an estimated 80,000–100,000 people were killed and 200,000 displaced.

Figure 3.11 further shows that lack of attention is the norm, as well as the power of violence in getting an issue on the agenda in the Global North. Despite all the violence and displacement for more than two decades we see almost no attention whatsoever to Sri Lanka's plight until a handful of stories in 2006 when we see the worst violence since the 2002 ceasefire. More than 200,000 people were assumed to have been displaced in four months. Later that year the LTTE expelled all European truce monitors at the Sri Lankan Monitoring Mission due to the EU labeling it a terrorist group. In 2008 the UNHCR announced that more than 12,000 families were displaced in just a few months.

But it is in 2009 when government forces made a final push bombarding rebel forces (and innocent civilians in the vicinity) until they retreated to the northern beaches of the island and then killed the rebel leader. In May 2009, the government of Sri Lanka declared victory over the LTTE. In the year after the victory, however, 100,000 remained in camps while the government sought to interview everyone and weed out former LTTE combatants, the majority of 150,000 that were allowed to leave internment camps were not able to return home but were held in "transit centers" (Patten 2010). Critics argued that President Mahinda Rajapaksa's policies exacerbated grievances rather than responded to them, and observers argued that the peace was tenuous as long as Sinhala majority parties continued to fail to incorporate Tamils into mainstream politics (ICG 2010). The strong NGO presence continued as the post-conflict conditions remained fragile. Some international media attention continued, covering the presidential election that took place on January 26,

2010 between the president that brought about the end of the war, President Mahinda Rajapaksa, and the general that led the army to the victory over the Tamils, General Sarath Fonseka (Polgreen 2010).

While the escalating violence is the primary focus of the coverage, there is also mention of high-level advocacy by US and European government officials. In April 2009, the *New York Times* began to write almost daily articles, often mentioning Hillary Clinton, the UNSC, and Indian government critiques of the Sri Lankan government. This same month the UN Under-Secretary-General for Humanitarian Affairs, as well as the French and British foreign ministers (representing the EU) visited Sri Lanka, and while their missions were unsuccessful, they did achieve some attention. The allegations of massive war crimes on both sides definitely spurred many of the articles in May. After the LTTE leader was killed, and the war officially over, the media coverage decreased. There are no articles at all in June, and in July the main discussion is international actors feeling culpable in the internment camps since they are providing the funding for them. This case is the most striking in the attention to extreme displays of violence and apathy otherwise.

Colombia

Violence and displacement in Colombia have a history that dates back to *La Violencia*, or "the Era of Violence," a period of conflict from 1948 to 1965 between the Colombian Conservative and Liberal parties. The violence began in 1948 with the assassination of the Liberal leader Jorge Eliécer Gaitán in April 1948; the fighting that ensued left an estimated 200,000 dead (ICG 2002, 2).

The FARC (*Fuerzas Armadas Revolucionarias de Colombia-Ejército del Pueblo* – Revolutionary Armed Forces of Colombia) rose out of the "Era of Violence" with support from the USSR in 1965 but underwent a significant transformation from its Communist roots. At the same time, the ELN (*Ejército de Liberación Nacional* – National Liberation Army) was also formed with close ties to Cuba (ICG 2002). In addition to these two leftist insurgency groups, a number of other smaller guerrilla groups also sprang up including the Maoist *Ejército Popular de Liberación* (EPL) and M-19 (ICG 2002, 4).

In response to the activities of these leftist groups, the "paramilitaries" mobilized, ostensibly to protect landowners from attacks, kidnapping and extortion, but the growth of the paramilitaries was intimately tied up with the growth of the drug trade throughout the 1980s. The "death-squad *Muerte a Secuestradores* (Death to Kidnappers), founded by the Medellín cartel in 1981, constituted a precursor of today's AUC (United Self-Defence Groups of Colombia)" (ICG 2002).

International Crisis Group researchers followed FARC developments through the 1990s:

After the collapse of the Soviet Union in 1991, the FARC went its own way in the vast isolation of rural Colombia. Bereft of any meaningful ideological ties and financed mostly by extortion, kidnapping and "taxes" obtained in exchange for protecting drug traffickers and thousands of small and large coca farmers – perhaps their only remaining true rural support base – the FARC significantly expanded its ranks, consolidated its territorial control, including in smaller urban centres, and enhanced its military capability. It became a national insurgency, with military fronts in almost all parts of the country. (ICG 2002)

Throughout the 1980s and 1990s, the drug trafficking business expanded, primarily cocaine, with all armed groups benefiting from the profits, and during this period many attempts at peace building were initiated and failed. A number of presidents proposed peace plans, ceasefire agreements and amnesty programs but with little success, the demobilization of some small insurgency groups was coupled with the increasing strength of the FARC. By the early 2000s, there were an estimated 155,000 soldiers in Colombia's regular military, 17,000 fighters and 10,000 militiamen in FARC, 3,500 in ELN, and 8,000 paramilitary fighters in the AUC – a total of 220,500 armed parties to the conflict in a population of 40 million.

By the beginning of the 2000s Colombia provided most of the cocaine and an estimated 75 percent of the heroin to the American market. Rapidly expanding drug production and the continuing violence led the US and Colombian governments to devise the 1999 "Plan Colombia," which was to be a peace plan and aid package that supported economic development and counter-narcotics programs roughly 50/50. The plan came under intense criticism however when the Clinton administration failed to release all of the promised US$7.5 billion and of those funds that were transferred 80 percent were for counter-narcotics and only 20 percent went to economic development (ICG 2002, 13). "Colombia has advanced from receiving barely US$17 million in narcotics assistance and virtually no other economic or military aid in 1996 to being the top recipient of US anti-narcotics assistance world-wide and the third-largest recipient globally (first in Latin America) of US combined economic and security support" (ICG 2002). The Bush administration continued and increased funding for "Plan Colombia."

The election of President Alvaro Uribe in 2002 ushered in a new and much more hard-lined approach to the insurgents and armed groups. It was during the campaign for that election that Ingrid Betancourt, who was running against Uribe, was kidnapped by the FARC and held in captivity until she was rescued by a bold Colombian security forces operation in 2008. Uribe increased security forces, cracked down on the FARC and demobilized the paramilitaries through the 2005 "Justice and Peace Law" (ICG 2007; 2008b). While many credit him with the increased security in urban areas and decreased kidnappings, the "demobilized" paramilitaries and insurgents morphed into "New Illegal Armed Groups" (or NIAGs) – narco-traffickers that continued to terrorize civilian populations and displace communities from their land (ICG 2012).

By June 2008, 2,649,139 people were displaced according to government figures, and 4,361,355 people according to one of the key Colombian NGOs advocating for displaced rights, *Consultoría para los Derechos Humanos y el Desplazamiento* (CODHES). The Internal Displacement Monitoring Center noted: "an alarming trend of rising internal displacement has been registered since 2006, and the highest rate of displacement in 23 years was recorded in the first semester of 2008" (IDMC 2008, 8).

The pattern of violence is similar across the country, armed groups, whether leftist insurgents, rightist paramilitaries or NIAGs murder, rape and threaten civilians to push them off the land for economic gain (through narcotic cultivation) or for strategic gain vis-à-vis other armed groups. "Human rights defenders and representatives of internally displaced populations are regularly targeted; at least eight leaders of IDP organisations were killed in the first six months of 2008" (IDMC 2008, 11). The vast majority of displacement is from rural areas to the outskirts of urban areas. The displaced live in squalid conditions, with sub-standard housing, lack of access to income-generating activities and without the resources to provide food or medical care for themselves or their families. These "land invasion" urban slums are controlled by paramilitaries in parts, and beset with drugs and violence.

New York Times journalist Juan Forero interviewed residents in Soacha where I did fieldwork for the chapters that follow, and describes the scene:

[Soacha] is a kind of halfway house between urban slum and refugee camp. The inhabitants live as "internally displaced persons," a term the world's bureaucrats use to describe refugees who stay in their own country, victims of war who were abruptly uprooted from homes elsewhere in Colombia, either by Marxist guerrillas or right-wing paramilitaries ... the ethnic background of the inhabitants is the first indication that they came from elsewhere. Many are Afro-Colombians from Choco, a jungle region near the Panamanian border that could not be more different from the windswept Andes location of Soacha, which has a population of several hundred thousand.

The migrants say they face discrimination when they seek jobs, which are always hard to find in Colombia. They were poor where they came from, but they did not need money in the countryside, nor jobs, for that matter. "Things were easy," said Roberto Camacho, 54, a community leader. "We had farms. We had fish. We could hunt. Here everything is about money. You need it for everything." (Forero 2004, 4)

More than 15,000 displaced persons are living in the slums that are Soacha, the stories of what drove people there are similar, as one interviewee described to me: armed men come at night and ask a man to sell them his land for a small sum, if he refuses they tell him his widow will sell it for less tomorrow. "These families have borne witness to massacres, detentions, and the disappearance of family members or their neighbors," explains an MSF aid worker. "They have been harassed by armed groups, 'taxed' for money and property, and in some cases they have been forced to flee to save their children from forced recruitment" (MSF 2005).

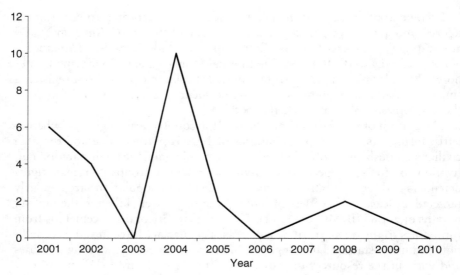

FIGURE 3.12. Attention to displacement in Colombia (2001–2010)

Despite the scale of the displacement and the level of the violence, as seen in Chapter 2 – there was no coverage in 2010 in any of the European or American papers about this massive displacement crisis. However, earlier in the decade there was some attention to the issue with nine articles appearing in the *New York Times* in 2004 (see Figure 3.12).

But there was no particular increase in violence in 2004, nor in displacement, this happened in 2008, the year I was conducting fieldwork. There was no major policy change; there was a short visit by a UN official and a quick few-hour visit by President Bush. What is interesting is that this increase in attention does not seem to be attributable to anything other than the Latin American Desk Officer from the *New York Times* being a native of Colombia, writing out of the Bogota office. He left for the *Washington Post* in 2006 and we see a drop off in coverage of the Colombia displacement situation. As Joachim argues, successful advocacy is the result of a myriad of factors, chance being one of them. In the case of Colombia, there is not a strong social science theory that can explain when the international community bothers to shine a light on the violence and displacement there – it is not driven by violence, geopolitics or advocacy, but rather a lone desk officer with a concern for his country.

Conclusions

This chapter has shown that when it comes to getting an issue of massive displacement on the global agenda, failure is the norm. The majority, 60 percent of these massive displacement crises, get no agenda space whatsoever. For those that do achieve some level of attention, maintaining it is even harder. The handful of cases that do receive a good amount of coverage – Palestine, Afghanistan, Iraq, Pakistan, Chechnya and Lebanon – do so because of their geostrategic importance in the global war on terror.

Most "medium sized" cases go forgotten, as we saw in detail in the cases of Bosnia/Croatia and Bhutan. Most shocking is the massive cases, Somalia (400,000 suffering in displacement), Uganda (1.9 million) and Colombia (4 million), that go ignored, largely un-advocated for in the international arena. The best chance a displaced community has of getting attention to their plight is if there is a sharp up-tick in the violence, as in the case of Sri Lanka. The sole success story of the seven cases is Burma/Myanmar where public advocacy by government representatives and NGOs shone a light on the plight of the Karen and Karenni refugees, and paved the pathway to a long-term durable solution to be resettled in a third country. Another advocacy success story is that of Bhutan, but it was a behind-the-scenes negotiation, with Norway taking the lead in brokering an agreement to find a new home for the displaced Lhotshampas who clearly had no other alternatives. After 20 years of paying for aid maintenance the US and EU governments, realizing that the Lhotshampas would never be locally integrated in Nepal and never repatriated to their homeland in Bhutan, made the decision to resettle them, mainly to the United States.

Of the universe of issues, the case of Darfur too points to a ray of hope that advocacy can keep an issue on the agenda, but it is difficult to parse out what can be attributed to the Save Darfur Coalition's constant efforts and what can be attributed to a scale of violence that was designated genocide.

Overall, Chapters 2 and 3 have demonstrated how incredibly difficult it is to carry out advocacy on behalf of these populations at the global level. First, advocates are up against a packed global agenda, vying for space against humanitarian disasters, public health epidemics, wars and countless other crises. Second, many of these populations are so marginalized and resource-poor they have no organized advocates focusing specifically on their cause. The major international human rights and refugee rights organizations attempt to cover it all, but they are under-resourced and over-stretched. They tend to focus on increasing overall US and EU budget support for these crises and don't have the bandwidth to advocate for political long-term durable solutions to each individual crisis. Third, even if an issue gets on the international agenda, moving from attention to action is a massive leap, which governments of the Global North often fail to make.

This is why advocacy at the national level, in the countries hosting displaced populations, becomes so critical – this is quite possibly the only place we will see some progress on improving access to rights for the world's displaced. It is this I turn to next. This chapter introduced the broad contours of the conflicts that have led people to run for their lives in the seven cases that will be the subject of the rest of this book. Chapters 4 and 5 will present evidence from the fieldwork about the nature of advocacy in these seven cases.

4

Frontline advocacy

Lobbying for refugee rights at the national level

Advocates in Washington DC, Brussels and Geneva have a well-formulated strategy. They have decided how to frame their position, drafted policy proposals aimed at achieving their goal, devised a set of direct lobbying tactics to communicate their message, talked with like-minded groups – often divvying up tasks to be completed by each coalition partner, and considered whether a public education campaign and media outreach would bolster their position. They are specialists in advocacy; it is their round-the-clock task to persuade government officials to bring reality in line with their goals.

Take for example the fight for LGBTQ (Lesbian, Gay, Bisexual, Transgendered and Queer) rights in the United States. LGBTQ and allied groups were mobilized across the country fighting for equal rights for LGBTQ citizens. They strategically worked at state level and federal level to expand and protect equal rights for marriage and benefits. They were creative in their messaging with frames like "Love is Love" to highlight the universal nature of their goals. They were creative in their tactics, using stunts like "glitter bombing" (where glitter is sprayed on anti-gay politicians) and flash mobs to shame anti-gay politicians and achieve media coverage of their cause. As public support for equal rights and same-sex marriage grew, politicians were under increasing electoral pressure to support equal rights. Advocates continued to publicly protest and work for justice through the judicial system. The Supreme Court was finally responsive in 2015 with the ruling on *Obergefell* v. *Hodges*, which confirmed the right of all citizens to marry (S.C.O.T.U.S. 2014). Gay rights groups' mobilization, strategizing, coalition-building and activism created political pressure that ultimately achieved responsiveness on the part of governing institutions.

The picture just painted is a far cry from the type of advocacy being carried out on behalf of the displaced on the frontlines. First, many of the organizations we might imagine would pick up the gauntlet of refugee rights, do not. Second, those that do are often not advocacy organizations – they are humanitarian aid

Who is advocating?

organizations, whose primary mission is to provide life-saving food, materials and medicine. Advocacy is a distant secondary activity that is done if there is time and resources, both of which are in severe short supply. Third, where traditional advocacy groups, targeting policymakers in developed democracies, have some leverage through the well-known power of "votes and money," international humanitarian and human rights NGOs working in conflict zones have no such leverage. Furthermore, they are fighting for people the governments, to put it bluntly, don't care about and they are fighting in a context of limited capacity and corruption. To lay it out more formally, there are at least four significant barriers to effective advocacy:

1. Advocacy is not the priority of most organizations aiding the displaced, saving lives is.
2. Even if humanitarian relief groups could find the resources to divert toward advocacy, they are fighting for non-priority citizens.
3. Any humanitarian relief groups that do try to press for freedom to work or freedom to move are doing so in a context of no political leverage.
4. Not only do aid groups not have any political or economic leverage, the pressure being applied is often in the opposite direction. Corruption leads government officials to be extracting concessions from aid groups, not the other way around.

Based on the fieldwork in Bosnian refugee camps in Croatia, Burmese refugee camps in Thailand, Bhutanese refugee camps in Nepal and Somali refugee camps in Kenya, this chapter explores what organizations are advocating for the displaced vis-à-vis local and national authorities in the countries hosting refugee populations, how they go about it and to what effect. In case after case, we see evidence of these four substantial hurdles to effectively advocating for the rights of the displaced.

Who is advocating and what are they up against?

The UNHCR carries out its mandate to protect and advocate for the displaced with the help of an army of Implementing Partners (IPs) and Operating Partners (OPs). This includes the large international NGOs primarily based in the United States and Europe that specialize in refugee affairs and humanitarian aid such as: the ARC, the NRC, the DRC, the IRC, the JRS and CRS. Many national and local NGOs also partner with the UNHCR to aid the displaced. These include local bar associations who aid with legal representation of the displaced, as well as local health workers and national human rights groups. These organizations primarily focus on providing life-saving food and medicine for the displaced. In so far as they advocate for the rights of the displaced, it is for a set of constrained rights that only address their rights within their camp/confinement. Generally, these constrained rights include the right to food, water, sanitation, health care and education; the right to not be raped by security forces; the right to a lawyer if involved in a criminal proceeding in the host country. Rarely does their advocacy focus on changing the confinement regime: for the freedom to work and the freedom to move.

While many of the humanitarian aid organizations working with the displaced attempt to plead their case to national authorities, their advocacy often falls on deaf ears. "Advocacy" is largely constrained to face-to-face meetings with authorities, which are usually monthly, though sometimes less often. These are meetings where aid organizations mainly discuss aid delivery logistics, but add on some points about police or military brutality or exploitation. They rarely broach broader policy change goals like the freedom to move or the freedom to work. Across the following four refugee cases we see a good deal of variation as to whether the displaced are given a voice through international and national NGOs. I discuss each in turn – from the essentially no-voice situation of Bosnian refugees in Croatia, to the relatively better-represented situation of Bhutanese and Burmese refugees.

Bosnian refugees in Croatia

There is almost no advocacy being conducted on behalf of Bosnian and Kosovo refugees (and Croatian IDPs) in Croatia. There is no international humanitarian aid presence left since it is years since the conflict subsided. This means that there are no international NGOs advocating for the refugees and IDPs still in limbo after the breakup of Yugoslavia to be able to move freely, work, naturalize or be resettled. There is only the UNHCR and their implementing partners in Croatia: the Croatian Red Cross (CRC) and the Croatian Law Center. The Center for Peace is not funded by the UNHCR but is providing legal aid to refugees in the country as well. As a UN official explained:

The Croatian government has always been in charge of the refugees here, they formed a special office for Displaced Persons, Refugees and Returnees (called ODPR). It is strange – it is under the Ministry of Tourism and a few other things that don't really make sense. It was formed mainly to deal with the Bosnian refugees when the war broke out there. At first in the early days there were some problems, they were accepting women and children but there was *refoulement* of the males, they didn't know, we educated them and it got better. There was never the regular UNHCR registration process, the Croatian government set up there own process; their own documents. (Interview March 10, 2008, Zagreb)

In the camp of Mala Gorica where I conducted fieldwork, 20 minutes north of the town of Petrinja, near the small city of Sisak, there were no permanent staff stationed at the camp, just visits from time to time by UNHCR, CRC or Croatian Ministry of the Interior staff. The population of 158 refugees and IDPs lived in pre-fabricated houses donated by the Japanese International

Cooperation Center when the camp was established in 1995 – they were nearing their end as they were only designed to last 15 years. A UN staff person described the situation:

> This was a spontaneous settlement of Bosnians, the Croatian government surrounded the spontaneous settlement and secured it, at first only the UNHCR were allowed in and out, the only NGOs that could get access were ones that worked through the UNHCR … There were later IDPs from Croatia as well and with that there were discrepancies in how the government dealt with different people in the same camp, the Croatian IDPs would get food assistance while the others would not, it lead to a lot of discrepancies. Even now, that the government is closing other camps and sending and relocating people to different camps, the newly arriving ones are not getting food aid, the government says it is too difficult to change procedures at this point so they just aren't getting fed, so the UNHCR and CRC are having to step in and pay for and provide food aid as if there was a humanitarian crisis. Also, since there are a mix of IDPs and refugees it is difficult because the Croatians are allowed to work, whereas the refugees are not. (Interview March 13, 2008, Mala Gorica)

The UNHCR has worked in partnership with the government of Croatia as they consolidate and close camps, but it also has to constantly push for improved access to rights. The UNHCR, however, faces a worst-case advocacy scenario. It has no supporting international aid organization to partner with so is essentially alone in its fight. Additionally it is fighting on behalf of people that the Croatian government does not see as its first priority. Moreover it has other priorities, like keeping the displaced alive with life-saving food and materials. Finally, it has little leverage that it can use to get the Croatian government to change policies regarding the freedom to move or the freedom to work.

Somali refugees in Kenya

From an advocacy perspective, the situation in Croatia is difficult. Yet from a humanitarian perspective, however, while there is a shortage of food for the displaced, at least the conflict has ended, there are no new refugees arriving, and the overall conditions are depressing but not deadly. The situation in the Somali refugee camps, on the other hand, is horrific. As mentioned in Chapter 3, the Dadaab refugee camp complex consists of three camps on the Kenyan–Somali border, housing 400,000 refugees as of 2012. The UNHCR, in its 2009 funding appeal, describes the dire situation:

> The Somali unrest and displacement to Kenya is straining the resources of the Kenyan Government and humanitarian agencies. New arrivals are accommodated in camps in Dadaab (Dagahaley, Hagadera and Ifo) which host three times the number of people for which they were initially designed … the needs are enormous and the current level of funding is insufficient … Acute malnutrition, anaemia, poor sanitation, aged camp infrastructures, poor shelter and shortage of non-food items are posing a great challenge to UNHCR and the NGOs who work together to assist Somali refugees in Dadaab. (UNHCR 2009a, 1–3)

The humanitarian response to this crisis is large, with 14 NGOs partnering with the UNHCR and eight international organizations and agencies. These 22 large organizations, which include CARE, IRC, Lutheran World Federation, Norwegian Refugee Council, Action Against Hunger and Médecins Sans Frontières, have decades of experience in massive crisis response: delivering supplies, organizing food distribution, setting up health clinics and managing sanitation.

The UNHCR's 2009 annual appeal highlights the first major barrier to effective advocacy on behalf of the displaced at the national level: *Barrier #1 – Advocacy is not the priority, saving lives is.* Any humanitarian aid worker you speak within Dadaab wants improved access to rights for the refugees – for them to be able to move freely, work, or to be able to go home. Unfortunately, home is an endless war zone and the rights to food and water are not even being met. Advocacy takes a back seat when the basic necessities are lacking. One of the lead Implementing Partners I interviewed in Dadaab described where they were directing their energy:

For a long time we have been working with the UNHCR, we were one of the first agencies to work in Dadaab, actually we started all the way back in Liboi, that was in 1991, when the first group of Somalis came to the country as refugees. We assisted them a lot in Liboi, and then after the camps were established, we moved as well. For a long time there were just four partners, there was UNHCR, GTZ operating medical services and then CARE doing a variety of activities in the camp.

Now with the growing number of people in the camps and the increasing population, we have had many more partners coming in and we have had to give out part of what we've been doing to other partners, especially to those with a specialization in that area. So as of now, we have five sectors, four sectors specifically target the refugees, but the fifth sector is the Local Area Program which targets the host communities around the refugee camps, and that program covers an area of about 50 kilometers radius around the camps.

So one of the biggest sectors in terms of numbers and size is WatSan [Water and Sanitation], we are the ones that are responsible for the distribution of water, for all the refugees in the three camps and all the Implementing Partners, so we are doing that through a system of bore holes, we have about 16 of them right now, we pump water for about 18 hours a day, to make sure refugees are getting sufficient amount of water, that has gone down with the influx of people, but when we had 200,000 refugees, we were providing 18 liters of water per person per day, now with the increase in refugees that has not been matched with an increase in resources, which means our water capacity per person has gone down, we are currently managing 14 liters per person per day, in some camps we are doing the 18 per person, so we are falling short of the Sphere standards. (Interview July 1, 2009)

The humanitarian community launched Sphere Project in 1996 to develop metrics for "minimum requirements for sustaining human life in dignity, which in turn, are meant to meet basic human needs" (UNHCR 2006, 14). The minimum standards have to do with:

1. water supply, sanitation and hygiene promotion;
2. food security and nutrition;
3. shelter, settlement and non-food items; and
4. health action (Sphere Handbook 2011).

In Dadaab, arguably one of the largest humanitarian crises in the world, it is not only in the area of water that Sphere standards are not being met. Sphere benchmarks are being missed in all sectors. Dozens of infants die each day due to severe malnutrition, maternal mortality is high, and security is low.

Another interviewee described their work trying to prevent violence in the camp – with nearly 400,000 people packed into a 50-km^2 zone, only a few hundred international humanitarian aid staff, and possibly recuperating unarmed Al Shabaab militants, security is tenuous.

For Security the program is called Community Security and Safety, we enable the community to take control of their safety themselves. We do trainings and capacity building. We have what we call the CPST, the Community Peace and Safety Teams, they work on a voluntary basis and there is a member from each block, well ideally there would be a member in every block, we don't have them all covered yet but that is the goal. We trained 14 last year and are training 92 this year. So they work on a voluntary basis and they learn how to control, monitor, report and resolve incidences. They are trained how to identify incidences, and those incidences that violate human rights, like rape or physical attack, they report those to the police. (Interview July 10, 2009)

The displaced are not the only victims of violence. The summer I was in the field, Al Shabaab abducted boys from a rural Kenyan school as well as two international aid workers. In October 2011, two Spanish women working for Médecins Sans Frontières (MSF – Doctors without Borders) in Dadaab were abducted by armed men. Then in January 2012 they were reportedly sold by Al Shabaab to Somali pirates for US$200,000 (McConnell 2012). Aid workers continue to be abducted, with four international and one national staff abducted from Dadaab, an NRC truck stolen, the driver murdered and four others injured in the attack in July 2012 (CNN 2012). Al Shabaab continues to abduct children across the border in Kenya and within Somalia as documented in an in-depth report *No Place for Children* by Human Rights Watch (Spillius 2012). For the report HRW interviewed

164 newly arrived Somali refugees in the Dadaab refugee camps and in Nairobi in May and June 2011. Interviewees included more than 81 girls and boys who were under age 18 at the time. While the presence of children in fighting forces in the 21-year-long Somali conflict is not a new phenomenon, there has been an unprecedented upsurge of al-Shabaab forced recruitment of children since mid-2010; attacks on students, teachers, and schools have also been prevalent in the last two years. Although al-Shaabab has long relied on spreading extremist propaganda and material rewards to coerce children to join, since mid-2010 it has increasingly recruited children forcibly to replenish its

dwindling ranks. Children have nowhere to hide. Al-Shabaab has abducted them wherever they congregate: schools, playgrounds, football fields, and homes. (HRW 2012)

The reports of the level of violence used against abducted children are disturbing: a 46-year-old teacher from Mogadishu interviewed by HRW described the fate of one girl they took from the school who resisted a forced marriage:

> She was given to a commander. He was an old man. She was taken to El Ashabiya. He told his men to kill her and they filmed it and sent it to mobile phones. My students saw it. They saw the mutilation. They brought back her head to the school and assembled all of the girls and said, "This is an example of what will happen if you misbehave." The girl was 16 years old. (HRW 2012, 57)

HRW calls for an end to the violence. Yet the only tool it has is its argument, which, without leverage, is a weak plea:

> Human Rights Watch urges all warring parties in Somalia to immediately end violations of the laws of war, in particular indiscriminate attacks against civilians. On children specifically, we call upon al-Shabaab, the TFG, and TFG-aligned militias to end the recruitment and use of children within their ranks. Al-Shabaab should publicly order its commanders to end the recruitment and use of children, and immediately hand over children within its forces to a civilian protection body, cooperating with the United Nations Children's Fund (UNICEF) and child protection actors to ensure their safe release. It should also immediately end targeted attacks on students, teachers, and schools.

It is difficult to imagine that people who decapitate children will heed this call.

International aid organizations are stretched to the limit just trying to keep people alive, such that opportunities for advocacy vis-à-vis local or national Kenyan authorities are limited. One NGO described the tensions with the local community: "Our relation with the local government has been hard, the host community is coming very strongly that they want the same services as well, the pressure from the host community is very strong, they are very aggressive. The local leaders bring politics in to some of these issues, they say we have been hosting these refugees we want a development package" (interview, Dadaab, July 9, 2009). This leads us to the second major hurdle facing humanitarian aid organizations advocating for refugees: *Barrier #2 – Fighting for non-priority citizens.* Somali refugees are citizens – of Somalia and of the world. They are entitled to all of the rights laid out in the Universal Declaration of Human Rights, but since they are not in the nation of their "habitual residence" (even though many of them are – to the children that have been born and raised in the camps, this is the place of their "habitual residence") there is no process by which they can demand them. Kenya is a developing country with infrastructure, health and sanitation needs – it has responsibilities to its own citizens that it does not yet have the capacity to provide. Providing rights to refugees is not a priority.

In all official publications by the UN agencies and NGOs, the Kenyan authorities are described as partners and in many respects they are – the

Kenyan government has been hosting hundreds of thousands of refugees from Sudan, Somalia and Ethiopia for decades. But the Kenyan government is also at a point of frustration: first authorities will not allow the displaced to move freely or work, and second local integration for Somalis in Kenya is out of the question (UNHCR Global Appeal 2008–2009, 149). In 2007 Kenya passed the Refugee Act, which established the DRA (Department of Refugee Affairs) and laid out a plan for transferring management of the camps from the humanitarian aid organizations to the government of Kenya. Many described the Kenyan authorities' growing interest in managing the camp complex as driven by concerns about border security and Al Shabaab. A raid by authorities of the Somali slum in Nairobi in the summer of 2009 led to many arrests of suspected Somali Islamic militants, so there is a basis for the government's concerns. While the Kenyan government had been content with the international aid community's management of the camps throughout the 1990s and early 2000s, by late 2006 they were taking a much more active role in Dadaab. Aid workers saw this as more of a hassle than help and described DPA officials as trying to micro-manage what was happening in the camps.

Whether one views the Kenyan government as a friendly key partner that lacks capacity or as a more unsympathetic host government that views Somali refugees as security threats, one thing is certain: refugees are not the priority of the Kenyan authorities, Kenyans are. This is reasonable, of course, and yet it renders advocacy at the national level exceedingly difficult. NGOs and UN agencies already have too many other matters to tend to – life-saving services – and they are targeting politicians with their own constituents to attend to.

Bhutanese refugees in Nepal

The 100,000 Bhutanese refugees live in stick huts in a floodplain of a river valley in eastern Nepal. The camps have been there for more than 20 years. Entire generations have been born and raised in leaky stick huts, with mud floors, stick platforms for beds, no windows or doors, no privacy, pit latrines, and swarming insects. All of this is made worse seasonally by monsoons, fires and cholera outbreaks.

With the help of six graduate students and four UNHCR translators, we interviewed 100 refugees in their huts to get a sense of daily life and better understand the community activities they engaged in and the income-generating activities to which they had access. The Nepali government does not allow them to move freely or to work. Some of the men work illegally in India and send back money, and the children crush stones by hand along the river and sell them to construction companies in the area. Some men worked illegally in the construction sector in the nearby town, but this was a small minority. Most people sat around all day, every day, completely dependent on aid. Most did not even choose to gather in the communal areas, but rather stayed in their huts, and performed basic chores – washing what little clothes they had, gathering water, and cooking their rations.

The UNHCR, the 11 Implementing Partners and the 4 NGOs working as Operating Partners, including CARITAS, Lutheran World Federation, IRC and the International Catholic Migration Commission, assist the refugees, as do a range of UN agencies. They, like the aid organizations in the Somali camps, must focus their energies on life-saving food and medicine. They too must deal with the tensions with the host community and a government that see Bhutanese refugees as an extremely low priority. Nepal is one of the poorest countries in the world, with an annual per capital GNI of US$490 (UNICEF 2012). It has also suffered from a decade-long civil war (1996–2006) and Maoist insurgency, which claimed 15,000 lives and internally displaced more than 100,000 Nepali citizens. It also hosts a politically sensitive Tibetan refugee community of 20,000 (CIA World Factbook 2012).

It was in this climate that the UNHCR and humanitarian aid groups had to advocate for over a decade for refugees to be allowed to return home to Bhutan or integrate locally in Nepal – to no avail. Bhutan refused to take the refugees back and Nepal refused to allow them to naturalize. This struggle highlights the third major barrier to effective advocacy at the national level: *Barrier #3 – No leverage*. When advocates lobby for a certain policy in democratic systems, they usually have two points of leverage: votes and money. Advocates can threaten to mobilize votes or resources against a policymaker during the next election cycle if they don't do as the advocate proposes (these threats of course can be more or less credible – the more credible, the more influential). International NGOs and the UN can make no such threats – all they have is their arguments, to which the governments of Nepal and Bhutan have no interest in listening. As discussed in Chapter 3, there was a breakthrough but only with the leverage brought to bear by Norway and the United States.

Once the breakthrough happened though, violence erupted. This time in the camps and targeted at refugees that signed up to be resettled, at the IOM and the other aid agencies helping in the resettlement. Those throwing the Molotov cocktails feared that a massive resettlement operation would empty the camps and release any pressure on the Bhutanese government to ever let them return home and reclaim their land. With thousands of refugees leaving every month to be resettled in the United States, the camps were becoming disorganized, with empty huts becoming breeding grounds for drug abuse and gender-based violence. Our research team conducted a GPS mapping of empty huts, so that refugees from farther away camps could be relocated to the more central camps and move into huts in better condition.

This case provides empirical evidence for each of the major barriers to effective advocacy discussed so far: humanitarian aid organizations must focus on life-saving food and medicine, advocacy is not the priority, the Bhutanese refugees are non-priority citizens to the Nepali government, and non-citizens to the Bhutanese, and finally, even if aid organizations mobilized the time and resources to engage in advocacy, they have very little leverage to pressure host governments to change their policies. The Nepali government argues that it has its own unemployed and impoverished citizens to worry about; it cannot take on the Bhutanese refugees as well.

Karen and Karenni refugees in Thailand

The coalition of organizations aiding Karen and Karenni refugees from Burma/Myanmar in the camps in Thailand is arguably the best organized and most established of the humanitarian responses discussed in this chapter. The CCSDPT (Committee for Coordination of Services to Displaced Persons in Thailand) consists of 18 (20 at the time of fieldwork) humanitarian aid organizations and has been working in the country since 1975. Originally, they were primarily operating on the eastern border of Thailand during the Cambodian genocide, which lasted from 1975 to 1979. In 1981 it reached its peak size of 52 agencies "serving refugees from Laos, Vietnam and Cambodia" (CCSDPT 2012). A UNHCR staff member I interviewed noted the exceptional nature of the CCSDPT's role:

> It is a unique situation here, probably the only one in the world where UNHCR is not in charge of food, commodities, all that the CCSDPT does, that has been in place since the 70s, originally formed to handle the Cambodian refugees, and it changed in the 80s and 90s, the first Burmese crossing was in 1984, and UNHCR wasn't allowed to open an office until 1998. (Interview May 15, 2008)

A key member of the CCSDPT is the TBBC (Thai-Burma Border Coalition), which is a consortium of 12 international NGOs that has a deep understanding of the context and history of the crisis (TBBC 2012). The TBBC has been serving displaced persons from Burma since the first refugees fled to Thailand in 1984.

The CCSDPT organizes regular monthly meetings of the Executive Committee in Bangkok for all the international and national NGOs, international organizations and agencies and relevant Thai officials to share information and facilitate coordination. In addition each of the working groups and sub-committees meet regularly in Bangkok or Mae Sot – the main town among the nine refugee camps that acts as the center of operations for the organizations in the field. This monthly meeting and the meetings of the task forces are the primary opportunities to advance advocacy goals, but despite the regularity of communication with Thai authorities, influencing their position remains difficult, as discussed in more detail below. Just as in the cases already discussed, aid groups are focused on providing life-sustaining food and medicine, are fighting for second-class (non)citizens, but have no leverage – and perhaps even less leverage in Thailand than they may have in other countries.

While the organization of the aid groups is notable, conditions in the camps are on par with those in the Bhutanese refugee camps – poor land, bad drainage, pit latrines, stick huts with thatched roofs, mud floors, stick platforms for beds, no privacy, lines for food rations … in short, encampment. One of the interviewees whose organization was in charge of WatSan described the scope of the operation:

We've only been here for a year and we are only working in Mae La, this is the biggest camp – 50,000 people and so there were big sanitation problems, water, garbage, the people in charge couldn't cope. AMI took over from MSF in 2005 but not really sanitation just some vector control. They tried to find a local NGO (IRC, ARC, etc.) but none of them could handle it. So they began to look outside of Thailand and so they asked us. (Interview May 30, 2008)

He continued:

The sanitary conditions are not good. The site is not good; you really feel the absence of the UNHCR in the planning compared to camps in Africa, which are well organized. Mae La is 2 square kilometers for 50,000 people, it was organized and designed for a small population density in a large space, that has changed. There is not 2.6 square meters per person – far less. They live in squalidity, reducing the number of people is very important, resettlement is a good thing. The latrines – before were just holes, so it was damaging the water supply, and would overflow in the rainy season as the water table would rise. Also there is not 20 liters of water per person per day. People are fetching water from wells and there are health problems for children as a result. (Interview May 30, 2008)

The toll on refugee health is high from chronic malnutrition and unclean water, but just as in the Bhutanese camps in Nepal, the situation gets worse seasonally:

During the rainy season, which is just beginning, there are outbreaks [of cholera and other infectious diseases] and so we have worked on a plan for when the outbreaks come. Originally we had planned to come earlier in the year last year, during the dry season, but we were delayed, it took longer to get staff because of the difficulty of recruiting. There was a cholera epidemic at the end June. The Thai authorities didn't inform us in time, there were reports in Mae Sot, so it didn't start in the camp, but they like to blame everything on starting in the camps. This year there has been some cases of dengue, we have taken preventive action. (Interview May 30, 2008)

One of the NGOs I interviewed shared databases of the Sphere indicators in the camps while I was in the field. To take Mae La camp as an example, 1,897 babies were born in the camp in 2007, 5 percent of children were malnourished, access to health services was strained, with the goal of 10,000 people per medical facility being long surpassed with 24,415 being assigned to the clinic in Mae La camp. And the numbers continue to grow beyond the "official" numbers as the violence and oppression in Burma continues (despite recent indications by the junta that they are moving toward political reform). The abuse inside Burma leads to a steady stream of new arrivals in the camps, as one interviewee described: "In 2007 the Thai government said the camps were closed and stopped registering people but there are 200–300 new arrivals every day, so this is leading to a huge number of unregistered refugees in the camps" (interview May 15, 2008).

Who is advocating?

Refugees are not allowed to work so there is nearly complete dependence on international aid (in the case of Mae La – the percentage of refugees (of working age) employed or self-employed (engaged in income-generating activities) stood at 0 percent of 50,000). The UNHCR advocates for freedom to work, but while it seemed that made progress had been made, political instability within Thailand eroded it: "Many people in camp do nothing and so we argued to open the camps to the Labor Market – the former PM Taskin agreed but then there was the coup. So that is a main point of advocacy we have with the Thai government. The aid dependency is among the less educated." The UNHCR could be said to be even more limited in its leverage in Thailand since Thailand is not a party to the Refugee Convention:

> Thailand won't sign the Convention because it is a well off country surrounded by not well off countries, and so they think it would only increase their problems and they feel they have helped the refugees in the past from various wars and conflicts, and so don't need an outside organization to come in, they think they can manage. Also there is benefit at the borderline, gems etc., that the military benefits from – if the UNHCR came in they couldn't do that. (Interview May 15, 2008)

Another aid worker with an international NGO described the difficulties the UNHCR faces: "They are in a difficult situation, they were pretty much brought in to take the flack for the Thai failure, the border attacks in 1998/9 – to put an international face to a localized refugee issue. So the UNHCR has been working with its hands tied, they have no mandate here, very little budget" (interview May 23, 2008).

This is similar to the situation in Kenya, where the host government is both a partner and a problem. The Thai authorities have been hosting this refugee population for decades, and that must be recognized. However, at the same time, they refuse these refugees the right to work or move, and they are obstinate in the face of international pleas for improved access to rights. The difficulties with the government do not end there, which brings us to the fourth major barrier to effective advocacy in the field: *Barrier #4 – Corruption*. While some aid workers alluded to corruption of Kenyan officials, and I experienced it myself in the field, the aid workers I interviewed in Mae Sot, the field headquarters for organizations aiding the refugees in the nine camps along the Thai–Burma border, were very explicit about it. As an aid worker with a child-focused organization described:

> We have had a lot of trouble with the camp commanders. Especially in [one of the northern camps]. The Palat – the Thai word for camp commander – is very demanding. He makes demands on the NGOs and if they aren't met he tells the security forces not to let us in. So, to do your work you have to meet the demands. So for instance, he saw we were changing the tires on our truck, and said he wanted the old ones, tires are like 30–50,000 Baht, and we had to give them to him ... So we've had a lot of problems with MOI. He demanded something of [one of the other UN Implementing Partners] and they didn't comply and when they showed up the next day for work he

had commanded the Os-Ops to deny them entry. So you have to comply. And [another Implementing Partner] has also had problems, there is skimming from trucks, they show up with a shipment and the camp commander just says okay that's 10 sacks of rice for me and just takes them off the truck, the refugees see it, he does it right out in the open. They do it with bamboo too, every time there is a building material shipment they take 10 percent of it.

He described a number of other types of extortion specific to their programming, which are excluded to protect the organization's anonymity, but the message is clear – in the relationship between the host government and the aid organizations, it is the government that has the leverage.

The difficulties of advocating vis-à-vis the Thai authorities, at the local and national levels, is further complicated by a fact that most interviewees would only mention off the record: "And this is off the record, well, the first part isn't, that is known, but the second part is not so known. The Thai government has an economic relationship with the Burmese government, there is a lot of money there – in gems, oil, gas – and increasingly they've been providing incentives to Thai businesses that establish operations on the other side of the border" (interview May 22, 2008).

The barriers

The empirical evidence presented in this chapter shows that there are four clear hurdles standing in the way of effective refugee rights advocacy:

#1 Advocacy is not the priority, saving lives is

The organizations managing displacement camps are primarily, and understandably, large international humanitarian aid organizations that have the experience and expertise to organize, construct and manage massive displacement crisis response. Their primary task is life-saving food, water, shelter and medicine. The IRC's mission statement captures the fact that advocacy, necessarily, is secondary to life-saving interventions: "Founded in 1933, the International Rescue Committee is a world leader in relief, rehabilitation, protection, post-conflict development, resettlement services and advocacy for those uprooted or affected by violent conflict and oppression" (IRC 2007). Indeed, the largest American refugee organization, the ARC, doesn't even mention advocacy in its mission statement: "ARC works with its partners and constituencies to provide opportunities and expertise to refugees, displaced people and host communities. We help people survive conflict and crisis and rebuild lives of dignity, health, security and self-sufficiency. ARC is committed to the delivery of programs that ensure measurable quality and lasting impact for the people we serve."

In fact, the UN funds the IPs only to carry out activities related to "protection." Activities they want to do above and beyond the tasks agreed upon in the Partnership Agreements must be funded by their own budgets. Advocacy is not a core component of "protection," so it does not fall under any of the UN budget line items of: Agency Operational Support, Legal Assistance/Protection, Crop Production, Livestock/Animal Husbandry, Forestry, Domestic Needs, Household Support, Shelter/Other Infrastructure, Education, Health Nutrition, Income-Generation, Sanitation, Transport/Logistics, and Water (Non Agricultural). In short, most of the organizations we might expect to be advocating for the displaced do not see advocacy as their primary mission or even as part of their mission. Furthermore, international and national NGOs get no budget support for advocacy. If they want to engage in advocacy, they have to do it on their own time, with their own staff, funded by resources found elsewhere. This is in no way a criticism of these organizations – they are doing critically important work – but rather it is simply an effort to highlight that while there are organizations out there working to save the lives of the displaced, those organizations cannot be assumed to be effective advocacy organizations to advance the rights of the displaced. This same problem exists in virtually every single refugee crisis discussed in Chapter 2.

#2 *Fighting for people no one cares about*
In almost all cases, refugees are treated as if they are unwanted. They are socially excluded. They are a problem. National governments hosting refugee populations see them at best as a nuisance and a drain on resources, and at worst a security threat with embedded armed elements. Host governments don't want them there and they don't want them to stay. They have no incentive to improve their living conditions, and fear that if they improved the conditions then more refugees would come. Humanitarian organizations are fighting for unwanted constituencies. They are in an incredibly difficult advocacy position, and if they push too hard or act too politically, the host government can expel them. This phenomenon of governmental animosity for refugee populations does not only hold for the refugee cases studied in depth in this chapter. The same dynamics are at play in South Africa, Rwanda, Tanzania, Nigeria, Lebanon, Bangladesh, Burma/Myanmar, among many others, not to mention the public hostility to refugees and asylum seekers in Europe, the United States and Australia.

#3 *No votes and no money = no leverage*
During previous research on advocacy in the European Union (Mahoney 2008), a powerful American lobbyist said: "I'd never want to advocate in the EU, there is no leverage, there's no votes and there's no money." What he meant is that, at the supranational level in the EU, the European Commission and the Council are not elected in popular elections – member state governments appoint them. As a result, advocates cannot use votes as leverage in their advocacy, arguing for example that if a policymaker supports a policy alternative they will pay for it at the polls, come the next election. In addition, since there are no elections to those bodies, and no campaign financing for the European Parliament, money provides advocates with little leverage.

The result is that advocates have less power to get what they want. While this is not the place to go into the detailed workings of the European Union, there are some pathways for political leverage and pressure through elections. Advocates fighting for the forcibly displaced have even less leverage than advocates in the complex international governance structure of the EU. The only tool they have is the moral argument that we should do better by the displaced based on our common humanity. Unfortunately, this tool is not big enough for the job. This barrier to effective refugee advocacy goes for every refugee crisis listed in Table 1.1.

#4 Corruption

The difficulties international aid organizations have in interfacing with governments hosting displaced populations does not end with apathy or non-responsiveness. At times host government officials are more interested in aiding themselves than the displaced. As aid workers go about their day trying to deliver supplies and programs, they are often pressured to pay off corrupt local officials. When aid organizations are being forced to pay bribes just to get their primary mission tasks accomplished, they are in an incredibly weakened position when it comes to advocacy. The host governments are pressuring them, not the other way around. While it is hard to get aid workers to discuss corruption openly, we know many of the countries listed in Table 1.1 also suffer from high levels of corruption as measured by Transparency International. It is difficult to say which camps create the most difficult conditions for aid workers when it comes to corruption, but it is important to point out how this fact substantially hampers their ability to be effective advocates for the displaced.

As we will see in Chapter 5, many of the same barriers face advocates fighting for the rights of the internally displaced, and yet the hurdles before them are even higher: resettlement is almost never an option, and the target of advocacy is often the offending armed force as well.

5

Frontline advocacy
Lobbying for IDP rights at the national level

The situation of IDPs is at the same time incredibly similar and different from that of refugees. IDPs suffer denial of rights and horrific living conditions just as refugees do, but the fact that they have not crossed an international border makes their situation often worse than that of refugees. First, they are often closer to the violence and it is more difficult for aid to reach them, as with the case of Syrian IDPs in 2015 who were getting very little assistance compared to Syrian refugees in Turkey that were being assisted by the UNHCR and the international community. Second, they are not protected by international refugee law; they are technically citizens of the country in which they are being denied their rights. This chapter explores the particular difficulties that face the advocates lobbying on their behalf.

While the UNHCR and its team of Implementing Partners have a mandate to aid refugees that have fled across borders, they do not have a mandate to aid IDPs. There is no UN convention relating to the status of IDPs. Rather, the traditional idea of sovereignty still holds: what happens within our borders is our business. The doctrine of Responsibility to Protect has called for a redefinition of sovereignty from one of non-interference with internal affairs to one of government responsibility to protect their populations from ethnic cleansing, genocide, mass rape and starvation (R2P 2013). Anne-Marie Slaughter pushes further, arguing for a redefinition of sovereignty to one of capacity – capacity to protect, capacity to engage in a web of globally networked, responsible states (Slaughter 2004).

The UN developed a set of Guiding Principles on Internal Displacement in 1998, which are not binding but which are

> intended to serve as an international standard to guide governments, international organizations and all other relevant actors in providing assistance and protection to IDPs. The Principles identify the rights and guarantees relevant to the protection of the internally displaced in all phases of displacement. They provide protection against arbitrary

displacement, offer a basis for protection and assistance during displacement, and set out guarantees for safe return, resettlement and reintegration. (GPID 2013)

However, the guidelines make clear that the responsibility does fall with the national governments first: "Responsibility for the protection of IDPs rests primarily with national governments. One step governments can take to meet this responsibility is to develop a legal or policy framework on internal displacement based on the Guiding Principles" (GPID 2013).

Since the UNHCR does not have mandate over the protection of IDPs, the UN developed a "cluster approach" in 2005 to task different UN agencies with various life-saving tasks: "The United Nations High Commissioner for Refugees is responsible for Camp Coordination and Management, Emergency Shelter and Protection for conflict-generated IDPs. Other agencies with cluster lead responsibilities include: World Health Organisation (Health), United Nations Development Programme (Early Recovery) and the United Nations Children's Fund (Nutrition, Water/Sanitation). UNICEF shares the education cluster lead with the Save the Children Alliance" (GPID 2013). The cluster leaders have a difficult task, providing aid where they do not have a mandate, and forced to coordinate with national governments that are often involved in the conflict producing the displacement.

The Guiding Principles are a noble goal, but in reality conditions fall far short of the mark, just as refugee conditions fall far short of the rights laid out in the UN Convention on the Status of Refugees. The same four barriers to effective advocacy discussed in the last chapter hamper IDP activism as well:

1. Advocacy is not the priority of most organizations aiding the displaced, saving lives is.
2. Even if humanitarian relief groups could find the resources to divert toward advocacy, they are fighting for non-priority citizens. This barrier takes on a different form in IDP situations compared to refugees – refugees are often unwelcomed aliens. In the case of internal displacement, the displaced may be seen by the government as an enemy to be destroyed, as in the case of Tamils in Sri Lanka, or as a marginalized minority like the Acholi in northern Uganda.
3. Any humanitarian relief groups that do try to press for freedom to work or freedom to move are doing so in a context of no political leverage since they would be advocating in the name of marginalized or "enemy" groups.
4. Not only do aid groups not have any political or economic leverage, but corrupt government officials could be pressing them for concessions.
5. And finally, an additional barrier that is particularly relevant in IDP cases, especially those where the displacement is due not to the government's hostilities but from rebel group violence, is a lack of capacity. In some cases the government may have the will to improve the conditions of the displaced but do not have the capacity. In these situations, advocates are in a particularly difficult context.

Who is advocating?

Paralleling the last chapter, again I describe which organizations are advocating for the displaced vis-à-vis local and national authorities but in these cases within their own countries. I explore how they go about it and under what conditions they are effective at the local or national levels. The evidence presented in this chapter is based on 34 in-depth interviews and fieldwork in Croatia, Uganda, Sri Lanka and Colombia, four of the longest internal displacement crises in the world.

Who is advocating and what are they up against?

Though the UNHCR does not have an official mandate to protect IDPs, it has increasingly been taking on that task. In the four cases discussed here, the UNHCR had the most active role in Croatia, but largely because of the mixed nature of those camps – with IDPs and refugees living together. It also had a coordinating role organizing the clusters in Sri Lanka. However, the agency was not very involved in the response to the IDP crises in Uganda and Colombia. The UNHCR has a presence in both of these countries, but played more of a coordinating role, and in Uganda it focuses its efforts on caring for the refugees that are in the country as a result of other conflicts in the region: Rwanda, Burundi and Somalia. In each of these cases, national-level organizations played a more active role than in the cases of refugee displacement discussed in the last chapter.

Croatian IDPs

The displacement that resulted from the breakup of the former Yugoslavia highlights well the difference between refugees and IDPs as well as the absurdity of the distinction. In a place where everyone was once the citizen of the same country – Yugoslavia – during the war and then the breakup people became either "refugees" or "IDPs" depending on the random chance of geography and in which direction they fled. In the camp I visited, which had been in existence since 1995, there were Croatian IDPs, returnees from Serbia, Bosnian refugees and ex-refugee settlers from Bosnia (i.e. no plans for them ever to return home to Bosnia).

While the conflict has ended, the displaced suffer incredibly difficult living conditions; the small temporary dwelling units originally given by the Japanese government are falling apart now that they are being used long past what was intended. The water going into the units is poisonous, as an aid worker described:

This is a problem, the pipes that go into the units comes from a source that is polluted with heavy metals, so it can be used for cleaning but not for cooking. There is a clean spring nearby so refugees and IDPs need to walk to get water each day (the government has hooked a faucet up to the spring it seems) so they need to carry the bottles back. This is problematic for the largely elderly population so some members of the camp go and get the water for the older people, sometimes in exchange for a few kuna if the person has a pension (some do since some are IDPs). (Interview March 13, 2008)

In this case, the IDPs are better off than the refugees, and this goes for food aid as well, since as mentioned in Chapter 3 the government has been providing food aid to some populations and not others.

Aid workers said that it is impossible to have a vegetable garden because the land is a floodplain, the ground was soaked while I was conducting fieldwork and it hadn't rained significantly in days. Some people work on the black market, those that can work legally go to town to buy vegetables. There is a truck that comes every day and sells bread and milk, but only the displaced that can figure out a way to earn some income are able to purchase anything.

The aid workers described another nearby camp, CC Dumace, northwest of Petrinja. The camp was in use since 1993, set up through a Swedish Red Cross donation, Kosovo Croats had been flown in during the war and at the time of fieldwork the camp still had a population of 234 Kosovo Croats. A UN officer described the conditions: "the children are not taken care of, they have lice, and there have been difficulties, not everyone gets food aid, for different reasons – some have status some don't – and last week there was a small riot because the CRC [Croatian Red Cross] came to give the food out and some people were getting it and some were not and it is hard to explain why" (interview March 13, 2008).

As previously mentioned, there is nearly no international humanitarian aid presence aiding these displaced peoples other than the UNHCR and their national-level implementing partner. The advocacy capacity therefore to fight for improved access to rights for Croatian IDPs is essentially non-existent. The UNHCR attempts to do what it can with a small staff, few partners and no support from advocacy organizations at the global level bringing pressure to bear from the outside. In this case, there are not even enough humanitarian relief organizations providing food, shelter and medicine, let alone to engage in effective advocacy.

Ugandan IDPs

As discussed in Chapter 3, the Ugandan conflict and related displacement began in 1986, and over the next two decades violence escalated and displacement conditions deteriorated. We also saw there was very little attention to the Ugandan case on the global media agenda for the first decade of the twenty-first century. There were some advocacy being carried out in the United States and Canada, but that advocacy did not translate into attention or international action. There were also very low levels of advocacy being carried out by the aid organizations providing food, shelter and medical services in the camps. Of those that were engaging in some type of advocacy, most were humanitarian aid organizations.

While the UNHCR is present in Uganda, it is working with refugee populations (from Sudan, Rwanda, DRC, Somalia and Burundi) as well as IDPs and,

Who is advocating?

since it has a mandate for the latter, some aid organizations said it spent more of its resources doing so:

In the Kampala office [of UNHCR] there is a real dichotomy between refugee and IDP populations and there is a gap. I still wonder if Kampala even understands the IDP situation. With refugees it is much more well defined, there is a process, you go about the procedure, there is a mandate, but with IDPs none of that applies so they seem disinterested, they just spend their time and energy on the refugees. (Interview June 20, 2008)

Another aid worker mentioned that the "UNHCR is new in the IDP process, so they didn't ask so much of the IPs [implementing partners], so it's not really camp management."

Just as with refugees, we see strong evidence of the first barrier to effective advocacy on behalf of the internally displaced: #1 – *Advocacy is not the priority, saving lives is*. First, security in the camps remained a major issue through most of the 1990s and early 2000s. There were threats from LRA (Lord's Resistance Army) raids and as you moved north, closer to the border with Sudan, those threats intensified. In addition, rehabilitating people that have been the victims of violence is resource-intensive work, as one Ugandan program director for an international organization described:

We support children who are orphans and we help rebuild the community's capacity to take care of those orphans. Our country has had a history of violence, of these trends of violence that have led to many orphans and many widows, and the population has been traumatized and they don't have the capacity to take care. So this is what we have been doing. (Interview June 23, 2008)

There has been an active insurgency for 20 years, and this has continued and continued, so people would flee and settle in a camp and then they would return, and then would have to flee again and we worked wherever the people were, with the community. We have done two types of interventions Relief and Development. For Relief that is health care, sanitation, education, school construction. But when people move from place to place, it is wobbling work we do, it is very hard to coordinate when the population is constantly moving. If the people move, the school we built is left and we have to start over again. If a borehole was dug, maybe you can take the drilling machinery but that work is lost. So it leads to wobbling work. (Interview June 23, 2008)

Traditionally orphans were taken care of by relatives, families were big, they were clans, a child that was orphaned they would take in, there was always a father figure around, it was a clan issue. But now the community is incapacitated from this war, how can you expect a family with seven children of their own, that doesn't have basic necessities to say yes, we take pity on this child from our extended family and we will take him in, when there is already not enough. So people are incapacitated. (Interview June 23, 2008)

The needs for health care, sanitation, education and rehabilitation are so great. From March 1995 to 2008, this organization had received and rehabilitated 13,000 abducted children. He went on to describe how they arrived there:

At the height of the conflict we had 400 children here, there were two ways of escape, one the LRA forces were in Uganda and they escaped or two the LRA and government forces were in direct battle and they escaped and the soldiers would bring them here. We had one baby that a soldier found on the battlefield that was still sucking on its mother that was dead, we had another as well that the mother threw on the battlefield because it was crying and she was trying to run away. They abducted boys but girls as well and forced them to become their wives, well I should say wives in quotations, sex slaves is more accurate, so those girls had children by the rebels. So we would receive them, feed them, check their health, they would see a doctor and we would trace their families. Even those babies. (Interview June 23, 2008)

This interview sheds light on just how incredibly difficult it is to accomplish the organization's primary mission – receiving victims, nursing them back to health, and beginning the long process of rehabilitation – advocating for rights is a distant goal.

Aid workers described impossible conditions and attempting to accomplish just the bare minimum. To begin with the camps are poorly constructed which makes providing aid more difficult, as an international aid worker described:

All the camps were set up by the government, not the UNHCR, so they don't meet standards. The huts are so close together, fire has been a problem, if there is a fire and there often are in the dry season, one hut on fire will catch all the others. There are some boreholes in each, but not enough. There are decaying huts. (Interview June 20, 2008)

Then with 65 camps in Gulu District alone (one of three districts most affected by LRA activity) stretching up to the Sudanese border, many camps are simply inaccessible as one Ugandan aid worker described working for a European aid organization: "there are these very far away camps, they are a struggle to get to, there are little streams crossing the road, we only go during the dry season and then you can only get there by land rover, no other vehicle can make it, so the NGOs don't go there it is too hard to get to" (interview June 24, 2008). In the camps aid workers can reach, in addition to providing aid, they need to collect data to effectively carry out their work, another taxing task leaving little space for advocacy: "tons of information we are collecting, how many latrines, how many vulnerable women, how many people died, how many were born – we have field staff out collecting this data every day" (interview June 25, 2008).

And despite all the hard work, many aid workers were extremely frustrated with the situation, seeing little improvement in conditions, as one described:

Can I say my biggest frustration? That 20 months I've been here, still we're flagging the same problems and still we see the IDPs in the same deep shit, sorry for the language, but that's how it is. It is the same problems that were here a year and a half ago. Like a health center isn't working, money comes, and still it isn't working, what are we doing here?! (Interview June 20, 2008)

Another described the exhausted state of aid workers: "We've been here for a year and a half, it is very draining here when you work in Africa it is very

Who is advocating?

draining, all the international staff suffer from fatigue, you have to put so much more energy into things than you do in Europe. You have to work very hard for everything and then the outputs aren't what you wanted" (interview June 20, 2008). It is therefore not surprising that little advocacy is occurring above and beyond the required aid work. A Ugandan aid worker described the same fatigue that the international workers felt:

> When you go to swim across the Nile River, that is one thing, but when you go to swim across the Indian Ocean that is a different thing. Why? Because you can see the other side of the Nile River, you can see the end, you can calibrate your effort the energy you expend, but when you cross the Indian Ocean you can't see the other side, you don't know how to spend your energy. And that is fatiguing. That is my work. If you meet Kony in your work, ask him when he is going to stop, and let me know, so then we can know how to spend our energy, our motivation, what strategy to follow. That is the greatest problem: undefined strategy. (Interview June 23, 2008)

The heavy demands of delivering aid, the difficulty of the conditions to deliver that aid, the psychological toll of working with extremely victimized populations combine with an overall aid fatigue to make space and time for effective advocacy almost impossible.

The barriers, of course, do not stop there. In situations of internal displacement, the government often has the same attitude toward the displaced as host governments do toward refugee populations. Even though the displaced are citizens, internally displaced groups are often marginalized segments of society, the Tamils in Sri Lanka, the Acholi in Uganda, Durfuri in Sudan. Thus, we also see strong evidence of the second barrier to effective advocacy that we saw in refugee cases: #2 – *Fighting for people no one cares about*. Many aid workers described the government of Uganda, seated in the capital Kampala in the south, as discriminatory to the Acholi people in the north of the country. Some described outright discrimination others a more subdued form where government officials were simply not very interested in seeing conditions improve. One aid worker described the difficulty of working with local Ugandan authorities to move aid projects aimed at helping Ugandan IDPs forward:

> The local authorities it is very difficult to get any participation, it is hard to get them to take any action, you have to work hard for it. It is hard to even get them to meetings, you have to bribe them in a way with a nice lunch or something like that, and then they will agree to something very easily in the meetings but then it is very hard to get them to sign to it on paper. Working with the District level is the hardest, the lower levels, the sub-county and the parish level can be easier. (Interview June 20, 2008)

International organizations advocating at the national level did not fare much better. International organization staff describe countless meetings with officials, but often meetings and discussions don't translate into policy changes or changes on the ground. One national-level aid official described their work in Kampala:

> Cluster meetings happen on different days, UNDP leads GBV [Gender Based Violence], UNICEF leads protection – so different agencies lead different clusters. And the

coordinators for each specific cluster is the one that attends these meetings, so I'll attend if GBV is meeting. The last cluster meeting I was at we were preparing for the CAP – the consolidated appeals process – and that usually funds the agencies more than the NGOs but we were meeting to get more funding for GBV in the North. So sharing statistics, updates, what's the latest that's going on and what are the funding needs, the funding gaps, how are we going to lobby together to get more funding, there were no agencies before for GBV work, so we are lobbying for more funding. So it is a coordination meeting, what are people doing, what are the challenges, and then also a lobbying effort on a more national scale – rather than just what each individual organization is doing – so coordination and then lobbying both nationally and internationally. We have definitely been lobbying, on education, we meet with the Ministry of Education, the Ministry of Gender, for child labor, how are we combating it, how is the country trying to keep kids out of labor and focus on school, how does it compliment our programs. In Karamoja on Education, we'll have meetings with the District and all our other partners. Okay, teachers are not showing up to these schools we are working in. How can we lobby the government to actually place teachers in these schools and make it a priority? (Interview June 27, 2008)

Most aid organizations described this type of interaction with local authorities – both at the local and national level, meetings, discussion, sharing information but with seemingly very little impact. It is a similar barrier that we saw in refugee crises, when it comes to lobbying: #3 – *No votes and no money = no leverage*. International aid organizations can share data and suggest changes, but ultimately they don't have any power to hold government authorities accountable. Unfortunately, even though the displaced in the north are citizens of Uganda, they are not in a position to wield power through elections or money either.

Often though, difficult government relations went beyond apathy to outright obstruction, partly due to politics, partly due to the fourth major barrier to effective advocacy: #4 – *Corruption*. One aid worker alluded to the loss of funds and the difficulty of working with the Ugandan government:

We tried to work with them on a road mapping, which were national roads, which were local, which were community, which were impassible during the rainy season? It was too political, the Ugandan government has the last word. When you work in emergencies it is easier you only work with your own colleagues with other UN agencies, not with multi-actors. They blocked it, and I wondered why, it was clear they didn't want people to know what roads the LRA might be moving troops on. Also, there were big projects of road rehabilitation, roads that were supposed to be rehabilitate it turned out they were not, road restoration that was funded by one NGO turned out to also be funded by another, and so I don't think they wanted anyone looking into these things. It was trouble. We try to launch a lot of things but it doesn't go anywhere. (Interview June 20, 2008)

Thus we saw a significant humanitarian aid presence in northern Uganda for much of the later half of the conflict, but those aid workers were too overwhelmed with immediate emergency relief activities to engage in advocacy. Of those organizations that did try to advocate on behalf of the displaced they ran into the now familiar set of barriers: lack of leverage, and government apathy and corruption.

Colombian IDPs

Chapter 3 reviewed the more than 50 years of violence in Colombia. The continual insecurity has led to waves of displacement; often to the outskirts of cities and paramilitary activity in the urban areas often lead the secondary waves of displacements. While international and national NGOs are fully aware that violence and displacement continue, many argue that the government of Colombia has political reasons for claiming the contrary:

> The Colombian government and the President say that there is no armed conflict, that there is no displacement, but the situation is dire, more than anything in the regions where there remain combatants. There are areas where there is a conflict of power between the public force and the armed actors, such as the paramilitary and other armed groups. The government has a concept of these groups as bands of bandits. However, the most dangerous thing is that these bands of armed fighters are displacing people. Furthermore, this displaced population is encountering the narcotics trade. So, we are trying to affect the regulations and jurisprudences that drive the government, because Colombia is one of the countries with the most regulations and laws for the protection of the victims of conflict ...We are trying to redefine the concept of "victim" to include this population, because at the moment, they do not qualify. The displaced population's declaration said that paramilitary groups displaced them. The government officials did not look at the declaration because they asserted that there was no paramilitary displacement. Thus, the displaced people weren't registered, and consequently a lot of this population has not received any direct humanitarian aid from the government. (Interview December 12, 2008)

This was confirmed by nearly everyone that I interviewed, that displacement was occurring but was not being documented. One Colombian aid worker working for an international organization said aid to Colombia was declining because there is a perception that the conflict has ended because the paramilitaries have been officially demobilized, but the reports of violence and displacement continue:

> There are a lot of experiences that people are not included in the registry because they say they were displaced by new groups. Or paramilitary groups they maybe don't understand the difference and the person who is evaluating these declarations says that "paramilitary groups are demobilized in this city so you are not displaced." But these are the same groups, the same paramilitary groups with different names ... it is so difficult because now the national government is saying that there are no more paramilitary groups – that all the paramilitary groups have been demobilized. That we find now that there are new emergent groups – that there are more narco-traffic groups than paramilitary groups. The government won't recognize that we still have paramilitary groups. Because the big question is if there are only narco-traffickers why did they kill human rights leaders and IDP association leaders and union leaders? (Interview December 11, 2008)

The UNHCR reported that in 2012, "a total of 101 large group displacements had taken place affecting 6,650 families. The displacement was particularly acute in 11 areas of the country: Antioquia, Cauca, Chocó, Córdoba, Nariño, Norte de Santander and Putumayo" (UNHCR Colombia 2013).

Not only does displacement continue but a new phenomenon has developed with the rise of narco-terrorism: confinement zones. Essentially those who would have normally fled are no longer able to do so as armed combatants confine them by force and landmines, as one aid worker described:

There are still fighters in the guerilla groups as well as the paramilitaries. Both the guerilla forces and the public force confine them, and they, those forces, limit the entry and export of foodstuffs and medicines. This is another one of the causes of displacement. There are cases where the indigenous communities are confined, but that's a new situation. The guerilla forces control those zones, and any time someone needs to leave, they can only leave if they leave their family behind as collateral. That way if the person has information against them, the guerillas have his family. Psychologically, they are attacking him by forcing him to leave behind his family. This is another type of confinement. Before anyone leaves, he is asked where he is going, how long he will be gone. If the person is planning on being gone longer than he said, he remembers that the guerillas have his family. The guerillas also use landmines, which contribute to the confinement of the displaced people. After a community has been established, the guerillas will make a perimeter using landmines. The families usually must live within three kilometers of their crops, so the guerillas allow them to leave the landmined areas only within specific times. (Interview December 12, 2008)

While the violence and displacement continues, living conditions are harsh and it is incredibly difficult for the displaced to find jobs in cities already suffering from 20 percent unemployment, the government of Colombia does have a formalized process for documenting and aiding documented displaced persons. A displaced person makes a declaration to a public ministry and then that declaration is sent to Accion Social, the body in charge of aiding the displaced. Accion Social has 15 days to decide if the person and their family is included or not in the official registry – the RUPD (Registro Unico de Poblacion Desplacada). If you are included in the registry, you are sent to one of the local NGOs and are eligible for three months of aid.

If you have fled to a city, aid is easier to access. If you have fled from a rural area to another rural area, it is incredibly difficult to access aid:

So I think we need to always keep in mind the difficulty in reaching out to these communities especially now when we are in a year when a lot of displacement has happened in very, very remote areas, so even in some cases we had a helicopter operation so there we need to limit to do what is essential. We had a community that we assisted for four months and that was a helicopter operation so there we could not bring the whole kit so we had to select and look at the community to see what was most urgent and then also taking into consideration food needs and try to balance what needs are in terms of nutrition ... so we could only bring them rice and we would always try to balance rice, beans, and oil and salt and the basics. (Interview December 8, 2008)

While the situation is dire for the displaced of Colombia, this is one of the few cases were we see active and impassioned advocacy on their behalf and government officials especially the Constitutional Court do seem to deeply care about the suffering of these populations. I interviewed 14 organizations and all were advocating for the rights of the displaced on some level. And their efforts had paid off, in that the government did set up an entire system to aid the displaced (Accion Social and the RUPD) and was providing three months of aid when families were forced from their homes. One European aid worker captured well the movement for rights in the country:

the whole construction of public policy has evolved quite quickly since 2004 with the ruling of T025 from the Constitutional Court and I would say specifically in the past two years there has been many, many rulings and statements made by the court forcing the government to act and of course IDPs are more and more aware and more and more NGO organizations are also informing IDPs of their rights. (Interview December 8, 2008)

Through advocacy by NGOs, mostly Colombian, the Constitutional Court considered the case of displacement in Colombia and made a number of statements, as a UN agency staffer described:

the key definitive statement was on how the government was dealing with displaced populations and [the Court] declared an unconstitutional state of affairs. So in light of that, a monitoring commission was set up and it released a report on October 30th and that report is quite interesting actually because it's a whole survey ... 8,000 households or something like that. It was quite massive and lots of interesting data in it. Indicators and such, the Constitutional Court has developed indicators as well [to measure] if displacement has an effect on access to rights. (Interview December 9, 2008)

A Colombian aid worker described the official government board to oversee the situation of the displaced, as well as the series of advocacy events they organized to keep pushing the government for more effective response:

This year we have held 27 workshops where we have invited some of the organizations from each department. They were directed at different groups of the displaced population: indigenous people, afros, farmers, unionists. We have contacted churches and different government agencies. In Colombia there is a national board for the protection of displaced populations. It is made of 15 members from the displaced populations who were democratically elected by the population, so they have also been our allies. Apart from that, we work a lot in rural regions, so that has also allowed us to spread our mission, and the mission of the displaced people to restore their rights.

For each workshop, we planned on having around 50 people, but each one had almost 100 people. These workshops were very important to them because a lot of these people don't have information, or they have certain questions regarding the themes of the workshops. So, each workshop was led by an expert in that theme, and that was very important because there were both individual and collective questions that in one way or another, the experts were able to address. After all the workshops, we held an international seminar focusing on the theme of public policy. We invited 300 leaders from around the country. It was a very diverse group, so it was very important. We were able to get their suggestions, which came from all different regions, the work they have done in their regions, and the knowledge they have of their regions. We talked with them about which ideas we could bring to Congress, so that the regional leaders could start having exchanges with Congress. (Interview December 11, 2008)

Many of the advocates described a personal and often life-time commitment to advocating for the rights of the displaced, as the director of one of the primary displaced rights group described, hearing the countless stories of terror and escape, has been simultaneously traumatic (as described by the aid workers in Uganda) but also has strengthened her resolve to keep fighting. This is a somewhat lengthy quote but this aid worker articulated so clearly the sentiments of almost all the interviewees.

[Our organization] has a lot of responsibility; we assume a great deal of responsibility for these 4.5–4.6 million displaced people in Colombia. We are very clear about who the displaced populations are, however, they have put all their hope in us, and that is a lot for a person. And knowing the personal stories of each person is … first, it's very sad knowing the conditions in which they lived, and what conditions they still are living in, above all – the anemic social and spiritual situations they are in. One person can't do everything, but we can see what support systems aid these populations the most. It is very difficult not having the resources to get to regions where there is no institutional presence to help the populations, the same populations that are asking us for help. We want to do something, such as in the Western regions, but we just don't have the resources to travel to those zones. So, we try to identify which predicaments we can help people get out of, but we still have a lot to do. Those populations are human beings, and when you start talking with them, you think a lot, a lot, about them. You can have all the professional experience and capabilities, but it is still difficult. They had to leave everything, leave a loved one who they don't know where they are now, if they have been captured or killed, if their own children are still alive. Through all that, they maintain a faith that things will get better. It makes me want to do a lot for them. Apart from all the human weaknesses like sadness, uncertainties, and frustrations, I never forget about them because they keep moving forward, so we have to keep supporting them …

Psychologically, it affects us, because everyday we hear stories about how someone's husband or daughter has been killed. We heard a very disturbing testimony that a mother told us during a workshop about the victims. Her daughter, a nurse, was going to work by car when a paramilitary group intercepted her, tortured her, played with her mind. Imagine how hard that was for her family, here where the government has not put measures or administrators in place to deal with these issues. I learn a lot working with the victims everyday, but it's very hard to keep everything clear while not letting it affect you. I think that every project involving this population takes some kind of psychological toll, for both the victims and the workers. In many regions, these people don't have any psychological help. You go to these regions and you feel like a psychologist, journalist, lawyer, all of that. So, we keep fighting, and personally, whether through [this organization] or elsewhere, I'll keep fighting for them ...

I keep asking myself: Where are the local programs to help the elderly, the disabled? What are we doing in this country? What does the government do? We are telling the outsiders that Colombia has a program to deal with all this, but we really do not. People always say we're leftist, that we're guerrillas, but there is actually so much that needs to be done here. There are so many sad stories. I would get home at night and cry, cry, cry, cry and ask myself, "What is happening here?" All we can do is keep working, us from here and you from there. And I'll give you anything you need. (Interview December 13, 2008)

The government of Colombia is described by some as trying to aid the displaced, by others as shirking its responsibilities by not allowing large portions of the displaced to register as displaced. Regardless of one's perspective on the government's underlying interest in aiding the displaced, there does seem to be agreement that part of the explanation of insufficient response is simply a lack of capacity. This is the fifth of the five barriers to effective advocacy we see across the cases. In Colombia, NGOs exist that are specifically advocating for the displaced, the government has listened, shown concern, and been responsive in a number of ways (through the Constitutional Court and setting up the RUPD) but at the end of the day it simply doesn't have the capacity to deliver aid to all those that need it. This is evidence of the *Barrier #5: Lack of capacity*. Even though in the case of Colombia there are advocates lobbying for displaced rights, the issue is on the government's agenda, and there appears to be political willingness to do something, they simply do not have the capacity to solve the problem of four million people displaced.

As mentioned, unemployment is generally high in Colombia, and when the displaced flee from rural areas and an agricultural lifestyle to the city where they lack relevant skills, it is difficult to find jobs. Further, across the country in the towns and villages receiving displaced populations, they already have their own problems of poverty to deal with (as most host governments in refugee situations argue). One aid worker described the local governmental response:

We are trying to collect data but it is very difficult when the municipality does not have enough resources or funds to get their own people health and education services. What the mayors say is: "Well, I don't have enough money for education for all my people, so how can you tell me that I need more money or I must have more money to assist new people in my municipality. It is impossible, I have no money!" And it is true. (Interview December 11, 2008)

Thus, even in cases where the government could be argued to care about the people, and even in situations where there are advocates actively fighting for the rights of the displaced the government may simply not have the capacity and resources to provide an appropriate response. In Colombia, the Supreme Court has ruled in favor of displaced rights, requiring the government of Colombia to provide at least three months of aid for victims of forced displacement. Local human rights activists celebrated this victory but lack of capacity limits the Colombian government's ability to deliver on this promise.

Sri Lankan IDPs

Chapter 3 briefly introduced the contours of this two-decade conflict, which the international media largely ignored. While many Tamils fled to India and to other countries in Southeast Asia as refugees, I focus here on the internal displacement that happened on the island. The Sri Lankan army managed the camps, aid agencies supplied services but under the complete control of the army, as one aid worker put it: "The army basically tells us what to do and we just implement it" (interview September 18, 2009). There was no freedom of movement or freedom to work. The army decided who was allowed in and out, and IDPs were only allowed to leave for medical services, to give birth or to visit a loved one in a combatant detention center.

Conditions in the camps were described as incredibly crowded, and the land where the camps are situated as completely unsuitable, in one aid worker's words:

> these conditions that the people are placed in ... they are far below any kind of standards, Sphere standards, any form of humanitarian standards, legal instruments ... ICRC code of conduct, the guiding principles of Sri Lanka, the constitution of Sri Lanka, international humanitarian law ... So I would say we have managed the situation. Over the last nine months we have been able to provide humanitarian assistance of some kind. Still below the minimum standards ... because of no de-congestion plans and all these zones are very overcrowded, so we can't build the toilets, we can't have more shelters ... Still we have about 18 people living in each shelter, where there should be five individuals. Over the board in Manik Farm the toilets are below SPHERE standards. ICRC do not have access, MSF don't have access. So the longer we stay there the more uncomfortable it is in terms of our principles. So we need a much more stronger advocacy role in terms of freedom of movement, in terms of a transparent screening process. So people who are not seen to be a threat should be policed and allowed to go back to their places of origin or go back to host family situations. (Interview September 23, 2009)

IDPs were forced to stay in the camps, people thought to be LTTE, or LTTE sympathizers, would be regularly arrested (or abducted depending on the interviewee) by military forces. One aid worker described some of the programming they were doing and in his words you get a sense of the psychological toll of forced encampment: "We offer to implementing solar cookers, compost bins, and make some small vegetable gardens around their shelters ... home gardening so that at least for a month or two they can get something. For a child or even an adult to watch a plant grow is better than sitting there doing nothing" (interview September 25, 2009).

As with many of the other cases, most NGOs are primarily focusing on providing life-saving food, shelter and basic health care and do not have the bandwidth to engage in advocacy, if they do lobby the government it is for the most basic of things: improved access to camps for aid workers, not improved

Who is advocating?

access to rights for the displaced. This is due in part to limits in capacity but also a very palpable sense that it would fall on deaf ears. One Sri Lankan aid worker with an international organization described their position:

[Our organization] is not doing any advocacy work ... formally you can't say that you are unhappy with certain things in the environment that you are working in ... you know ... is not hundred percent you are happy with. Only so much that we can advocate. You advocate for greater access to these camps ... and it has improved in that sense, [advocacy] has worked but only to a certain extent. But we in [our organization] are not doing any advocacy work. (Interview September 26, 2009)

As with most of the refugee cases discussed in Chapter 4 and the IDP cases discussed here, the major barrier to effective advocacy is *Barrier #1 – Advocacy is not the priority, saving lives is*. One American aid worker described their mandate:

We are working on, saving lives, emergency response, and have a strong component on water sanitation. Earlier we did food, but we decided in April to phase out of that. We are working on shelter and we are also working on providing non-food relief items in terms of standard packs and infant packs, and in terms of hygiene packs. We have a strong hygiene promotion component to our water sanitation program where we try to work and engage as much with the local communities there. (Interview September 23, 2009)

Aid workers were busy providing aid, the little advocacy they did do was primarily to increase their own access to the camps so they could better do their work. This decision was partly due to their understanding that any advocacy around freedom of movement or freedom to work would likely fall on deaf ears.

The Sri Lankan case is likely the strongest example out of the four cases discussed here where *Barrier #2 – Fighting for people no one cares about* is most pronounced. The government of Sri Lanka was and is actively hostile to the displaced population, which it sees largely as synonymous with the Tamil armed rebellion. Aid workers described a range of government behavior from apathetic, to obstructionist, to outright hostility. On the apathy side of the spectrum, a number of aid workers found the government incredibly difficult to work with through the cluster meetings in which the government wouldn't work as a team play in the relief effort and would not share pertinent information:

So there are inter-cluster meetings that happen on a fortnightly basis both in Colombo and the Vavuniya levels. And I think what can be strengthened is the link between Vavuniya and Colombo. As you may know there is a big disconnect between what happens in the field and what happens at the Colombo level. The links have to become stronger because a lot of the decisions are made in Colombo and we should make sure that what we are supposed to adhere should have a strong impact on the ground. So there are inter-cluster meetings, there are deputation meetings ... there is a lot of meetings. There is a lot of coordination but without really knowing the position of the government ... and until we know what the governments' plans are ... and if they don't share these plans with the INGOs, and UN and the donors ... then it is really hard to plan the process and our way to engage in the future. And this still we are waiting for. (Interview September 23, 2009)

Relations between the government and the INGOs were described by most interviewees as strained or difficult, one aid worker described some of the reasons for that tension:

One reason why the government is distrustful about the INGOs is that they concentrate most of their efforts and their products in the north and east. And one of the things about them is branding ... so even if they have a toilet or a tent they will put their name on it. So when these things fall in the hands of the LTTE they take these things ... so when the army goes to the camps, they find these things with the brands names on it. So then they say, okay you have been giving these things. On the other hand, half the weapons they have are the weapons that they gave taken from the military. So that's a problem, the [NGOs] are humongous in this branding. So that has been one reason. And there has been empathy for the Tamil people who are the minority, and the Sinhalese people who are the majority has been seen kind of as the wrongdoers by the INGOs. There is also the issue of religious conversion and Western imperialism. And all of that has contributed to this whole thing. But, during the end of the war, when the NGOs were expected to praise the government for its efforts, they instead started questioning the methodologies ... There is pressure from the West, and seemingly nothing from India. The Indians have more or less agreed with the government policies but keep saying that something should happen for the recent displacement. So on one hand you have China and India and on the other hand you have the West. So it's a very interesting situation. When I talk to Indians they say that outside Tamil Nadu there is hardly any interest. So I have heard that 8 out of 10 people will be happy that the LTTE is not there because they posed a threat to everybody. But what I am talking about is that there is little concern among the people for their own people. (Interview September 25, 2009)

Not only did the government response range from apathetic to hostile but INGOs, NGOs and the displaced themselves had no leverage to pressure the government to action. There is a great deal of evidence of the third barrier to effective advocacy for the rights of the displaced: *Barrier #3 – No votes and no money = no leverage*. An international aid worker described how difficult it is to just get basic work done vis-à-vis local authorities. Aid groups do not have the power, local authorities have the power and aid groups are working at their mercy, having to be careful of what they say:

I think we are all in a kind of situation in Manik Farm where the biggest gap is the freedom of movement. If we look at the gap analysis the biggest is the freedom of movement. So we are working in situations where it is closed. In terms of an IDP camp we want it to be run by civilian authority. We don't have that. We have kind of a military authority. In terms of the safety and security of our staff ... they are not allowed to take their mobile phones inside. Which is also a concern of safety and security of our staff. In terms of access to the camps we do not get unrestricted access all the time. So in terms of what we are achieving there ... in terms of protection it's very, very

Who is advocating?

problematic ... when you open your mouth ... you have to be careful how you work. (Interview September 23, 2009)

This same aid worker went on to describe how some advocacy was being done at the international level since it was so difficult to do any on the ground:

> I think advocacy is happening both at the public and the private level. I mean there is a lot of things happening behind the scene, both here in Sri Lanka with different heads of agencies and things ... and over the last few months issues had been raised in terms of freedom of movement and the screening process and awareness about the impending floods that are going to happen, issues of staff security and safety, and release of the staff from the camps ... this has also been raised at the international level as well. So in terms of advocacy it happens at multiple levels – local, national and international. I think that a lot of people think that within the country at the moment it is really hard be articulate, or be public, in terms of advocacy because of the repercussions for the organizations. One organization recently put on their website some articles about some service that they did in Manik Farm ... they were told that if they do not detract their statement in the next two weeks they have to leave the country. For individuals it is all the more hard to take a stand on something ... I am speaking like this to you because you are coming from a university ... but I will not be speaking like this to anyone else ... for the situation in our organization and for others. (Interview September 23, 2009)

This interview so clearly demonstrates how constrained aid workers are from being advocates – if they speak out, they could be kicked out, and the displaced will not have any support at all.

That lack of leverage of the INGOs, national NGOs and the displaced themselves is clear in the case of Sri Lanka. One unique thing about this case is aid workers are at least talking about the need for freedom of movement, whereas in many of the other cases the immediate pressure of humanitarian response did not even seem to allow aid workers to think of such advocacy goals. In the case of Sri Lanka, likely due to the very strict enforcement of encampment by the government, we see the displaced pleading for freedom of movement and aid workers' recognition of the need to advocate for it – what is still missing is a positive government response to those requests. An aid worker described a needs assessment that was carried out with the IDPs, surveying them on what basic humanitarian needs they had:

> you know what they said? The most important thing for now is the freedom of movement. It could be linked to the monsoon ... we have two monsoons so we all know what we are going into ... people know the instability of the land in Vavuniya, people know about the level of water in Jaffna and what is going to happen in Mannar ... so, these things come down to political will ... do people have that voice to make decision? I hope we can ... I think things have started to happen now and I hope it will change. We have to have a multi-pronged approach to these very issues ... I mean this is a very precarious and difficult situation that we are in now with regards to the north. (Interview September 23, 2009)

A protection and advocacy advisor for a European aid agency echoed this frustration with the lack of progress in urging the government to act:

Monitoring is the more frustrating thing ... its hard to define ... people have different ideas of what the goal is ... and the goal for me for my position is to have more information to do advocacy work ... but the advocacy has resulted in very little actual change for the IDPs on the ground. And that's not because the protection monitoring has failed, but because of our lack of influence on government regardless of what information we have and what we do and that we do not have any ability to change at the moment. (Interview September 23, 2009)

Some instances of corruption were documented, but not in the sense that the government was extracting bribes from NGOs thus weakening their advocacy position but rather the government extracting bribes from the displaced. The aid workers were not at all surprised as this, which in itself is not surprising as I was told about such exploitation in every case where I conducted interviews: "And there has been rumors that they have been able to buy their way out of the camps, because some have money for bribes. It actually has been in the paper. And I think that's normal, that's normal behavior. There is nothing to be very surprised about" (interview September 25, 2009). He went on to note that they too have tried to do international advocacy or below-the-radar advocacy since there would be such strong negative repercussions for the organization's primary work:

If we have some information we give it to the relevant people if they can do something with it. All non-attributable. And we have done various kinds of international advocacy, but we have not done anything public because the security and repercussions on the programs would be drastic. So nothing public ... but a lot of private ... high level and low level advocacy, and it had been all very private and discrete. But I would say that it had been quite successful in that the issues that we think are very important had basically been taken up by the key stake holders. Like our message is what they are using, whether or not they had been successful in getting the results is still unclear. Well I will say there has not been any improvement, no change for IDPs in this country. (Interview September 23, 2009)

He described the main issues to be freedom of movement, a shift toward civilian control of the camps, improved access to the camps for NGOs and a more transparent and accountable process to screen out former combatants from the IDPs and to allow non-combatants to leave the camps.

A national aid worker working for an INGO felt there was evidence of some progress, though this is contradicted by others:

Advocacy is being done regularly both formally and informally at the local and Colombo levels. For example the NGOs working in the protection cluster, advocated the government make safe corridors for people when there was heavy shelling in the Vanni region. We had also been pushing the government to release people to their host families. Now host families in Vavuniya who are not IDPs can apply to take in IDPs for shelter. Freedom of movement is one of the main things we are advocating for. The government is slowly agreeing to this. (Interview September 18, 2009)

With this quote though we also see that often advocacy on the ground is for life or death needs – here, a safe corridor, in other cases protecting against gender-based violence, or getting basic food supplies through.

The barriers

This chapter has shown that the staff working for organizations aiding the internally displaced face many of the same barriers that those aiding refugees face. First, organizations tasked with providing humanitarian relief are concerned with keeping the displaced alive, providing food, shelter, water and medicine. Of the four cases discussed here, only in Colombia do national level organizations exist to primarily fight for the rights of the displaced and demand that the government provide for its citizens that have been forced from their land by armed forces. And in the case of Colombia we have seen some success, with the establishment of the RUPD and the 2011 Victims and Land Restitution Law, but the gap is massive between the rights laid out in the Guiding Principles on Internal Displacement and the conditions on the ground.

Second, Colombia is one of the "best case scenarios" when it comes to effective advocacy on behalf of the displaced, IDPs in Uganda and Sri Lanka fare much worse. These cases are clear examples of barrier #2 – fighting for non-priority citizens. If we consider the broader set of all IDP cases discussed in Chapter 2, host governments, or governmental units, are hostile to the IDP population in numerous cases including DRC, Somalia, Sudan, Central African Republic, Burma/Myanmar, Syria and Afghanistan. In other cases, they are apathetic, as in the case of Croatia, Nepal and East Timor.

Third, the international and national organizations aiding the displaced lack any leverage to encourage the national governments to reform their policies or implementation of those policies, as seen in every case discussed in this chapter, and essentially every IDP case globally. Fourth, even in cases like Colombia where the government has the will to support IDPs, it lacks capacity. This phenomenon can also be seen in Iraq, Azerbaijan, Chad and Congo.

Chapter 1 established the scale and the severity of the global displacement problem, Chapters 2 and 3 presented data showing that the displaced have few advocates in the powerful hall of governance in the Global North and little voice in the public arena of the Western media. Media saturation and the 24-hour news cycle drown out the few campaigns that do mobilize. And for the few that forge an effective coalition and campaign the "ask" is often unclear. What can policymakers in the US and European governments do, even if they were so moved? The displaced are powerless in the international policy arena.

Chapters 4 and 5 delved deep on seven cases of refugee and internal displacement. In case after case, we see evidence of seemingly insurmountable obstacles from resource limitations of aid organizations, to political and economic powerlessness of the displaced and their potential advocates, to lack of will and capacity on the part of hosting governments, to the outright violence and hostility of governments and rebel movements toward these vulnerable communities.

If the organizations aiding the displaced have no leverage, can the displaced themselves mobilize and advocate for their rights? It is to this question I turn next.

6

Frontline mobilization
Advocating for rights in displacement camps

More than 200,000 Darfurian refugees and IDPs waited for nearly a decade in camps on the Chad–Sudanese border. Conditions were described as overcrowded and squalid, food rations are in short supply, alcoholism and domestic violence are on the rise. Aid workers perceived a pervasive malaise among the displaced and an inability to engage, too war-weary to try to improve their situation.

In situations such as these, can the displaced mobilize to engage in collective action? Participating in collective action, or various types of community groups, can normalize daily routines, provide purpose and dignity to camp life, build skills, trust and social capital as well as solve collective problems. Collective action can help rebuild communities during displacement and provide a foundation for the displaced when they return home or are resettled. Political forms of collective action could give the displaced a voice to fight for a wide array of rights.

Examples exist to suggest collective action is possible even in the most trying conditions. In the Tham Hin refugee camp 10,000 Karen refugees have been living in a 1 km^2 camp for 10 years with no hope of returning to Burma; a football league has been established to provide the children with exercise, community building and a release.[1] The Karen Women's Organization has also been formed to advocate for the rights of displaced women and create opportunities for their children. In Djabal Camp, Chad, a school has been established by refugee teachers and girls are receiving an education for the first time.[2] Afghani refugees in the Katwai refugee camp in Balochistan, Pakistan have initiated a

---

[1] NineMillion.org, 2007, www.ninemillion.org/videogallery/videogallery.cfm?id=3.
[2] UNHCR, 2007: "Learning to be a leader, one task at a time," www.ninemillion.org/hotspot/hotspot.cfm?id=44&tab=1.

weaving cooperative, which involves nearly every family in the camp in the carpet production process.[3]

So the question becomes: When does collective action among the displaced occur and what explains it? The research presented here considers all types of collective action including those aimed at solving immediate infrastructure problems like digging wells and latrines and cleaning up camps; as well as organized educational groups, cultural groups, collective income-generating activities, health and psychosocial counseling groups and advocacy-related groups such as women's groups, victims groups and displaced-rights groups. I draw a distinction between non-political groups and these more political groups advocating for rights; since the receptiveness of authorities toward self-help collective actions may be quite different than their openness for political mobilization; resulting in great hurdles to political mobilization.

This chapter will, first, define collective action and describe the type of collective actions I seek to study. Second, I lay out the factors that are hypothesized to promote collective action and those factors that inhibit it. The theoretical approach will consider the barriers to mobilization that the collective action literature has traditionally recognized as well as the hurdles that are unique to situations of forced displacement. The factors that influence mobilization (either positively or negatively) can be grouped into four aspects of the displacement situation: the human security context; the legal context; the cultural/community context; and the duration context. In addition, NGO activity and leadership is a major determinant of collective action among the displaced and forms the fifth category of factors. In the second half of the chapter, I present the findings from the fieldwork in the seven cases which suggest that that context and NGO activity do indeed have an impact on collective action among the displaced, and importantly that there are contextual factors that can be changed to promote more collective action.

The definition and determinants of collective action

Explaining human cooperation, or lack thereof, is of interest to nearly every discipline in the social sciences. Collective action implies individuals making independent decisions to work together for some collective outcome. Collective action problems "occur whenever individuals in interdependent situations face choices in which the maximization of short-term self-interest yields outcomes leaving all participants worse off than feasible alternatives" (Ostrom 1998, 1). This is a more formal way of saying what Rousseau discussed more than 200 years earlier when he described the dilemma of the stag hunt: hunters can choose to go into the forest and work together to hunt a stag, and if successful will feed themselves and the entire village, or one hunter can choose

---

[3] UNHCR, 2007: "Feature: Eager weavers put a positive spin on refugee life in Pakistan," www.unhcr.org/news/NEWS/3e3a3e8ba.html.

The definition of collective action

to defect, in pursuit of his own short-term self-interest and hunt a hare for his own consumption, leaving the other hunters and the village without food. The allegory of the stag highlights the positive effects of human cooperation and the deleterious effects of uncooperative behavior. This definition of the collective action problem is critical in understanding what collective action is in the formal sense, and what is simply activity by a collective.

Collective action can aim to provide a public good (like roads, irrigation or sewage systems, or rules and regulations) or prevent a public bad (like the destruction of common spaces, or the depletion of common pool resources such as water and forests). Public goods can vary on two dimensions: exclusivity and "jointness" (Udéhn 1993). Many public goods are non-exclusive, such as roads, once they are built they are for the use of all. Some public goods are also characterized by "jointness" – "jointness means that the utility one person derives from a good does not diminish as a result of its use by other people. A lighthouse is one commonly cited example. Legislation intended to give us clean air would be another" (Udéhn 1993, 241). However, not all collective action problems involve the provision of a public good or the prevention of a public bad, the benefit of the collective action could only accrue to the participants in the collective action but the drive to maximize short-term self-interest still leads to sub-optimal outcomes for the group – the stag hunt is such an example. An income-generating project such as a plowshare, in which a group of people shares a plow and two oxen to plow their fields, would be another: Each participant has an incentive to not contribute to the costs of maintaining the plow and the oxen while reaping the benefit of easier harvesting.

Many of the scholars attempting to explain cooperation began from a rational choice perspective, as is evident in Ostrom's language, modeling the decision to engage in collective action at the individual level as a cost–benefit analysis (Olson 1965, Salisbury 1969, Moe 1980, Hansen 1985). The individual considers participation in the collective action, be it a neighborhood watch group, community clean-up crew, or women's rights organization or political protest and assess the costs (time, energy, resources, or the threat of backlash from the authorities) and the benefits (providing the collective good – like security; or preventing a collective bad – the destruction of the public spaces due to the tragedy of the commons). Sub-optimal outcomes (or Pareto inferior) occur for the collective because each rational individual, when faced with the decision to contribute to the collective action or to shirk and let others do the work, would decide to free ride. They do no work but still enjoy the collective benefits of security and a clean town square. If everyone decides to free ride, no collective action occurs and the collective problem is not remedied (or the collective good is not provided). While this theoretical framework would predict a dismal state of the world's societies, in reality we see much greater levels of cooperation and collective action.

The literature on collective action, stemming from political science, economics and sociology, has attempted to explain this seemingly "irrational" phenomenon. First, scholars have suggested that there are other benefits to engaging in the collective action other than the collective benefit, such as: selective material benefits of being in the group (the free t-shirt when one joins Greenpeace), selective purposive benefits (feeling you did your citizen duty by voting) and selective solidarity benefits (a sense of camaraderie with fellow protesters in a social movement) (Clark and Wilson 1961, Olson 1965, Salisbury 1969, Pollack 1997). Second, skillful entrepreneurs or leaders can influence the perceived costs and benefits associated with the participation in the collective action (Walker 1983, Nownes and Neely 1996). A well-organized leadership can lower the costs of participation, as we saw with the US President Barack Obama's revolutionary use of online mobilization during the 2009 election. A charismatic leader can make the success of a movement seem eminent or the threat of a government crackdown remote. Third, norms of cooperative behavior or reciprocal altruism can be developed that lead to increased collective action (Ostrom 1998). Fourth, repeated interactions or iterative games result in higher levels of cooperation as individuals realize they will deal with their fellow community members over a longer period of time (Axelrod 1984). Fifth, communication, especially face-to-face communication, builds trust and the opportunity for individuals to make promises to each other about their commitment to the collective action (Ostrom 1998, Udéhn 1993). And sixth, institutions can be developed to sanction those that do not engage in the collective good and to facilitate superior outcomes (Hardin 1968, Ostrom 1990).

Thus, the hard rational choice approach assuming self-interested short-term-maximizing individuals would predict no occurrence of collective action, while other scholars suggest there are reasons why we should expect to see cooperation and collective action. In reality, we see both outcomes and everything in between, from rampant free riding and sub-optimal collective outcomes like the destruction of public lands (Olson 1965, Ostrom 1990) to some of the most inspiring instances of human cooperation the world has ever seen including the overthrow of oppressive regimes and the liberation of nations (McAdam 1988, Tarrow 1998, Zhao 2001). Explaining this variation is fundamental, as Elinor Ostrom, the 2009 Nobel Laureate in Economics, puts it: "The really big puzzle in the social sciences is the development of a consistent theory to explain why cooperation levels vary so much and why specific configurations of situational conditions increase or decrease cooperation" (1998, 9).

Anecdotally we know that collective action occurs among the displaced in camps and settlements, what we don't know is what specific configurations of situational conditions, or *contexts*, increase or decrease that cooperation. This is the aim of the research presented here.

To do that successfully we must delineate our focus, to that end we concentrate on what could be considered normatively "positive" collective actions, in that they are the building blocks of civil society. Walzer defines civil society as "the space of uncoerced human association ... the set of relational networks – formed for the sake of family, faith, interest and ideology – that fill this space" (quoted in Edwards 2009, 20). I am interested in understanding how collective actions in displacement contexts can contribute to the rebuilding and strengthening of civil society. I therefore do not investigate the formation of militias, armies, terrorist cells, drug trafficking, human trafficking or gangs; while all of these groups require coordination and cooperation among the individuals involved in them, I argue these collective activities do not have positive externalities for the broader community. In addition, research on the formation of militias and armed groups has been done more thoroughly elsewhere (see Terry 2002, Muggah 2006).

I collected data on the formation of the full range of collective actions: from the very informal ad hoc groups to more formal CBOs; both those started by the displaced and those initiated by NGOs; and finally across sectors including those that have to do with infrastructure (water and sanitation), education and culture, health and psychosocial, livelihoods and income-generating activities, the environment, security, and "political" groups advocating for women's rights, child rights, victim's rights and displaced rights.

NGOs play a particularly important role in that they can be a catalyst for collective action by providing leadership, resources, communication, selective incentives and institutions to facilitate cooperation. In short, NGOs can provide many of the ingredients the collective action literature has been identifying over the past decades as conducive to collective action.

Life is occurring in these camps: political life, civic life and community life. It is imperative we study and understand those patterns since those that are displaced by violence are often embedded in a cycle of violence. If positively focused collective action in camps can be promoted, it can fill the vacuum that leads to more insidious types of collective action including militias and terrorist organizations.

Collective action contexts

Four sets of contextual factors (or components of the political opportunity structure) are expected to influence the ability of the displaced to engage in collective action: the human security context, the legal context, the cultural context and the duration context. The fifth category of factors concerns NGO work with the displaced communities. Factors in each of these categories are hypothesized to vary on a continuum from conducive to prohibitive of collective action.

Human security context

Maslow's (1943) famous article laying out the human hierarchy of needs provides a theoretical grounding to understand when people will be able to think about higher-order things like "the common or public good." Until basic physiological needs are met (food, water and shelter) and basic safeties are attained (security of body, health and family), individuals cannot prioritize other needs such as belonging to a social group, altruism, problem solving, esteem and self-actualization. Only once lower needs are satisfied can individuals shift their attention and energies to community building and problem solving.

These basic physiological and safety needs align well with the new concept of "human security." While the exact scope of human security continues to be actively debated, a number of scholars and international organizations have defined it as freedom from war, genocide and other forms of political violence on the one hand, and hunger and disease on the other (Human Security Report 2005). The expectation then is that low levels of human security related to physiological needs (food, water, shelter, health) and low levels of human security related to safety needs (political violence, military recruitment, abduction, rape, abuse) will result in lower levels of collective action among the displaced. The lack of human security creates a barrier to mobilization as individuals need to expend energy on attempting to secure these basic necessities.

Legal context
The legal context governing the lives of the displaced can have major implications for how empowered the displaced are and the likelihood they will mobilize and engage in collective action. The literature on resource mobilization (McCarthy and Zald 1978) and political opportunity structures (Kitschelt 1986, Kriesi 1996, Tarrow 1998) suggest how legal characteristics can influence mobilization for collective action.

First, whether the displaced are able to move freely, work freely and access education has implications for their ability to mobilize resources, which are important for the mobilization of collective action. Resources can be in the form of money, goods, skills, labor or facilities (McCarthy and Zald 1978, Marwell and Oliver 1993, Cress and Snow 1998) and resources can be mobilized from within, or derived from without from "conscience constituents." Access to education is important for skill development, and there is evidence that those who are more highly educated are more likely to participate in civil society (Morgan *et al.* 1975).

The degree to which the displaced can move, work and study freely varies significantly across displacement crises. When the displaced have crossed international borders, they are protected by the international refugee convention but are then often forbidden from working or moving freely out of refugee camps. Schools are often provided within camps but can be overcrowded, and constrained to primary education, with extremely limited opportunity for secondary education. When the displaced have been so internally, they are ostensibly still citizens of their home country and should enjoy the rights and freedoms of any other citizen of that country; this however is often not the case. In many internal displacement situations, the displaced are restricted in movement and limited in ability to engage in income-generating activities (or livelihoods). Laws governing whether the displaced are allowed to work and whether they are allowed to move freely in and out of camps, influence their access to resources and their vulnerability to exploitation. Strong movement restrictions are hypothesized to suppress collective action as camp residents cannot access resources, move between camps, and interact with migrant populations or local populations, which could be helpful in collective activities.

Another aspect of the legal context that is expected to have an impact on collective action, especially of the political type, is government oppression. Literature on political opportunity structures has highlighted the importance of the prevailing political conditions to the formation of social movement organizations, as Kriesi puts it, "the extent to which challenging collective actions will be facilitated or repressed" (1996, 168). High levels of government monitoring and intimidation in camps and displaced settlements is likely to suppress collective mobilization especially those that are aimed at advocating for the rights of the displaced.

Cultural and community context
The literature on social capital has shown that interpersonal trust is important for community engagement (Putnam 1993; 2003). The level of trust among the displaced population, both regarding the others that are displaced and regarding those that are "governing" the camp, is expected to influence their propensity to mobilize. The level of trust though, is related to a second important characteristic: diversity. Ethnic, nationalistic or religious diversity can make it difficult to form groups to solve collective problems. Two types of social capital have been identified: bonding social capital, which links homogeneous populations, and bridging social capital, which links heterogeneous populations. The expectation is that collective action is most likely where trust is high and the population is homogeneous, collective action should be slightly less likely where trust is high but the population is heterogeneous, and finally, collective action is least likely when trust is low, regardless of the composition of the population.

How intact the displaced community is will likely also play a role in the formation of collective endeavors. In some ways, studying collective action formation among the displaced offers a unique research setting quite different from studying collective action in long-standing communities that are not suffering from extreme stress. In certain situations it is a matter of studying community building in a virtual vacuum. In other situations this is far from the case. Depending on the nature of displacement, the individuals who find themselves in a camp may see most of the community structures, leadership, elder groups, and family ties intact; in other situations massive forced migration may result in families torn apart and social structures erased with little to no community on which to rely. It is important to understand the nature of the displacement, the composition of the camp and the degree to which collective actions are really being organized from scratch or be re-organized by the community structures that moved with the displacement.

Duration context
Lastly, the length of the displacement is critical. As Axelrod (1984) and Ostrom (1990) suggest, over time iterated interaction among members of a population can lead to norms of reciprocal altruism. Protracted displacement crises of course would allow more time for norm development, collective action formation, organization resourcing and implementation. While this study only focuses on protracted situations, expectations about how long the displacement will continue are also likely to have significant influence on the willingness of the displaced to engage in collective action to improve the immediate camp community. If people anticipate returning home or to a new home soon, they will be less likely to engage in collective problem solving in the camp. If people suspect the duration of the displacement could go on for some time, they should be more likely to cooperate in collective action in the camp.

NGO activity – projects/initiatives
While the difficult contexts surrounding displacement create barriers to mobilization, it is possible to overcome those barriers in certain cases. In some instances, the displaced overcome these barriers on their own and begin grassroots collective activities. However, since most collective actions require resources, and resources are in short supply, external intervention is often required. NGOs can provide many of the critical ingredients for mobilization highlighted in the collective action literature including incentives (Clark and Wilson 1961, Salisbury 1969), leadership (Walker 1983), resources (McCarthy and Zald 1978), and communication pathways and institutions to facilitate cooperation (Ostrom 1990).

In some displacement situations, there may be no NGO presence in camps at all or only infrequent visits for basic aid delivery. In other settings, NGOs are initiating creative and dynamic interventions but it remains unclear how NGO interventions intersect with displacement contexts to allow successful collective action.

Therefore, it is necessary to collect information on: the number and type of NGOs present; whether there is a coordinating mechanism in place to maximize the impact of the NGOs operating there; and whether that coordinating mechanism is functioning. The more NGOs and the better coordinated, the more external resources to aid in mobilizing collective action.

In addition, to gain a deeper understanding of how specific NGO programs promote (or fail to promote) collective action, it is also necessary to collect data on each project run by each NGO. Therefore, we gathered information on whether or not NGOs are implementing interventions that mobilize the

The nature of collective action

community; the type of intervention (agricultural, educational, recreational, rights-focused, etc.); the recruitment process to the intervention; whether and what type of incentives were provided to participate; and the leadership of the group or project.

Data collection

The case selection and interview requests process was discussed in detail in Chapter 4. Field interviews and collected materials are drawn on to establish the following indicators:

- **Collective action** – the types of collective action that are occurring (educational, political, economic, cultural, etc.); the degree of formalization (full-fledged CBO or ad hoc informal group); their structure and organization; the level of involvement in the collective groups; the initiation and leadership of collective action (displaced led or NGO led).
- **Human security context** – access to food; access to water; access to shelter; access to health care; level of violence outside camp; level of violence inside camp; threat of forced inscription, rape, abduction.
- **Legal context** – regulations regarding access to education in the camp; access to livelihoods; freedom of movement in and out of camp (de jure and de facto); government oppression.
- **Cultural and community context** – demographic information; race; ethnicity; religion; nationality; whether the community was largely intact upon arrival or dispersed; level of trust.
- **Duration context** – how long the displacement situation has continued and the general expectations about when repatriation or resettlement will occur.
- **NGO activity** – number of NGOs operating; coordination mechanisms in place; number and types of interventions; scope of participation; provision of incentives to participate.

The nature of collective action among the displaced

Each of the seven cases involves massive displacement, in the cases of Uganda and Sri Lanka the displaced are largely in IDP camps, though many have also fled to extended family in larger towns and cities; in the case of Kenya, Nepal, Croatia and Thailand they are in refugee camps, and in Colombia IDPs largely concentrated in "land invasion" settlements at the outskirts of the major cities.

Collective action, particularly political collective action, is quite high in Colombia and Thailand, quite low in Uganda, Kenya and Croatia and mixed in Nepal and Sri Lanka as shown in Table 6.1. We see higher levels of mobilization in Uganda during return, now that the violence has ended but it has to be fostered by NGOs, higher levels of mobilization among the Bhutanese earlier

TABLE 6.1. *Level of collective action among the displaced*

	Collective action
Croatia	Low
Kenya	Low
Uganda	Low/Mixed
Nepal	Mixed
Sri Lanka	Mixed
Colombia	High
Thailand	High

in the decade and less later in the decade once the resettlement process began, and higher levels of mobilization in the eastern Sri Lankan camps compared to the internment camps of the north where government spies and inquisition are rampant.

Why do we see such variation when it comes to collective action across the seven cases? Drawing on evidence from the field interviews and databases and reports collected in the field I discuss the factors that are promoting and inhibiting political and non-political collective action in each case.

Of the seven country cases the Karen, and to a lesser extent the Karenni, refugees in Thailand are forming CBOs and formal collective actions at an impressive rate. The majority of collective actions fall under the non-political umbrella but political collective action also occurs with groups advocating for the rights of the displaced before the Thai camp management, Thai local officials and the international NGO community, predominantly on day-to-day concerns such as the food basket, the language of instruction in camp schools or access to secondary schooling for their children.

An NGO staffer that regularly meets with residents in all nine camps has been compiling a list of CBOs and has identified some 280 organizations across the camps. As he described:

I'm trying to support the CBOs in their lobbying of the NGOs. We did a gap in services study/analysis. What came out were the gaps, what the NGOs weren't able to do. Then I sat down with the CBOs in Nu Po, Umpium, Site 1 and Ban Dong Yang. They identified their work plans for the coming year, then we compared their activities and we found there were areas where they would be filling gaps. Then we used that document to try to lobby the NGOs – with a message of "let's get together" you know. And I have to say the CCSDPT, and the TBBC I have to admit, but been embarrassingly unreceptive. I've only been doing it for six months, but in six months we could only get one meeting with the NGOs and even then they made no commitments. There is a lot the CBOs are doing, more they could be doing, we the NGOs are stretched to the limit – no resources, no time – so why not help them do this work? (Interview, Mae Sot, Thailand, May 23, 2008)

Mae La is one of the largest refugee camps in Thailand with estimates hovering around 38,000.[4] Mae La is bustling with multiple schools, libraries and boarding schools, a football field, NGO offices and black market shops.

NGO staff are aware of at least 34 CBOs organized and managed by the refugees including the Karen Women's Organization (KWO), the Karen Youth Organization (KYO), the Karen Student Networking Group, an organization of Buddhist monks, cultural organizations promoting traditional Karen dancing, music and arts, and a union of health workers. These groups organize events, run nursery schools, organize peer-to-peer trainings, collect dues and directly seek external funding. The KWO wrote for and received a grant from UNICEF and KYO was supported by the Soros Foundation.

Not only is the level of CBO activity very high, but the refugees manage the camps. The security is maintained by the Camp Commander and RTG and supplies are provided by the TBBC and the CCSDPT but it is the Karen Refugee Committee (KRC) that manages the camp, that distributes the food, and that pays the small stipends to refugees that aid in the distribution of supplies and other camp tasks. The KRC has a Department of Education, and a Department of Agriculture, an advisory body of Elders, oversees the CBOs and adjudicates less serious crimes in the camp. The KRC oversees the management of all seven Karen dominated camps (a Karenni Refugee Committee oversees the two Karenni dominated camps in the north) but each camp has its own Camp Committee which falls under the KRC. Each Camp Committee has 15–20 members that are in charge of different areas including education, health, food distribution, judiciary, women's issues, security and youth. The composition of the KRC and the individual Camp Committees is decided by regular elections for two-year terms.

In Colombia, we also see significant levels of mobilization; and particularly high levels of political mobilization, fighting for the rights of the displaced before local and federal authorities. IDP organizations have been formed in the departments most affected by the conflict (Chocó, Nariño, Arauca, Cauca and Putumyo), as well as in the major cities, advocating for rights of the displaced. A number of national umbrella organizations exist to organize regional and sub-regional IDP organizations. The *Mesa Nacional des Desplazadas*, the umbrella organization of IDP organizations, is consulted on all public policy debates, parallel structures exist at the regional and municipal levels. To better represent the rights and interests of displaced women there is also the *Liga de Mujeres Desplazadas* (League of Displaced Women); the *Fundación Mujer Familia y Trabajo* (Foundation of Women, Family and Work) and "Women and Armed Conflict in Colombia" which has a working group of 20 organizations

---

[4] This figure though is known to be imprecise since the Royal Thai Government (RTG) declared the camps "closed" in 2007 and stopped registering new arrivals even though new arrivals continue to stream in every day and fill the dwellings of the thousands that have been officially resettled.

working to raise awareness of the violent conflict in Colombia and the violation of the rights of women. Similarly, there are specialized groups representing indigenous peoples and Afro-Colombians who are disproportionately affected by the conflict. *Opcion Legal*, one of the primary implementing partners of the UNHCR, has 140 IDP organizations in its database, which it assists through capacity building.

Levels of mobilization in Uganda are very low despite the fact that the displaced population encompasses the full range of population demographics – young, old, able, disabled, males, females, etc. – since nearly 80 percent of the population of northern Uganda is displaced. The only grassroots collective action identified were small savings groups where the displaced would pool small bits of resources and give it all to one member of the collective who would then engage in an income-generating activity like brick making; the next month, resources would be pooled again and given to another member of the collective, and so on. Other than this, most NGOs complained of an inability to mobilize the displaced to help with camp maintenance tasks, community health programs and education programs without some type of incentives or payments.

A similar description applies to the Somali refugee camps in Kenya, the hundreds of thousands of refugees residing there have fled constant war, across long distances, only to arrive at under-resourced, overcrowded camps in desolate and remote land at the edges of the Sahara Desert. Collective camp organization for political purposes or otherwise are hard to find. Refugees participate in food distribution, Non-Food Item (NFI) distribution and a number of other NGO activities required to maintain the camp but these are all incentive positions, where the refugees receive some modest payment, often in the form of NFIs, for their participation.

Mobilization was even lower in the camps in Croatia. The refugees and IDPs still left from the 1991 war are the most vulnerable individuals; the elderly and disabled that have not been able to start over. There are no groups, no mobilization, no NGO projects. Some residents will help the older residents by getting water or cutting wood for a few kuna, the local currency, but no form of organized or informal collective action could be identified. Mala Corica settlement, 20 minutes north of the small town of Petrinja, provides a clear example of the character of the Croatian camps. It is a small collection of pre-fabricated temporary dwellings donated by the Japanese government in the 1990s. There are 158 people (refugees from Bosnia-Herzegovina and Serbia and some Croatian IDPs) residing in small wooden buildings. Each plot has space enough for a small garden but residents complain the land is bad, as it is located on a floodplain and things do not grow. The water source that feeds the pipes into the dwellings is polluted with heavy metals and so residents must walk to get access to clean drinking water. Residents get a small allowance to buy food; some supplement this by working illegally or legally depending on their status. If they are ill, they can go to town and go to doctors who have been arranged to treat those with refugee status. Camp life is quiet and desolate.

Human security context and collective action

Human security levels are higher in the camps in Croatia and Thailand than in the camps and settlements in Uganda, Sri Lanka and Colombia. Access to food, water, shelter and health services are moderately good in the camps in Croatia and Thailand. In the case of Uganda and Sri Lanka, there is a greater lack of access to basic services, little access to clean water and sanitation. The settlements at the outskirts of cities in Colombia are not recognized in any way by the government and therefore services are not provided there. Aid to the displaced in Colombia is on an individual basis for those individuals who are registered with the central registration system called the Unitary Displaced Population Registry (*Registro Único de Población Desplazada*, or RUPD). Generally, though, conditions regarding access to food, water, shelter and health care are fairly comparable, ranging from at or below Sphere standards in each case.

Regarding conflict near the camp and violence within the camps the highest level of insecurity occurred in Uganda during the period of encampment with attacks on camps common (IDMC 2008). Raids on the camps to abduct boys to serve as child soldiers and girls as sex slaves were regular occurrences. The threat of abduction was so great that children would walk miles every evening to sleep on the streets of the larger towns to avoid the raids. The security situation has drastically improved in Ugandan camps since the Cessation of Hostilities agreement. Colombia marks the other case with high levels of insecurity, land-invasion encampments are often ruled by paramilitary/narco-terrorist gangs, threats to IDPs living in these areas are high and the inability to know who is a paramilitary or not suppresses collective action in the neighborhoods. NGOs operating in these areas are forced to negotiate with paramilitaries simply to move their staff in and out safely and implement programs for the displaced.

In most of the interviews and primary data collected in Sri Lanka, the issue of human security (in the northern camps, especially Manik Farm) or more precisely the lack of it, had been of overwhelming concern. Most NGOs agree that a sudden influx of a large number of war-torn and devastated people had created a humanitarian crisis.

The conditions of food, water and shelter, as many interviewees put it, "were below Sphere Standards." This was a tired and exhausted population living under closed camp conditions with heavy military presence outside the camps. One of the INGO workers, a native to Sri Lanka, also mentioned there was police presence within the camps, and there were rumors about police officials moving around camouflaged as IDPs. This had led to mistrust among the IDPs, as any open critique of the government repression and camp conditions were not possible even in privacy. According to many officials, NGOs were not officially allowed to do protection monitoring within Manik Farm. As one aid worker said:

Protection monitoring and protection activities are not officially allowed in the north ... you are not really allowed to talk directly to IDPs ... which is something that particularly affects the protection sector ... it affects everybody ... because that means you cannot do things like needs assessments or evaluations of assistance ... we do not have access to the beneficiary data ... to the IDP registry. So it is impossible to tailor programs. So I mean a clear example would an example of Save the Children ... how can they plan a program if they don't even know how many children are in the camps or have any access to the information ... not even the numbers but where they are ... we just don't know ... so it's completely ad hoc all of our response.

This confirms the theories of collective action that emphasize the importance of trust among members of the group for collective action to occur. The general lack of human security, and the lack of trust, created conditions where sustained political collective action is not possible. However in many of the interviews, NGO workers have also mentioned non-political collectives concerned with basic humanitarian needs of survival but in other cases the military was in full control:

In every zone they have camp management committees. They are taking a much more active role in this ... and even most of our casual labor is through the camps themselves ... so in zones there are skilled people within the camps and they are utilized for building the shelters ... and for working in the wash they have committees. There are hygiene promoters and volunteers are really looking at the public health issues and environmental issues within the camps.

And:

I mean when you say camps you mean camps with respect to the north, as in Jaffna and Vavuniya. I think it's almost entirely militarily administered. I think you have kind of elements of civilian officials ... public officials working like from Health, Education and sectorally ... but I think that the command I would say is still very much in the hands of the military. And they still do come under the competent authority which is again a kind of diversion from civilian authority ... because the competent authority to date has been military.

Legal context and collective action

Freedom of movement and freedom to work was restricted in almost every case with the most extreme cases of confined encampment occurring in Uganda, Kenya, Thailand, northern Sri Lanka. Restrictions on movement were much lower in eastern Sri Lanka, and were eased in Uganda following the Peace Agreement. Freedom of movement in Croatia was quite lax for both refugees and IDPs and fairly lenient in Nepal, with some men leaving the camp for various types of construction and demolition jobs in the nearby town. Movement and work are open to Colombian IDPs, and while the displaced often do face discrimination when seeking jobs they do have the ability to work odd jobs in Colombia's large cities. Across all the cases Colombian IDPs had access to relatively higher levels of resources due to the lack of restrictions on their movement and the ability to tie in to other networks of extended family and to networks of those who have been displaced for a greater period of time.

The nature of collective action

Restrictions on access to livelihoods clearly had a toll on collective mobilization with the most restricted encampment cases of Kenya, Uganda and northern Sri Lanka showing the lowest levels of mobilization. During the height of the conflict in northern Uganda, the government of Uganda ordered all citizens into the "protected villages" where they were forced to remain, under threat of being shot if they attempted to leave the camps. The internment camps of northern Sri Lanka were equally locked down. While de jure restrictions on movement and livelihoods existed in the Karen camps in Thailand, a de facto system of payments for movement in and out of the camp, and payoffs to officials to look the other way when the displaced engage in income-generating activities allows the Karen access to resources. In practice, a large number of residents work outside the camp in agriculture and factories. Access to education, and thus skill-development which could be used for mobilization purposes, was roughly the same across all the cases and did not appear to have any significant effect on collective mobilization other than the fact that many of the NGO initiatives were targeted at school children such as Right to Play's soccer clubs and Shanti's libraries and book clubs in Thailand.

The extinguishing power of government oppression could be seen most in the cases of Uganda and the camps in northern Sri Lanka. As mentioned in both cases, government enforcement of internment was done with an iron fist and respondents alluded to this suppression as a reason for generally low levels of mobilization. Though legally all the IDPs were citizens of Sri Lanka, from the pragmatic standpoint IDPs in Vavuniya did not have any rights enjoyed by other citizens, the most important being the freedom of movement and livelihood. One of the INGO officials wanted to qualify the closed nature of the camps.

People can leave the camp for specified reasons. You can leave the camp if you have a medical emergency.so you can go to the hospital. If you are about give birth ... pregnant women are supposed to be able to leave at 37 weeks. Mostly they had been leaving much later than that but they had been allowed to leave the camp to give birth. You can leave the camp it seems quite recently now to visit a member of your family who has been separated out as a former combatant in one of the rehabilitation centers. So the military have started organizing family visits from IDPs to those sites. And ... that's it. For all of those reasons you have to come back to the camp. It's not permanent leaving.

The main reason for the lack of freedom of movement (which was only instituted after the last 2009 offensive in Vavuniya and Jaffna and was non-existent in the previous cases of displacement in Sri Lanka[5]) was attributed to the government's paranoia regarding LTTE extremist infiltration within the general populations. However, in Manik Farm, there were spontaneous protests against restriction of movements across different Zones in Manik Farm. When

---

[5] For example in eastern camps like Trincomalee and Batticaola from previous waves of displacement.

the army bussed in the displaced to Vavuniya, many families got separated into different zones. So it was important for them to visit them in other zones of Manik Farm. There were big demonstrations, as a result of which the Sri Lankan army had started allowing people to move around among the different zones by using a pass system. Similarly in a different case government violence has also been a point of mobilization as one NGO staffer in Sri Lanka recounted:

There was a demonstration on Wednesday morning in the College of Education ... which is one of the school sites ... they have been there since February ... one of the last school sites to be decongested and moved to Manik Farm. The demonstration was because there was an IDP who escaped and was caught by the SLA and beaten very severely. IDPs remaining in the site had heard that he was killed and they started protesting, demonstrating, and then demanding to see the boy (who escaped) as a proof that he was alive. So the SLA had to bring him to the camp and showed him. He was hospitalized with severe injuries but he was alive ... so that kind of subsided things.

One can then theorize from here that even within the context of a severe lack of basic human security and freedom of movement, spontaneous political collective action among IDPs can occur within camps, if the level of tolerance (or passive acceptance) toward existing coercive techniques deteriorates because of excesses of power (i.e. significant deviations from perceived norms of control). Any form of repression is unjust in itself, yet some forms of repression are more unjust than others.

This situation can be contrasted with that of the eastern camps in Sri Lanka, which were established previously. These were always completely open camps where the people were free to go out of the camps for livelihood activities ("you could do anything you wanted in the east") and there were visits allowed by family members. The interviews generally revealed that collective action occurred in these open camps and led to the formation of CBOs instrumental in providing legal assistance for procuring different documents needed in Sri Lanka's National Identity Card (NIC) and other government support which requires NIC. There are older camps from where people have not returned and have started to build their lives and communities in and around the camps. There was also the possibility of extensive host community participation:

We are doing a much more long-term engagement and we work in a predominantly an agriculturally based livelihood project. We try and work with existing community based organizations and work with farmer field schools ... its a kind of methodology that's really trying to get them look at the lived experience and empowerment, through a process of problem solving and critical thinking and analysis within an agricultural framework. And then utilize the skills in other areas and elements of life so that they can make more informed decisions about various different things. With regards to that project we do a lot of functional linkages so the project actually links up to the different government structures at the district level and we work with the

The nature of collective action 117

Rural Development Foundation, women development centers. We work with the agricultural extension officers, we work with the social services officers in terms of CBO (Community Based Organizations) strengthening and promote accountability and governance within them. So we are really trying to set up more civil society organizations which will advocate not just for their rights but the rights of people within the communities.

Why were the camps in the east open and the ones in the north not? It was difficult to get a definitive answer from aid workers, one replied:

I don't know … I don't know … I guess the government think that the people in the north from Vanni were much more hardcore LTTE that that in the east. In the east the population was slightly more mixed … though they were majority Tamils there were a significant Muslim and some Sinhala people. Of course there were no Muslims in the Vanni region because the LTTE have driven them out. I suppose the government thinks that all of the people in the north are either LTTE or supporters of LTTE. But whatever be the case it's illegal and there cannot be any justification for that.

Thus, we can argue that freedom of movement among the IDPs is the single most important predictor of sustained community based collective action among IDPs. And in turn freedom of movement, at least in the context of Sri Lanka, is a function of trust among the government and the displaced, where the trust is located along the axes of ethnic composition of IDPs and the perception (among authorities) regarding the nature of the displaced persons in terms of the threat they may pose to the sovereignty of the nation-state.

In Colombia, high levels of political mobilization remain despite intimidation. In this case, it is difficult to determine who the culprits are – the government, FARC, paramilitaries or narco-terrorists, but the *Instituto Latinoamerianos de Servicios Legales Alternativos* tracks threats and attacks against IDP leaders. At least eight IDP leaders were killed in the first six months of 2008 (IDMC 2008) and many more since 2002. A government agency exists to protect IDP leaders advocating for the human rights of the displaced but many argue the government is infiltrated by paramilitaries and being on the list could put leaders in even greater danger.

Why are the displaced able to have strong voices even in the face of masked intimidation? Perhaps the most important factor aiding the mobilization of the displaced in Colombia is the strong legal basis Colombia has to protect the displaced and the Court's proactive incorporation of displaced voices into the national debate. The Constitutional Court has been extremely progressive in condemning the government for not doing enough to aid the displaced, going so far as to declare an "unconstitutional state of affairs" in 2004 with ruling T 024 and calling for a follow-up committee to monitor public policy on forced displacement (CODHES 2008). That follow-up committee released a report, which further pushed for firm deadlines by which the government needs to take action to improve the conditions of the displaced, as well as take into consideration the special case of women and girls, indigenous groups and the

Afro-Colombian population. In each of these public policy debates, national and local NGOs and displaced CBOs have been incorporated in the process. As mentioned, the 2005 Justice and Peace Law was a process of demobilization of the paramilitaries but it was also a law to promote reconciliation and reparations for victims of paramilitary atrocities (Crisis Group 2008). This process, though slow in its implementation, had victim and displaced rights groups integrally involved.

Cultural/community context and collective action
There was evidence that the nature of the displacement and the level of trust were significant drivers in the ability of the displaced to mobilize. In Thailand, one of the reasons the KRC, the Camp Committees and the CBOs are so well organized is that many of the structures were transplanted from the autonomous Karen State in Burma. When the refugees fled, with them fled much of the leadership of the KNU – the Karen National Union and some of the leaders of the KNLA – the Karen National Liberation Army. Karen State maintained a well-developed government with, as mentioned, ministries of education, agriculture, defense, forestry, etc. Much of these structures were reinitiated after the displacement and provided a foundation on which to build the camp structures facilitating collective action.

The nature of displacement, however, intersects with the human security context as well, in a setting where resources are low, communities that move en masse may be at an advantage, but the displaced that find themselves in societies with relatively higher levels of resources may be at an advantage if they migrate in smaller groups, as is the case in Colombia. Displacement normally occurs on an individual basis there and since Colombia has a stronger infrastructure than many developing countries, it can absorb the influx of people. Most of those displaced move to urban areas and move in with extended family. This provides them with a basis of resources and networking opportunities with other displaced individuals that have access to further resources, be they financial, knowledge about the aid system, connections for employment, or legitimacy vis-à-vis the government as it relates to advocacy for the rights of the displaced.

In Uganda, the lack of interpersonal trust was highlighted by a number of respondents as a barrier to mobilization. A number of NGOs were attempting to institute "plowshares" where a set of oxen and a plow was given to the village and shared amongst the members of the village during harvest time. This traditional practice once worked quite well in Uganda, but today "plowshare cooperatives" have tended to break down, with free riding rampant. Oxen were not fed, plows left broken, the only way they came to work is if one person took control and responsibility for both and rented the team out for a monetary fee. The number one reason identified by interviewees for the inability for the "plowshares" to work, or to get people to work together, was the lack of trust, of neighbors and even family members, which came from the war. The Lord's Resistance Army's practice of abducting children and forcing them to become child soldiers, in the process often being forced to kill family members and neighbors, has led to rampant mistrust so pervasive that it has broken down the family unit. Further complicating the situation is the dismal state of human security; there is little access to clean water, reliable food sources or adequate shelter in the camps. Instability on the border with Sudan continues to instill fear in those traumatized by 20 years of civil war.

All of the displaced in Manik Farm in Sri Lanka are Hindu Tamils and they fled the LTTE-controlled areas in the north during the final stages of the war. The displaced in the east (as we have mentioned before) were somewhat little more heterogeneous in religious affiliation, with some Muslim and Sinhala among the displaced as well. Yet, contrary to the theories that propose high levels of collective action among a more homogeneous population, we find more mobilization in the east than in the north. This can be attributed to low levels of trust among the population in the north camps because of the threat of persecution and punishment by the army. Also, as many NGO staff stated, in the northern camps people have fled individually rather than in village units and they have become separated from their families.

Because of what happened before they came out ... it has led to almost complete community breakdown. So people from ... for example Mannar ... spent almost nine months being continually displaced ... as the frontline moved and moved. So they moved from Mannar up through Mante west ... across the north they hit Kilinochi ... then they moved to Mulativu and then ended up in that very thin strip of land in the east coast of Mulativu. So the people who started from Mannar over nine months the communities became smaller and smaller and increasingly fragmented. During the last month on the strip which is during May 2009 all the shelling led to further community disintegration. People fled starting from February 2009 onwards and they made the decision as individual nuclear families they did not make them as communities to leave the LTTE. So February, March, April there had been much more community fragmentation ... just individuals basically coming out. May you have some but not really ... so when you go to the camps ... it's another issue, because people have been cramped into tents and to a large extent they do not know the people they are sharing the tent with or people in the tents in the either side of them, which has also been an issue for building trust etc. It is much more prevalant in Zone 2 and 4. Zone 4 has a much larger presence of LTTE as they were the last to come out and hence related to that there is a much larger presence of police intelligence in the camps, and people since they do not know who they have come out with they also do not know who are the intelligence agencies. So there is a much higher level of paranoia and fear in Zone 4 and Zone 2 as they were the last people to come out essentially. (Interview September 2009)

The breakdown of community networks, combined with a lack of trust had led to low levels of mobilization, even though the displaced were all Tamils.

Duration context and collective action

Expectations regarding when the displacement will end do have implications for interest in mobilizing for collective action, this could be seen most acutely in Croatia, where there is no hope for a future: a future to return home, to be resettled or to integrate. The aging population has no real alternatives, they do not have family or connections back home and they do not have the skills to settle in a third country. Many still suffer psychological effects of the war and the displacement. The camp manager at one camp described them as "waiting to die" and that it was a retirement home of sorts. Further, the Croatian government has carried out a process of consolidating existing camps, with the aim of closing all camps by 2010. In doing so they have moved those who were displaced to eastern or central Croatian locations to other locations in the past few years. This has resulted in a mix of individuals, from different original locations, and different displacement locations being grouped in settlements with people they do not know. Residents ceded that being moved so many times made them less inclined to get to know the others, assuming they would be soon moved again.

We see the impact of displacement expectations in a different form in Thailand; here the hope of a new life is leading to a disintegration of a vibrant camp community. In 2004 the United States said it would accept up to 60,000 Karen refugees and a massive resettlement campaign has begun, Mae La camp is one of the first being depopulated.[6] By the end of April 2008, Mae La had resettled 2,996 of its residents (IOM 2008). Through the interviews, it became clear that this is one of the biggest factors suppressing collective action. This speaks specifically to the duration context – how long people think they will be in the camp affects their likelihood in engaging in collective action as one NGO staffer noted: "They aren't interested in Karen culture or traditional music any more, they are going to be in Missouri or somewhere next year so the young people are no longer interested in learning these things." As mentioned, in the past 10–15 years a number of strong groups were created passing down traditional Karen ways, with resettlement these groups are seeing less participation and interest.

Another NGO staff person, working on camp sanitation, described the difficulty in getting workers for NGO-sponsored sanitation projects:

We started working in May 2007, but in May 2007 Resettlement began in Mae La – in Dec 2006 was the announcement of Resettlement and so when we tried to start recruiting in May 2007 we found it very difficult, we were competing with other NGOs and they were known and we were not – we didn't have an office, and expectations had changed, people knew they were leaving soon and they didn't want to contribute to the camp since they wouldn't be there the next year.

A number of NGO representatives emphasized the negative impact resettlement was having on camp life, community organizations, health conditions as

---

[6] Between 2004 and 2007, 39,670 refugees had departed Thailand, so far in 2008, 5,230 more refugees were added to that number resulting in a total of 44,900 resettled (IOM 2008).

The nature of collective action

trained health workers leave and education as trained school teachers leave. It is both that there is a bias in receiving countries for better-skilled individuals and a selection bias on the part of the better educated who know about resettlement and want to apply. All NGO staff recognize the positive effect of resettlement on the individual but also recognize the difficulties it creates in camp management.

Since the conflict in Sri Lanka has continued on and off for about 27 years there were different waves of displacement, return and resettlement. The displaced in the older camps have mostly been returned sometimes forcefully and there are many national and international organizations (CARE, NRC, Sarvodaya and IOM) working on resettlement of the returnees. In the case of Manik Camp, the displaced knew that they would be allowed to leave in 180 days:

People know it will be going to be 180 days ... because that's what they have heard. The time had started in June ... so by the end of the year. So people have heard it because there are news papers available and quite a lot of people for some reason have access to radio. So people have been listening to BBC Tamil Service quite a lot ... and also Surya FM which is a national Tamil radio station. So that's what the government has announced ... 180 days and that's what people are thinking. (Interview September 2009)

But it was also obvious that resettlement was possible only after extensive de-mining in the north and screening by the government. From previous cases, it was obvious that resettlement without proper infrastructure would lead to further destitution, and meaningful resettlement generally takes a great deal of time.

Almost none of the returns have had infrastructure it's almost always been return coupled with emergency shelter and the whole infrastructure and community building etc. happens afterwards. So people do return to places where there isn't a functioning school etc. which is why you often see re-displacement ... or people would often return home but then would kind of informally move back into towns so that their kids can continue going to school. One of the big issues regarding returns in the east has been lack of access to education. People not wanting to return home because their kids are in schools in the town where the IDP camps are. It's also a big issue why people don't really want to accept the relocation in the east, for people cannot return home for high security zones, 6,000 people have been affected by the and the areas that the government had suggested have been basically rejected by the IDPs for a whole host of reasons. One of them is access to education. There is lots of other reasons but education is a priority for the people in this country. (Interview September 2009)

These comments show that resettlement in itself is sometimes not truly a durable solution and may not lead to any community mobilization and rebuilding as expected.

NGO activity and collective action

We see a wide range of NGO engagement and supportive mobilization from nearly no NGO presence in Croatia to a strong, well-resourced and well-coordinated one in Thailand. While the Croatian Ministry of the Interior, the UNHCR, the Croatian Red Cross and local groups of women helping the elderly get water and firewood visit the camps from time to time in Croatia, on a daily basis there is no NGO presence in the camps, no activities, no projects. There are no community groups, no CBOs, no informal collective actions.

Juxtapose this with the situation in Thailand where a highly organized consortium of 10 NGOs called the Thai-Burma Border Consortium (TBBC) distributes the bi-monthly food ration, which includes rice, fish paste, beans, oil, flour, sugar and chilies. An even larger consortium of NGOs, the Committee for Coordination of Services to Displaced Persons in Thailand (CCSDPT) organizes the work of 20 NGOs working up and down the border on a wide range of projects including education, health care, women's issues, disability issues, sanitation, literacy, justice and legal services, landmine awareness, HIV/AIDs awareness, GBV trainings among others. In Mae La specifically there are 15 international NGOs providing a range of services. In short, the human security context is comparatively good, with basic needs of food, water, shelter and health care provided, and basic safeties protected though there have been some incidence of abuse with the camp guards. Sanitary conditions and access to clean water are not up to international standards in Mae La due to its large size and the fact that it was designed for a much smaller population.

In the case of Sri Lanka, the interviews revealed a very complex relation between NGO activity and collective action. In Sri Lanka, there were many coordination meetings among NGOs at the local (Vavuniya) and the national (Colombo) levels. The coordination is organized through what is called the cluster system, where there are expert committees for each cluster/sector, for example, health, washing, food, education, etc. Each of these sector heads is chosen from an agency, and some agencies are entrusted with leading particular sectors. This has been done to avoid replication of the assistance within the camps. NGO activities helped foster collective action among the IDPs most during the resettlement and return phase, especially in terms of community support in the provision of property rights over land and other necessary legal documents related to birth, marriage and death. The older INGOs and the local NGOs have been most successful in accomplishing these tasks since they incorporated the local governments in this process.

Conclusions

There is a great deal of variation across the seven displacement crises in the level of mobilization and participation in collective action. The relationship between the five sets of contextual factors and the level of collective action is complex. Relatively higher levels of human security in Thailand and Croatia would predict higher levels of community building; we see this in Thailand but not in Croatia, which involves an elderly population with little hope of new beginnings. The low levels of human security in Uganda would lead us to

Conclusions

expect the low levels of mobilization we witness there, but through the expert interviews the lack of trust is a more important factor, a difficult situation brought about by 25 years of terrible tactics of war. Finally, the low levels of human security but relatively better access to livelihoods and freedom of movement in Colombia, which come with the country's relatively developed infrastructures, produce a vibrant displaced civil society. However, through the field interviews the legal structure and government promotion of civil society participation seems to be an important catalyst in the development of IDP groups.

While we see variation in the mobilization of the displaced within camps, the overall level of CBO formation, and especially CBOs aimed at fighting for displaced rights, is quite low. Considering the contextual factors that make mobilization difficult, the resource barriers and the lack of access to local or national policymakers that could potentially respond to displaced requests, this is understandable. The question then becomes: if the displaced cannot effectively advocate for themselves, the aid organizations on the ground have no leverage, and there is no space for their plight on the international agenda – what can be done? A new strategy is laid out in Chapter 7, one that looks realistically at the status quo and proposes the use of new tools to mobilize new leverage and directly improve the lives of the displaced.

7
An innovative global campaign for action

A broken system at every level

Advocacy campaigns exhibit a wide array of tactics, strategies, coalition formations and argumentation. However, there are a few necessary conditions for advocacy (rather than revolution) to be effective. At the most basic level Advocacy leads to Awareness (and political or economic pressure), which leads to Action (some type of policy change or behavior change on the part of the target of the advocacy – usually a government or corporation).

Advocacy > Awareness > Action

This advocacy chain is broken at each level of governance when it comes to fighting for the rights of the forcibly displaced. First, at the international level there is a breakdown even in the first step: there is a lack of advocates advocating for refugee rights before the governments of the Global North and international institutions. Most of the organizations that are engaged on displacement issues use their campaigns to raise humanitarian relief funds, not argue for a change to warehousing policies or an end to the displacement. In the few cases where large-scale advocacy campaigns have been organized like those around Tibet and Darfur, that awareness failed to turn into any real action on the part of US or European governments.

Even in the extremely rare cases where a campaign is mobilized and some level of media attention is achieved, it is nearly impossible to maintain a focus on the issue in the face of a thoroughly saturated media landscape. Advocates for the victims displaced by the rebel group M23's attacks on civilians in the Democratic Republic of the Congo, need to vie for attention with governmental collapse in Syria, suicide bombers in Paris, shooting rampages in the United States, and planned and unplanned plane crashes. Even if a campaign does gain attention, it would only maintain it for hours or a day, not long enough to result in pressure and action on the part of policymakers.

Second, at the national level in the countries suffering from refugee or IDP crises, there is also a breakdown at the first step. International aid organizations and national aid and human rights organizations cannot be effective advocates for the displaced. There are four primary barriers to these groups effectively advocating for rights, such as the right to move and the right to work: First, advocacy is not the priority, saving lives is – organizations that are on the ground to provide life-saving food, medicine and shelter are already under-resourced and overstretched, they simply don't have the bandwidth to do more than their mission. Furthermore, if they become too political they could be kicked out, as Doctors without Borders has been in Sudan and Burma, thus not being able to achieve their primary mission. Even those groups that do find some staff and resources to argue for rights before national authorities in the capitals of countries with displacement crises, they quickly realize they are, second, fighting for non-priority citizens. Conflict and poverty are intimately related (Collier 2007). The developing countries that are often the sites of refugee and IDP crises have a great deal of other problems of poverty, and their own citizens are in great need. In the best case, marginalized displaced populations are not a priority; in the worst cases, host governments are actively hostile to them.

For the advocacy causal chain of Advocacy – Awareness – Action to function, there is one other requirement: leverage. Once you achieve awareness there needs to be a way to put pressure on the target to get them to act in a different way. Leverage can be political or economic, in the US system this is often referred to as the levers of votes and money. In traditional advocacy, organizations can mobilize the masses, and use the political leverage of votes to get policymakers to respond to their demands. Other organizations use the economic leverage of money to help swing elections, and the threat of the use of economic leverage can be the lever that can sway policymaker action. In the case of international aid and human rights organizations operating in countries with displacement problems – they do not have either, which brings us to the third barrier: No leverage. International organizations cannot wield any political power in the country, and have limited resources. While we might be able to imagine a scenario in which international aid organizations withhold aid (economic leverage) to get host governments to change behavior, this in reality never occurs because aid organizations are supposed to be providing humanitarian relief to vulnerable individuals. And, in any case, many host governments would not mind if the marginalized groups are not cared for, indeed in IDP crises it is often the government that is the primary perpetrator of violence against civilians, as in the case of Syria, Sri Lanka and Sudan.

Furthermore, while national human rights advocates might be thought to have political leverage in their countries this is often not the case in nations with weak democratic institutions and unstable political parties (or alternatively overly stable, one-party rule). Since displaced populations are often minorities either outside their country of origin or inside their country of origin (in the case of IDPs) it is difficult for national human rights organizations to mobilize enough local support to bring pressure on government officials to improve conditions, or allow freedom of movement, freedom to work or a range of other rights like access to education or health care. Lastly, if national human rights advocates push too hard for displaced rights they could be killed, as many have been in Colombia, Burma and Sri Lanka.

The general weakness of democratic processes in many countries with displacement crises is not the only governmental barrier; there is one additional major impediment to effective advocacy for the displaced: Corruption. The presence of corruption in a political system turns the process of pressure around – instead of citizens putting pressure on policymakers to change policy or behavior, pressure is applied the other way around. National and local officials are putting pressure on international aid and national human rights organizations for a range of payoffs, often in-kind. If aid and human rights organizations don't comply, they are denied access, denied visas and permits and generally hampered from doing their work.

Third, at the local camp level there is also a breakdown in the advocacy causal chain. Again, at the very first step: the displaced themselves cannot be effective advocates for their own rights. They have lost everything, fled war, are often starving and traumatized, they are rarely in the position to mobilize a movement and engage in effective human rights advocacy on behalf of their people. Just like the aid organizations seeking to serve them, they have no leverage and if they become too political they could be kicked out or killed. Indeed, the displaced know how vulnerable their situation is, and as a result we see almost no mobilization by the displaced across all the cases.

At the international, national and local level, the most basic requirements of effective advocacy are not met. At every level, there is a lack of organizations even giving voice to the displaced needs for freedom of movement, freedom to work and a range of other rights. At every level, there are barriers that make effective advocacy nearly impossible even if there were organizations with the resources and the bandwidth to advocate for rights full time. These barriers are not going to change. The saturated media landscape at the global level is not going to change. The non-priority status of minority-displaced populations is not going to change. The lack of political leverage for international aid organizations, national human rights organizations and displaced representative groups is not going to change. And unfortunately, weak democratic systems and corruption are also not going to change any time soon.

If it's broke, fix it

The only way you achieve influence is with leverage, to get leverage you need to mobilize political or economic power. Mobilizing political power is difficult,

Real-world solutions

refugees have no political power in host countries, international aid organizations have no political power in host country, and IDPs are often marginalized groups that have no de facto power in their country even if they might legally have rights on paper.

There is a way forward. Concerned global citizens can mobilize economic leverage through person-to-person micro-finance and crowd-funding campaigns. Corporate matches can magnify that power. The unresponsive governments of the Global North and ineffective global institutions can be bypassed. This strategy is detailed after a discussion of some alternative strategies that I argue will not work.

Not empty critiques, but rather real-world solutions

This book has made clear that the tens of millions of people are living in conditions that no human should be forced to endure. The international community is largely unaware of their plight. The international organizations working on refugee issues focus mainly on mobilizing life-saving resources from wealthy governments. The old international refugee convention and the new global IDP guiding principles are routinely ignored. Organizations providing humanitarian relief are in no position to advocate for their rights. Unable to move freely and unable to work, they wait hopelessly for year upon year, decade upon decade. Living imprisoned, with nothing to do, no goals to achieve, no future to envision, breaks the spirit and destroys the mind.

The academic literature on refugees is frustrating; there is a strong sense that it is written by preachers and they are preaching to the choir. Further critiquing the work of the UNHCR and the international and national aid agencies that are just scraping by seems inauthentic at best and destructive at worst. We know international and national aid organizations are short on resources, staff, supplies and leverage; saying they should have more resources, while appropriate, does not improve the situation. Governments in North America and Europe are under fiscal austerity pressure and are cutting their spending, they not going to be significantly increasing their aid to displacement situations. Likewise, pointing out that the UNHCR and other UN agencies are bureaucratic, hierarchical and at times difficult to work with, which nearly all of my NGO interviewees pointed out, is also not going to be game-changing in the lives of the forcibly displaced.

Advocating that national host governments simply let the displaced work and move freely and integrate is naïve and thus doomed. Some of the international refugee advocacy organizations have advocated for this in specific cases but *realpolitik* still reigns. Sovereign nations will decide whom they will grant citizenship status to, and its related rights to work, move, vote and live a life of dignity. Governments with internal displacement situations often have tense relations with the minorities that are displaced, controls on freedom of movement and work are often pitched as a security measure for the safety of the displaced though there is often more nefarious reasons for the lock down. Any amount of lobbying by American and European embassy workers or campaigns by concerned citizens is unlikely to change that. National governments hosting refugee populations are never going to just allow these people to work, they haven't for 60 years, and economic conditions in many places are getting worse not better. Powerful countries like the United States are never going to introduce conditionality about refugees and IDPs into US foreign policy – conditionality related to corruption or major human rights violations is rarely effective, conditionality related to a marginalized population or foreign minority is definitely not going to work. Whether dealing with refugee populations or IDP populations, these countries are poor, with high levels of unemployment and simply do not have the capacity to do what needs to be done.

Pushing for freedom of movement and freedom to work at the global level through global institutions is likewise doomed to failure. For the past 60 years, as we've sought to deal with global problems the first inclination was to do so through the international organizations – the UN, the EU, the World Bank and the IMF. This was a direct extension from the domestic context where we solve national problems through national governing institutions. The idea has been to get norms transcribed into international agreements and conventions and then pressure misbehaving governments into implementing those norms. But there is a problem with the approach of national policy change through global norm change propagated by global institutions. Global institutions are intergovernmental in nature – that is they only have as much power as their member state governments choose to cede to them, and in nearly every case other than the EU, this has been, in effect, not much. When global institutions are tasked with "solving" critical global problems and yet don't have the power to enforce the global policies they develop – the result is inspiring rhetoric backed by policies with no teeth.

Instead, what is needed is a way to leverage the resources of the developed world, through a coordinated global advocacy campaign, to mobilize resources in innovative ways to empower the displaced directly through economic development and incentivize host governments to change their policies around freedom of movement and freedom to work.

A better route: the many to the many

In the early years of accelerated globalization – starting in the 1970s – transnational institutions may have been the most effective means to diffuse new norms, with the advent of the Internet, though, and the exponential growth of the proportion of the global population that is online, global advocacy campaigns have a new weapon in the arsenal. Many activists in the social justice movement have realized the power of direct mobilization of the public. The advocates for displaced rights, however, have not yet harnessed that power to its full potential.

A better route

Rather than mobilizing the public to press wealthy governments to give more aid, admit a few thousand more resettled refugees, or shaming national governments into allowing the displaced to move freely or work, I am suggesting that we mobilize the public to invest – invest in a new future for the displaced, whether IDP or refugee. This is not a call to divert funds from the life-saving activities carried out by international and national NGO implementing partners, rather it is a call for a new advocacy push, by new actors (I propose a new backbone organization in partnership with international refugee aid organizations) to harness a new untapped source of funds: the global public.

Through an innovative advocacy campaign, the backbone organization can catalyze person-to-person giving and lending to help the displaced begin rebuilding their lives. In the past 15 years, the rise of micro-finance and social entrepreneurship has demonstrated that the poor can effectively help themselves and create pathways to prosperity and improved living conditions if they are given access to micro-investments to start micro-enterprises and small businesses. To some readers with background in advocacy or displacement, this area may be unfamiliar territory; therefore I discuss this emerging field in detail in the next section after laying out a proposed structure for the mobilization and deployment of these new funds here.

This new mobilization of capital could be done through two different methods:

1. person-to-person micro-financing;
2. crowd-funded conditional micro-grant pools.

The platforms already exist; we simply need to bring together a coherent advocacy campaign with branded fundraising portals.

Using modern social media platforms and a social media campaign to reach a large audience of concerned global citizens (similar to KONY 2012), the campaign can communicate the plight of the displaced. The goal, however, is not just awareness or writing letters to government officials – but rather a clear and simple ask: giving a small sum to help empower the displaced.

These small funds will be used in two alternative ways, depending on whether the national host government is friendly or hostile to the displaced population. In cases where the host government is hostile to the displaced, and unlikely to be swayed by an international campaign encouraging freedom to work, even with an economic incentive, the campaign can support the displaced directly. Small sums could be mobilized through P2P (person-to-person) micro-finance sites to directly empower refugees and IDPs to start small businesses and begin providing for their families, improving their quality of life and giving them a pathway to purpose and dignity. These investments could be in the form of grants or loans. I would recommend grants in very unstable displacement situations, since they are easier to administer (tracking and repayment are not necessary) and loans in more stable situations (loans are logistically more demanding, but also financially more sustainable). The first, most well-known and largest

P2P micro-finance site is Kiva. Since Kiva invented the concept of person-to-person micro-finance and launched its platform more than US$789 million has been lent and more than 90 percent of low-income borrowers were able to successfully run their small business and repay their loans. More than US$10 million has been lent and repaid to refugee entrepreneurs in Palestinian refugee camps. So we know it is possible. As loans are repaid, individual small investors in the developed world can support new displaced entrepreneurs in the same camp or other camps.

In cases where the host government is friendlier, and might be more amenable to allowing the displaced to work and move freely, the micro-grants could be aggregated through crowd-funding giving platforms (like Indiegogo, Crowdrise and Kickstarter), to create a new pools of economic development funding which would be *conditional* – that is they would only be released for a given displacement crisis if the host government would change its policies to allow the displaced to move and work freely. I would propose mobilizing corporate sponsor matches to these crowd-raised pools. Kickstarter, one of the best-known crowd-funding platforms, has raised more than US$2 billion for entrepreneurial start-up projects. Individual campaigns for everything from watches to cat game card decks have raised between US$10 and $20 million. These publicly raised funds could be matched dollar-for-dollar by corporate donors. For example, the founder of Chobani Yogurt, Hamdi Ulukaya, has committed US$700 million to the plight of refugees. More corporate partners and wealthy individuals could be inspired by his leadership. By matching individual donations, it encourages the small givers to give more, since every dollar they donate is doubled.

These aggregated micro-grant pools would not be given to the host governments, they could be managed by international aid organizations already operating on the ground, but the carrot of an additional US$125 million in development aid, for example, for an area of the country suffering from a displacement crisis should be enough of an economic incentive to encourage host governments to allow freedom to work.

Various sub-negotiations could be agreed upon, for example designating that half of the new pool of funds go to local hosting community citizens and half to the displaced. In this way, host governments can be incentivized to allow the displaced to work through the appeal of new flows of direct investment. Tensions between host communities and the displaced can be ameliorated. Local communities can begin seeing the presence of displaced citizens as an opportunity for economic growth. With both the displaced and host communities having access to new business investment, local economies will grow (see Figure 7.1).

In situations of very long protracted displacements organizations already aiding the displaced could administer some of the funds in the camps as an MFI (micro-finance institution) would – as micro-loans rather than micro-grants. This would create even more financial sustainability in the model, as displaced

Scaling up social entrepreneurship

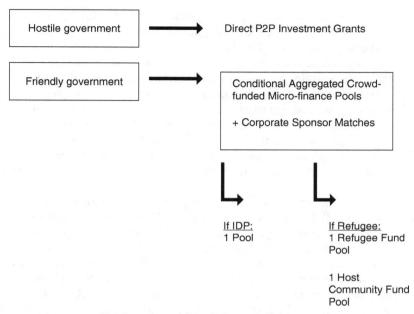

FIGURE 7.1. Proposed structure of fund flows depending on context

entrepreneurs and host community entrepreneurs pay their loans off and the funds can be lent again, to a new cohort of displaced entrepreneurs. With access to capital, the displaced can begin earning income again, provide for their families and living lives of purpose and dignity.

Social entrepreneurship is happening – let's scale it up

Social entrepreneurship is the idea of using market-based solutions to solve intractable problems. Over the past 30 years, this sector has gained significant traction as international aid and governmental approaches have systematically failed to solve problems. Mohammad Yunus won the Nobel Prize in 2007 for his market-based solution of using micro-loans and micro-banks (or micro-finance institutions – MFIs) to lend to the poor to support them as micro-entrepreneurs. His organization, Grameen Bank (meaning "Village Bank"), was founded in 1983 in Bangladesh to help poor small business owners get access to non-exploitative credit. Before Grameen Bank, if a poor entrepreneur needed a loan to buy material, supplies or inventory, their only option was to borrow from a loan shark, who charged exorbitant interest rates, upward of 200 and 300 percent. The poor did not have any assets to use as collateral so they could borrow from more established banks with more reasonable interest rates. Yunus' idea of providing loans, at reasonable interest rates, without collateral to lending circles was so innovative and impactful, that it has spread around the world (Yunus 2001; 2011). Grameen Bank and a similar organization in Bangladesh called B.R.A.C. (Bangladesh Rehabilitation Assistance Committee) have both lifted tens of millions of people out of poverty. Through access to small loans women have been able to purchase a chicken and sell eggs in the market, by successfully paying off that loan, they were able to graduate to a larger loan, for example to buy a goat, and sell the milk at a higher price point in the market. Successful repayment of that loan allowed them to graduate to yet a larger loan. I led an educational study abroad trip to Bangladesh in 2006 where we met a woman in rural northern Bangladesh who had graduated all the way to a pharmacy kiosk loan, and through the profits earned on her small business, successfully sent both her boys to college in the capital of Dhaka.

When the poor are provided with small sums of capital (as either loans or grants) to launch small businesses the results can be remarkable, with millions having been lifted out of poverty as a result of social entrepreneurial approaches. The body literature and case studies have been growing for over a decade (Bornstein 2007, Polak 2008, Bornstein and Davis 2010). Prahalad's *The Fortune at the Bottom of the Pyramid: Eradicating Poverty Through Profits* (originally published in 2004 and now in its fifth edition) shows through case after case that the poor, even the extremely poor, do still have some income and they make choices about how to spend those resources. Those entrepreneurs who create products and services for the poor in mind, create a financially sustainable way to solve the problems they face (access to medicine, access to nutritious food, access to clean water and sanitation, etc.). Elkington and Hartigan's *The Power of Unreasonable People: How Social Entrepreneurs Create Markets that Change the World* (2008) highlight the work of more than 50 entrepreneurs working around the world to solve social problems. They note that the funding of those social innovators can be philanthropic, market-based or a hybrid blending the two. Many social entrepreneurs need some type of venture philanthropy (so start-up funding that is a grant not a loan) to get started. In the case of massive displacement, where people have often lost everything, it is likely that micro-grants will be the most reasonable pathway forward. With support to start small micro-enterprises refugees and IDPs will be able to help care for themselves and their families.

Most of this book has laid out the horrors of the conflicts that have displaced millions, the terrible conditions people endure in the camps and the barriers to effectively advocating for governments to behave differently. But among all the stories of loss, there are stories about amazing ideas, innovation and hope, and there is a way for those good ideas to be scaled up.

This first great idea can be found in the Dadaab refugee camp complex on the Kenyan border. As discussed Somali refugees in Kenya are not allowed to work, not allowed to leave the camp, and as is the case all over the world, refugees are forced into idleness. There is a social enterprise that is providing jobs for women and a way to care for their families beyond the meager subsistence rations provided by the international community. Samasource is a creative cutting-edge social enterprise started by a young American, Leila Janah, in 2008. Sama means "equal" in Sanskrit. Samasource outsources data entry tasks to low-income people around the world, through a unique microwork model that harnesses the untapped potential of the world's poor. Samasource connects poor women and youth to training and employment in the digital economy. With successful microwork outposts in other parts of East Africa, Samasource opened a microwork station in the Dadaab refugee camp, powered by generators and solar. Samasource trained Somali refugees on digital tasks and provided them with dignified digital work through the Internet and a chance to earn income for themselves and for their families for the first time. Janah's idea seeded a broader movement called Impact Sourcing, a fair trade take on outsourcing.

Another example of innovation comes from the same camps, by another social entrepreneur, Paul Polak, which he describes in his book about social business, *Out of Poverty: What Works When Traditional Approaches Fail* (2008). Polak was an early mover in the social enterprise space – he invented the treadle pump, a low-cost water pump made with local materials that provided access to safe drinking water, as well as a low-cost drip irrigation system for farmers to irrigate their crops, doubling their yields and dramatically increasing their incomes. In each of these cases, he designed the product for extreme affordability and then provided micro-loans to families, which they were then able to pay off since the interventions increased their household wealth. With huge success in India and Nepal, he took his idea of extreme affordability and micro-loans to the Dadaab refugee camps in Kenya. There he provided micro-loans and supplies to Somali refugees to build donkey carts, which served as taxis. The refugee entrepreneurs increased their incomes, could pay back their micro-loans, provide better for their families and begin regaining a sense of autonomy.

The humanitarian aid organizations that are aiding the displaced in camps have also started some income-generating projects for the displaced: like the small hanging garden initiatives I saw in paramilitary controlled zones in Colombia or honeybee keeping and the farming cooperatives near the Karen refugee camps in Thailand. These interventions, however, are limited in scale since the aid organizations need to target the bulk of their budgets toward their main mission, usually food, water, shelter, education or health care, and they realistically cannot divert significantly more resources to these types of projects. In a camp of 400,000, it is a minuscule percentage that will have the opportunity to take part in an income-generating project started and funded by an aid organization. Furthermore, NGOs are unlikely to get new sources of funding as governments in the United States and Europe, under fiscal austerity pressures, are cutting back on foreign aid, not increasing it.

Importantly, the displaced do not need NGOs or external social businesses to come in to provide jobs; they can be incredibly savvy entrepreneurs. They invented the "pop-up." Small markets pop up in the camps if they were able to flee with some resources, as one aid worker in Sri Lanka described: "There are also little shops run by people from outside. There are ice cream stands. There are barbershops. Vendors come in with supplies and sometimes the IDPs sell the products. Bank of Ceylon and People Bank opened branches there and people deposited money" (interview September 18, 2009). Others start small production facilities based on traditional skills like carpet making or tapestry weaving like the Karen loom weaving in the camps on the Thai–Burmese border and the Afghani carpet weaving operations in camps in Pakistan. A journalist in one of the older camps in the border of the Democratic Republic of the Congo describes a range of small business: "There's a sense of permanence to Mugunga. Tents and shacks have been transformed into small restaurants and bars. Tailors and carpenters have set up businesses. Hardly anyone here believes that they will leave anytime soon. When one militia is ousted or leaves an area, another quickly emerges" (Raghavan 2013).

Refugees are masters of invention and innovation, because when you have lost everything, you have to come up with ingenious ways to build a business from scratch. With small grants or loans, more displaced citizens could start micro-enterprises that would provide income for their families as well as supplies or services for their neighbors.

The campaign

The mobilization of new capital to displaced entrepreneurs would require an accompanying advocacy campaign and backbone organization to run it. Advocacy campaigns to raise awareness about the plight of the displaced are clearly insufficient, most people in the developed world do not know about the millions of people languishing in protracted displacement crises as seen in Chapters 2 and 3. If they are aware that it is an issue, they have often only heard of one or two cases – like Syria or the Palestinian camps. A major global advocacy campaign is needed, similar to the KONY 2012 campaign run by Invisible Children that reached millions in months about the conflict in northern Uganda. This new campaign will raise awareness and mobilize a response for all the world's displaced – both refugees and IDPs. Such a campaign could leverage partnerships between human rights organizations and refugee aid organizations to reach traditionally concerned citizens. In addition, the backbone organization could forge new innovative partnerships with social media dominant partners like celebrities, musicians and forward-thinking corporations.

The KONY 2012 campaign proved that there is a deep altruistic vein that can be tapped. The biggest challenge is that the "ask" is often unclear. A creative campaign that alerts concerned citizens to a cause but which does not provide a clear pathway for them to take real, impactful action is destined to fail. KONY2012 was criticized for this – viewers were moved to post and share the viral video through their social media networks, but despite the millions of views, there was no real action concerned citizens could take.

Some refer to this as "slacktivism" – a phenomenon where seemingly meaningless Facebook status updates and online petition signing makes people feel good about themselves but does not to translate into real world policy change. Critics of slacktivism charge that participants don't actually care about the causes they claim to care about (Gladwell 2010). However, as we saw with the unprecedented charitable giving in response to the humanitarian disasters of the earthquake in Haiti and the tsunami in Southeast Asia – if there is a clear pathway for people to take action (giving) they often will. The success of Kiva also shows the willingness of concerned citizens to give.

People are more easily mobilized to take action when they can understand the causal chain and see the outcome of their contribution. Concerned global citizens don't trust, and rightly so, that they will have much of an impact writing a letter to a distant policymaker that might try to influence policy through a multilevel international governance system. However, they can help the displaced rebuild their lives one small business at a time. Through small contributions, ranging from US$5 to US$25 a concerned citizen could give a displaced entrepreneur a chance at a life of dignity and by pooling contributions we can create economic leverage where previously there was none.

8

Conclusion

In December 2015, Western media outlets celebrated the announcement of a UN Security Council Resolution that laid out a peace process for Syria. By that point France, Russia, the United States and the United Kingdom were all flying air raids over Syria and Iraq. The problem was that there were still major disagreements over whom to bomb: Russia was primarily targeting rebel groups opposed to Assad, while the United States, United Kingdom and France were focused on fighting ISIS. The Turkish downing of a Russian fighter jet exacerbated an already tense situation between NATO members and Russia. Finally, absent from the UN negotiating table was Assad who, following the announcement, seemed amused by the unanimous decision taken by the UN about his country without his country's input (Sengupta and Sanger 2015).

As discussed in the introductory chapter, Syria is an outlier. Rarely do we see every major world power engaged in trying to stabilize a region producing massive displacement. And yet, as unique as the Syrian case is, in the attention garnered and action mobilized, the story on the ground is all too familiar. Reports coming over the wire from journalists inside Syria continue to document regime attacks on civilian areas and schools in rebel-controlled territory. Photographs depict overwhelmed field hospitals trying to treat victims while being bombarded by both Russian and Syrian regime missiles. Entire cities have been reduced to rubble. Refugees continue to flow across the borders to escape the violence.

In December 2015, refugees in Turkey were moving into their fifth year in displacement. The lives of millions have been put on hold, indefinitely. Having lost everything, or nearly everything, they are living in white UNHCR-issued tents. Facing yet another winter, and little protection from the cold, more will be lost to exposure every year. They have run for their lives, but they are still not safe. Not safe from hunger, disease or hypothermia. They cannot return home, they are not allowed to move on and they lack access to investments, which

Conclusion

would allow them to use their skills and ingenuity to rebuild their professions, their businesses and their lives.

Syria is just another case of a failed international policy; one of 65 crises worldwide, involving 60 million people living in a state of precarious insecurity. This book has systematically documented that failure is the norm when it comes to global displacement. Instead of looking at the exception case of Syria alone, I have studied every major case of massive protracted displacement and the advocacy on behalf of those vulnerable citizens. Through this unique research approach, we see more clearly than we have through any previous research on global advocacy, that most disadvantaged populations have no voice. The displaced are powerless not only in the places they have fled from but at every level of governance where advocates might take up their fight.

Chapter 2 showed that at the international level, the majority of the displaced populations around the world do not even have advocates fighting for their case in particular. The general refugee rights and human rights groups are working on tight budgets, trying to sound the alarm about hundreds of crises simultaneously. They do not have the bandwidth to carry out prolonged campaigns on behalf of specific displaced communities. Even when there is a mobilized campaign like the Save Darfur Coalition or the International Campaign for Tibet, activists have a very difficult time breaking into the thoroughly saturated media landscape. Maintaining attention is even more difficult as seen with even hyper-viral campaigns like KONY 2012. The result is that the majority of cases of massive displacement receive no attention at all. Since most social problems only see governmental or intergovernmental action when there has been significant attention paid to the issue by the media and mass public, there is no pressure to act. Syria is the exception that proves the rule: Western powers only moved beyond words to actions when hundreds of thousands of refugees started showing up on the shores of Europe and European citizens started pressing governments to do something about the migration crisis.

In most cases, the governments of the West are unlikely to respond in a similar fashion. We have not seen similar mobilization in further afield conflicts, such as the Democratic Republic of the Congo, Central African Republic, Colombia or Sudan. Without clear national security implications for the West, military intervention aimed at stabilization is unlikely. In cases where there are not millions displaced but merely hundreds of thousands, Western powers are unlikely to have their foreign policy driven by concerns of a minority. For example, US foreign policy with China will not be determined by questions of Tibetan rights, nor will US trade policy with Thailand be determined by the rights it bestows on refugees fleeing Burma.

Data presented in Chapter 3 underscored that few cases that do receive coverage by the Global North do so because of their geostrategic importance in the global war on terror. Displaced populations in the Palestinian Occupied

Territories, Afghanistan, Iraq, Pakistan, Chechnya and Lebanon see the most coverage, but it is often a secondary mention, with the focus of the coverage being the conflicts that led to their displacement.

Exploring the trends in coverage of all 61 protracted displacement crises for a decade in the *New York Times* further confirms that most issues receive little to no coverage. Even when millions are displaced for decades, there will be often none or just a handful of news stories on their plight. Content analysis of the articles that do appear makes clear that if it is not geostrategic importance driving attention, it is violence. Violence sells, and only particular spikes in violence or new types of violence seem to warrant coverage of massive displacement by the Western media.

In-depth content and context analysis of the seven cases demonstrated further that, in each case, there are few advocates advocating for displaced rights, and when there were those activists were up against a saturated media landscape and struggled to get and maintain attention long enough to mobilize political action.

It is clear that the displaced are powerless in the arenas of the Global North. Unfortunately, they and their international advocates are also powerless in the countries hosting displaced communities. Chapters 4 and 5 documented how difficult advocacy is on the frontlines for both refugees and IDPs. There are five major barriers to effectively advocating for the displaced. First, advocacy is not the priority, saving lives is. Most of the organizations working with the displaced are humanitarian aid groups: they are short on staff and resources, and rarely have the bandwidth to spend fighting for more long-term rights like the right to work or the right to move freely. In cases where they have criticized governments or advocated too forcefully, they have been kicked out of the country. Second, the humanitarian and national human rights groups that do try to take up the fight of the forcibly displaced find that they are advocating for non-priority citizens. The level of marginalization ranges from bad (the displaced are an unwelcome drain on resources) to worse (the displaced are seen as harboring rebel elements or are themselves a group targeted for ethnic cleansing by the ruling regime). Third, organizations that do or might attempt to advocate for the displaced have no leverage. They have no political leverage, often being foreign aid workers granted access by a host government to do their work. And they have no economic leverage, being already under-resourced to do their primary life-saving work and unable to use those resources as a bargaining chip to get host governments to behave differently. Fourth, many governments hosting displaced populations suffer from problems of corruption. When government officials are habituated to working within a system of bribes and payoffs, they often are asking for concessions from aid workers (who are often viewed as resource rich in very resource poor contexts). This corruption flips the traditional leverage equation on its head, where the government officials are pressuring the aid organizations rather than the other way

Conclusion

around. And finally, fifth, there is a problem of capacity in many cases. Host governments are often overseeing underdeveloped economies, with a large informal sector and thus low levels of taxation. The lack of a tax base results in lack of governing capacity, which means even if host governments wanted to do a better job providing for the displaced, in say DRC or Colombia, they are unable to do so.

Chapter 6 showed that there is no better hope for effective advocacy at the level closest to the displaced – the local camp level. When people have fled for their lives, often only with the clothes on their backs, and arrive traumatized in displacement camps, the conditions are not ripe for rich community mobilization. Though we do see glimmers of hope, in cases like the Karen in Thailand and the internally displaced in Colombia we see community organizing and advocacy by the displaced on behalf of the displaced. These are both cases where the host government has created conditions for positive mobilization – self-help groups, lending circles, camp clean-up crews and even forums for self-advocating. These cases are promising in that they show host government policies vis-à-vis the displaced can be revised to foster and support positive types of collective action. This in turn can fill the vacuum that leads to more detrimental mobilization like terrorist and militia recruitment.

The evidence that the displaced engage in self-help groups, small markets and community groups provides support for the idea laid out in Chapter 7. A campaign targeted at concerned citizens of the Global North could mobilize new pools of investment. The impressive amounts of giving during humanitarian disasters show that concerned global citizens are willing to act, if the ask is clear. The complicated political workings of global policy challenges are too difficult to convey to the public. And in any case, the "experts" working the foreign policy desks of the Western powers rarely know what to do themselves. Take again the case of Syria, should the United States join forces with Russia and support Assad, choosing the lesser evil between his regime and ISIS? Should the United States arm opposition rebels and try to simultaneously take out Assad and ISIS? Will that strategy backfire and arm jihadists that the United States will meet on the battlefield somewhere down the line? The answer is anything but clear. Trying to run global advocacy campaigns to mobilize the public to get involved in the politics of displacement is futile.

Mobilizing concerned global citizens to invest in the future of the displaced is more feasible and more promising. A thoughtful, well-executed campaign targeted at citizens of the wealthier countries of the world, could convey the plight of the world's displaced as well as a clear and simple ask: donate US$5–$25 to invest in the displaced. Aggregating these small individual contributions could create significantly sized micro-finance grant pools. Partnering with corporate sponsors to match crowd-funded pools could double the resources available.

These micro-finance pools would then be deployed in two different ways depending on the context and the nature of the host government. Hostile host governments like the Syrian regime would be bypassed. Partnerships with aid organizations on the ground would be used to distribute and support micro-entrepreneurs in refugee and IDP camps.

Friendly host governments would result in advocacy and negotiation. A centralized campaign backbone organization would communicate that new pools of resources are available to displaced and host community populations but the release of those funds will be conditional on the host government allowing the displaced to work and move freely. Again, the funds will be deployed through partnerships with aid organizations already operating on the ground. Through this new campaign of investment, the displaced could begin rebuilding their professions and small business, empowering them to care for themselves and their families and moving toward a life of dignity and independence.

The international community is faced with two options. One, do nothing. Allow the status quo policy to continue. As millions remain displaced, and hundreds of thousands follow in their footsteps in the coming years, disillusionment will turn into despair. If the wealthy world stands idly by while the displaced are forced to live at the edge of existence, it will breed rebellion, extremism and endless cycles of violence. To echo Franklin D. Roosevelt: "People who are hungry and out of a job are the stuff of which dictatorships are made."

There is another path. One in which the West stands up to support some of the most vulnerable communities in the world. The displaced have fled war, persecution and violence to save themselves and their families. Their stories are harrowing and inspiring. They want to begin anew, rebuild their professions and live lives of dignity. We have the opportunity to invest in their future, in the development of countries in crisis and ultimately in a more promising future for us all.

References

The Atlantic. 2015. "What's Next for Migrants After Paris? Friday's Terrorist Attacks have Intensified an Ongoing Global Debate on Accepting Syrian Refugees." November 14. www.theatlantic.com/international/archive/2015/11/migrant-crisis-paris-attacks/416067/.
Amnesty International (AI). 2009. "Unlock the Camps in Sri Lanka: Safety and Dignity for the Displaced Now – A Briefing Paper." www.amnesty.org/en/library/asset/ASA37/016/2009/en/5de112c8-c8d4-4c31-8144-2a69aa9fff58/asa370162009en.html#1.1.1.RIGHT%20TO%20LIBERTY%20AND%20FREEDOM%20OF%20mOVEMENT%20outline.
Amnesty International (AI). 2012. "Bhutan Human Rights." www.amnestyusa.org/our-work/countries/asia-and-the-pacific/bhutan.
ARC. 2013. "American Refugee Committee International – About." www.arcrelief.org/site/PageServer?pagename=index_about_arc.
Axelrod, Robert. 1984. *The Evolution of Cooperation*. New York: Basic Books.
Baumgartner, Frank R. and Bryan D. Jones. 1993. *Agendas and Instability in American Politics*. Chicago: University of Chicago Press.
BBC. 2015. "Migrant Crisis: Migration to Europe Explained in Graphics." November 9. www.bbc.com/news/world-europe-34131911.
Beech, Hannah. 2007. "Laura Bush's Burmese Crusade." *Time Magazine*. September 5. www.time.com/time/world/article/0,8599,1659170,00.html#ixzz1zsebRCya.
Bieri, Franziska. 2010. *From Blood Diamonds to the Kimberley Process: How NGOs Cleaned up the Global Diamond Industry*. Burlington, VT: Ashgate Publishing.
Bob, Clifford. 2005. *The Marketing of Rebellion: Insurgents, Media and International Activism*. New York: Cambridge University Press.
Bornstein, David. 2007. *How to Change the World: Social Entrepreneurs and the Power of New Ideas*. New York: Oxford University Press.
Bornstein, David and Susan Davis. 2010. *Social Entrepreneurship: What Everyone Needs to Know*. New York: Oxford University Press.

Brown, Ben. 2011. "Horn of Africa Drought: A Vision of Hell at the Dadaab Refugee Camp." *Telegraph*. July 9. www.telegraph.co.uk/news/worldnews/africaandindianocean/kenya/8627548/Horn-of-Africa-drought-A-vision-of-hell-at-the-Dabaab-refugee-camp.html.
Burma to New York. 2007. "Number of Burmese Refugees Coming to the US and New York State." http://fromburmatonewyork.com/infographic_refugees3.swf.
CCSDPT. 2012. "Committee for Coordination of Services to Displaced Persons in Thailand – About US." www.ccsdpt.org/aboutus.htm.
CIA World Factbook. 2012. "Nepal." www.cia.gov/library/publications/the-world-factbook/geos/np.html.
Clark, Peter B. and James Q. Wilson. 1961. "Incentive Systems: A Theory of Organizations." *Administrative Science Quarterly* 6: 129–66.
CNN. 2012. "Aid Workers Abducted from Kenyan Refugee Complex." http://edition.cnn.com/2012/06/29/world/africa/kenya-aid-workers/index.html.
Cobb, Roger W. and Charles D. Elder. 1983. *Participation in American Politics: The Dynamics of Agenda-Building*. Baltimore: Johns Hopkins University Press.
CODHES. 2008. CODHES – Consultoría para los Derechos Humanos y el Desplazamiento. "Comisión de seguimiento de seguimiento a la política pública sobre desplazamiento forzado." www.codhes.org/index.php?option=com_content&task=view&id=39&Itemid=52.
Collier, Paul. 2007. *The Bottom Billion: Why the Poorest Countries are Failing and What Can Be Done About It*. Oxford: Oxford University Press.
Core Working Group. 2007. "Communique of the Core Working Group on Bhutanese Refugees in Nepal." May 16. www.international.gc.ca/genev/new-nouveau/20070516.aspx?view=d.
Cress, Daniel and David Snow. 1998. "Mobilization at the Margins: Organizing by the Homeless." In *Social Movements and American Political Institutions*. Edited by Anne Costain and Andrew McFarland. Lanham: Rowman & Littlefield, pp. 73–98.
Edwards, Michael. 2009. *Civil Society*. Second Edition. Malden, MA: Polity Press.
Elkington, John and Pamela Hartigan. 2008. *The Power of Unreasonable People: How Social Entrepreneurs Create Markets that Change the World*. Boston: Harvard Business Review Press.
Essa, Azad. 2011. "Dadaab, the World's Biggest Refugee Camp." *Al Jazeera*. July 11. www.aljazeera.com/indepth/features/2011/07/201171182844876473.html.
Fackler, Martin. 2010. "South Korea Experiences a Stirring for Revenge." *New York Times*. November 27. www.nytimes.com/2010/11/28/world/asia/28island.html?_r=0.
Forero, Juan. 2004. "Colombia's 3 Million Refugees, Hidden in Plain Sight." *New York Times*. September 12.
Gladwell, Malcolm. 2010. "Annals of Innovation – Small Change – Why the Revolution Will Not be Tweeted." *The New Yorker*. October 4.
GPID. 2013. "Guiding Principles on Internal Displacement." www.idpguidingprinciples.org/.
Gross National Happiness (GNH). 2012. "The Center for Bhutan Studies." www.grossnationalhappiness.com/.
Guardian. 2015. "Bodies of 11 Refugees, Most of Them Infants, Recovered off Greece." November 1. www.theguardian.com/world/2015/nov/01/bodies-of-11-refugees-most-of-them-infants-recovered-off-greece.

References

GuluWalk. 2012. www.guluwalk.com/.
Hansen, John Mark. 1985. "The Political Economy of Group Membership." *American Political Science Review* 79: 79–96.
Hardin, Garrett. 1968. "The Tragedy of the Commons." *Science* 162: 1243–8.
Hochschild, Adam. 2005. *Bury the Chains: Prophets and Rebels in the Fight to Free an Empire's Slaves*. New York: Mariner Books.
Hollenbach, David. 2008. *Refugee Rights: Ethics, Advocacy and Africa*. Washington, DC: Georgetown University Press.
Human Rights Watch. 2012. "No Place for Children: Child Recruitment, Forced Marriage, and Attacks on Schools in Somalia." February 20. www.hrw.org/report/2012/02/20/no-place-children/child-recruitment-forced-marriage-and-attacks-schools-somalia#page.
Human Security Report. 2005. Human Security Center, The University of British Columbia, Canada. www.humansecurityreport.info/.
Internal Displacement Monitoring Center (IDMC). 2008. "COLOMBIA: Rate of New Displacement Highest in Two Decades, a Profile of the Internal Displacement Situation." October 17.
  2013. "Yemen." www.internal-displacement.org/countries/yemen.
International Crisis Group (ICG). 2002. "Colombia's Elusive Quest for Peace." Latin America Report N°1. March 26. www.crisisgroup.org/~/media/Files/latin-america/colombia/colombias-elusive-quest-for-peace.
  2007. "Colombia's New Armed Groups." Latin America Report N°20. May 10. www.crisisgroup.org/home/index.cfm?id=4824&l=1.
  2008a. "Somalia: To Move Beyond the Failed State." Africa Report N°147–23. December. www.crisisgroup.org/en/regions/africa/horn-of-africa/somalia/147-somalia-to-move-beyond-the-failed-state.aspx.
  2008b. "Correcting Course: Victims and the Justice and Peace Law in Colombia." Latin America Report N°29. October 30. www.crisisgroup.org/home/index.cfm?id=5753&l=1.
  2010. "Sri Lanka: A Bitter Peace." Asia Briefing No. 99. January 11. www.crisisgroup.org/library/documents/asia/south_asia/sri_lanka/b99_sri_lanka___a_bitter_peace.pdf.
  2012. "Dismantling Colombia's New Illegal Armed Groups: Lessons from a Surrender." Latin America Report N°41. June 8. www.crisisgroup.org/en/regions/latin-america-caribbean/andes/colombia/041-dismantling-colombias-new-illegal-armed-groups-lessons-from-a-surrender.aspx.
International Organization for Migration (IOM). 2008. Resettled Myanmar Refugees by Location (as of 30 April 2008). Presented at the CCSDPT monthly meeting, Bangkok, Thailand, May 14.
International Rescue Committee (IRC). 2007. "Mission Statement." www.rescue.org.
International Rescue Committee Uganda. 2007. "Annual Report." www.theirc.org/resources/annual-report-06.pdf.
Joachim, Jutta M. 2007. *Agenda Setting, the UN, and NGOs: Gender Violence and Reproductive Rights*. Washington, DC: Georgetown University Press.
Jones, Bryan D. and Frank R. Baumgartner. 2005. *The Politics of Attention: How Government Prioritizes Problems*. Chicago: University of Chicago Press.
Keck, Margaret E. and Kathryn Sikkink. 1998. *Activists Beyond Borders: Advocacy Networks in International Politics*. Ithaca: Cornell University Press.

Kingdon, John W. 1995. *Agendas, Alternatives and Public Policies*. Second Edition. Boston: Little Brown.

Kitschelt, Herbert P. 1986. "Political Opportunity Structure and Political Problems: Anti-Nuclear Movements in Four Democracies." *Journal of Political Science* 16(1): 57–85.

Kiva. 2013. "Kiva – History." www.kiva.org/about/history.

Klotz, Audie. 1995. *Norms in International Relations: The Struggle Against Apartheid*. Ithaca: Cornell University Press.

KONY 2012. http://invisiblechildren.com/kony-2012/.

Kraft, Michael E. and Scott R. Furlong. 2010. *Public Policy: Politics, Analysis and Alternatives*. Washington, DC: CQ Press.

Kriesi, Hanspeter. 1996. "The Organizational Structure of New Social Movements in a Political Context." In *Comparative Perspectives on Social Movements: Political Opportunities, Mobilizing Structures, and Cultural Framings*. Edited by Doug McAdam, John D. McCarthy and Mayer N. Zald. Cambridge: Cambridge University Press, pp. 152–84.

Loescher, Gil, James Milner, Edward Newman and Gary Troeller. 2007. *Protracted Refugee Situations and Peacebuilding*. No. 1 Policy Brief. United Nations University.

Mahoney, Christine. 2008. *Brussels vs. the Beltway: Advocacy in the United States and the European Union*. Washington, DC: Georgetown University Press.

Marwell, Gerald and Pamela Oliver. 1993. *The Critical Mass in Collective Action*. New York: Cambridge University Press.

Maslow, Abraham H. 1943. "A Theory of Human Motivation." *Psychological Review* 50: 370–96.

McAdam, Doug. 1988. *Freedom Summer*. New York: Oxford University Press.

McCarthy, John D. and Mayer N. Zald. 1978. "Resource Mobilization and Social Movements: A Partial Theory." *American Journal of Sociology* 82: 1212–41.

McConnell, Tristan. 2012. "Al Shabaab sold Doctors Without Borders Hostages to Pirates?" *Global Post*. January 10. www.globalpost.com/dispatches/globalpost-blogs/africa-emerges/kenya-news-shabaab-sold-doctors-without-borders-hostages-.

Moe, Terry M. 1980. "A Calculus of Group Membership." *American Journal of Political Science* 24: 593–632.

Morgan, J.N., R.F. Dye and J.H. Hybels. 1975. *A Survey of Giving Behavior and Attitudes: A Report to Respondents*. Ann Arbor: Institute for Social Research.

Morrison, Keigh and Tim Sandler. 2005. "Children of War in Uganda." Dateline NBC. August 22. www.msnbc.msn.com/id/9006024/ns/dateline_nbc/t/children-war-uganda/#.T_oZF5gW_7I.

MSF – Medicines Sans Frontier. 2005. "Displaced Colombians Struggle to Survive in Urban Slums." www.doctorswithoutborders.org/news/article.cfm?id=1547.

Muggah, Robert. Ed. 2006. *No Refuge: The Crisis of Refugee Militarization in Africa*. London: Zed Books.

Nelson, Paul J. and Ellen Dorsey. 2008. *New Rights Advocacy: Changing Strategies of Development & Human Rights NGOs*. Washington, DC: Georgetown University Press.

New York Times. 2009. "Somalia: More Than 100,000 Have Fled, U.N. Says." The Associated Press. June 9. www.nytimes.com/2009/06/10/world/africa/10briefs-Somalia.html.

References

Nownes, Anthony J. and Grant Neely. 1996. "Public Interest Group Entrepreneurship and Theories of Group Mobilization." *Political Research Quarterly* 49: 119–46.
Olson, Mancur. 1965. *The Logic of Collective Action: Public Goods and the Theory of Groups*. Cambridge, MA: Harvard University Press.
Ostrom, Elinor. 1990. *Governing the Commons: The Evolution of Institutions for Collective Action*. Cambridge: Cambridge University Press.
  1998. "A Behavioral Approach to the Rational Choice Theory of Collective Action." *American Political Science Review* 92: 1–22.
Papadopoulos, Renos and Ana Ljubinkovic. 2007. "Report on Assessment of Psychosocial Needs at the Dadaab Refugee Camps." Center for Trauma, Asylum and Refugees, University of Essex, UK.
Patrick, Erin. 2005. "Little Protection in 'Protected Villages': IDPs in Northern Uganda." Migration Policy Institute Working Paper. May. www.migrationpolicy.org/research/uganda_two.php.
Patten, Chris. 2010. "Sri Lanka's Choice, and the World's Responsibility." *International Herald Tribune*. January 13.
Polak, Paul. 2008. *Out of Poverty: What Works When Traditional Approaches Fail*. San Francisco: Barrett-Koehler.
Polgreen, Lydia. 2010. "President of Sri Lanka Is Re-elected by Wide Edge." *New York Times*. January 27.
Pollack, M. 1997. "Representing Diffuse Interests in EC Policy-Making." *Journal of European Public Policy* 4(4): 572–90.
Prahalad, C.K. 2014. *Fortune at the Bottom of the Pyramid: Eradicating Poverty Through Profits*. Philadelphia: Warton School Publishing.
Putnam, Robert. 1993. *Making Democracy Work*. Princeton: Princeton University Press.
  2003. *Better Together: Restoring the American Community*. New York: Simon & Schuster.
Raghavan, Sudarsan. 2013. "In Traumatic Arc of a Refugee Camp, Congo's War Runs Deep." *Washington Post*. November 7. www.washingtonpost.com/world/africa/in-traumatic-arc-of-a-refugee-camp-congos-war-runs-deep/2013/11/07/22de1dbe-470b-11e3-95a9-3f15b5618ba8_story.html.
R2P. 2013. "Responsibility to Protect." www.responsibilitytoprotect.org/.
Ressler, Mattie. 2007. InterAction: Somalia – Guide to Humanitarian and Development Efforts of InterAction Member Agencies in Somalia.
RI. 2013. "Refugees International – Who We Are." http://refugeesinternational.org/who-we-are.
Risse, Thomas. 2002. "Transnational Actors and World Politics." In *Handbook of International Relations*. Edited by Walter Carlsnaes, Thomas Risse, and Beth A. Simmons. Thousand Oaks: Sage Publications, pp. 255–74.
Salisbury, Robert. 1969. "An Exchange Theory of Interest Groups." *Midwest Journal of Political Science* 13: 1–32.
Scholte, Jan Aart. 2002. "Civil Society and Democracy in Global Governance." *Global Governance* 8(3): 281–304.
S.C.O.T.U.S. 2014. "Supreme Court of the United States. Obergefell et al. v. Hodges, Director, Ohio Department of Health et al. October Term." www.supremecourt.gov/opinions/14pdf/14-556_3204.pdf.

Sengupta, Somini and David E. Sanger. 2015. "After Years of War in Syria, UN Passes Resolution on Talks." *New York Times*. December 18. www.nytimes.com/2015/12/19/world/middleeast/syria-talks-isis.html?_r=0.

Shirky, Clay. 2008. *Here Comes Everybody: The Power of Organizing Without Organizations*. London: Penguin Books.

Slaughter, Anne-Marie. 2004. "Disaggregated Sovereignty: Towards the Public Accountability of Global Government Networks." *Government & Opposition* 39(2): 159–90.

Sphere Handbook. 2011. www.sphereproject.org/handbook/.

Spillius, Alex. 2012. "Al-Shabaab Militia Abducting Teenage Girls to Marry Fighters." *Telegraph*. February 21. www.telegraph.co.uk/news/worldnews/africaandindianocean/somalia/9096315/Al-Shabaab-militia-abducting-teenage-girls-to-marry-fighters.html.

Subba, S.B. 2008. "The Bombing of IOM Office in East Nepal Sheds New Light on Resettlement of Refugees in a Third Country." Refugee Watch Online (A Co-Publication of Refugee Watch). http://refugeewatchonline.blogspot.com/2008/07/bombing-of-iom-office-in-east-nepal.html.

Swarns, Rachel L. 2006. "US Eases Curbs on Resettling Burmese Refugees." *New York Times*. May 5. www.nytimes.com/2006/05/05/us/05refugee.html.

Tarrow, Sidney. Ed. 1998. *Power in Movement: Social Movements and Contentious Politics*. New York: Cambridge University Press.

      2006. *The New Transnational Activism*. New York: Cambridge University Press.

TBBC. 2012. "Thai Burma Border Consortium – About Us." www.tbbc.org/aboutus/aboutus.htm.

Terry, Fiona. 2002. *Condemned to Repeat? The Paradox of Humanitarian Action*. Ithaca: Cornell University Press.

Udéhn, Lars. 1993. "Twenty-Five Years with 'The Logic of Collective Action'." *Acta Sociologica* 36(3): 239–61.

UNHCR. 2006. "Practical Guide to the Systematic Use of Standards & Indicators in UNHCR Operations." Second Edition. February.

      2008. "Nepal: UN Agency Condemns Attacks on Refugees." www.un.org/apps/news/story.asp?NewsID=26582&Cr=nepal&Cr1=refugee.

      2009a. "UNHCR Emergency Assistance Programme for Somali Refugees in Dadaab, Kenya." January–December.

      2009b. "Handbook on the Protection of Internally Displaced Persons." www.unhcr.org/4c2355229.pdf.

UNHCR. 2015. "Worldwide Displacement Hits All-Time High as War and Persecution Increase." June 18. www.unhcr.org/558193896.html.

UNICEF. 2012. "Nepal Statistics." www.unicef.org/infobycountry/nepal_nepal_statistics.html.

UNSC. 2004. "United Nations Security Council Resolutions 1564 – Darfur." www.un.org/ga/search/view_doc.asp?symbol=S/RES/1564(2004).

      2006. "United Nations Security Council Resolutions 1701 – Lebanon." www.un.org/ga/search/view_doc.asp?symbol=S/RES/1701(2006).

USCRI. 2013. "US Committee for Refugees and Immigrants – Who We Are." www.refugees.org/about-us/who-we-are/.

Vogler, Pia. 2007. "Into the Jungle of Bureaucracy: Negotiating Access to Camps at the Thai-Burma Border." *Refugee Survey Quarterly* 26(3): 51–60.

Wade, Francis. 2009. "50,000th Burmese Border Refugee Resettled in the US." *Democratic Voice of Burma.* July 1. www.dvb.no/news/50000th-burmese-border-refugee-resettled-in-us/2715.

Walker, Jack L., Jr. 1983. "The Origins and Maintenance of Interest Groups in America." *American Political Science Review* 77: 390–406.

Yunus, Mohammad. 2001. *Banker to the Poor: The Autobiography of Muhammad Yunus, Founder of Grameen Bank.* Oxford: Oxford University Press.

   2011. *Building Social Business: The New Kind of Capitalism that Serves Humanity's Most Pressing Needs.* New York: PublicAffairs.

Zhao, Kingzin. 2001. *The Power of Tiananmen. State-Society Relations and the 1989 Beijing Student Movement.* Chicago: University of Chicago Press.

Index

abducted children, 59, 71–72, 85–86, 119
abduction, 58, 106, 109, 113, *see also* kidnapping.
activism/activists, 1, 3, 11–12, 24, 38, 45, 53–54, 66
advocacy, 2–4, 16–19, 40, 43–46, 64–67, 78–80, 94–95, 124–25
   advocates and challenges, 67–78
   barriers to, 74, 77, 78–80, 82, 87, 88, 95, 96
   campaigns, 4, 11, 19, 24, 124, 128, 134, 139
   chain, 124–26
   effective, *see* effective advocacy.
   frontline, 66
   global, 3–5, 12, 137
   groups, 17, 21, 23–24, 43, 55
   national, 81–100
   organizations, 3, 21–23, 25–26, 34, 38, 44, 66, 84
   and priority of saving lives, 78–79
   transnational, 3–4, 5, 11–12
   and unwanted nature of refugees, 79
Afghanistan, 6t1.1, 9, 15t1.3, 25, 29–34, 29t2.1, 35, 40t3.1
Afro-Colombians, 63, 112, 118
agenda, 3–4, 21–24, 34, 36–38, 42, 43–44, 60, 65
   attention, 13, 23, 26, 33f2.7
   global, 21–23, 25, 29–31, 35, 39, 51, 56, 64–65
   international, 11, 46, 53, 59, 65, 123
   space, 18, 27, 31, 36, 64
aid organizations, 67–68, 74, 75, 84–85, 96, 125–26, 133, 138–40
   international, 50, 69, 72–73, 80, 88, 125, 126–27, 130
aid workers, 77, 80, 83–85, 86–87, 88, 92, 93–96, 97–98
Al Shabaab, 48, *see* al-Shabaab.
altruism, 104, 106, 108
American Refugee Committee, *see* ARC.
Amnesty International, 34, 50
apathy, 61, 80, 88
ARC (American Refugee Committee), 8, 34, 67, 76, 78
armed groups, 62–63, 89, 105
Assad, President Bashar, 1, 136, 139
asylum, 1, 20, 45
   seekers, 5, 26, 29t2.1, 79
attention, 18, 21–29, 35–46, 54f3.9, 59f3.10, 64–66, 124–25, 136–38
   to displacement crises, 21–37
   global, *see* global attention.
   spikes in, 40–42
   and violence, 64
Aung San Suu Kyi, 53, 55
Australia, 9, 22, 25, 51–52, 79
awareness, 32–34, 39, 45, 122, 124, 125, 129, 134
Azerbaijan, 6t1.1, 15t1.3, 29t2.1, 99

backbone organization, 129, 134, 140
bandwidth, 65, 94, 125, 126, 138
Bangladesh, 6t1.1, 14t1.2, 28t2.1, 79, 131–32
barriers
   to effective advocacy, 74, 77, 78–80, 82, 87, 88, 95, 96
   to mobilization, 102, 106, 108, 118

Bhutan, 6t1.1, 10, 28t2.1, 35, 45,
    50–53, 65, 74
  ethnic Nepalese, 50
Bhutanese refugees, 15–17, 19, 51, 52–53, 54,
    67, 73–76
births, 50, 94, 115, 122
Bosnia-Herzegovina, 6t1.1, 28t2.1, 35, 40t3.1,
    45–46, 65, 67, 83
Bosnian refugees, 16, 32, 68
bribes, 80, 87, 98, 138
Buddhist Monks, 54, 111
Burma, 26, 29–31, 29t2.1, 40t3.1, 56, 75,
    76, 99
  Aung San Suu Kyi, 53, 55
  government, 55, 78
  Saffron Rebellion, 38, 54
Burmese refugees, 15–16, 54, 56, 68
Burundi, 6t1.1, 14t1.2, 28t2.1, 83, 84
Bush, Laura, 39, 54, 55
Bush Administration, 54, 62
businesses, small, 19, 129–30, 132, 134,
    135, 140

Cambodia, 6t1.1, 28t2.1, 75
camp life, 101, 112, 120
camp management, 85, 110, 121
campaigns, 3–4, 54, 55, 56, 99, 124, 129, 134
camps, 17, 46–49, 56–58, 68–71, 74–77,
    83–86, 105–9, 110–15
  internal displacement, 5, 7, 10, 57, 96, 109,
    121, 140
  internment, 61, 110, 115
  refugee, *see* refugee camps.
Canada, 9, 22, 51–52, 84
capacity, 10, 72–73, 81, 82, 85, 93, 95, 100
  building, 71, 112
Catholic Relief Services (CRS), 8, 67
CCSDPT (Committee for Coordination
    of Services to Displaced Persons in
    Thailand), 75, 110–11, 122
Central African Republic, 6t1.1, 14t1.2,
    29t2.1, 56, 59, 99, 137
Chad, 6t1.1, 14t1.2, 28t2.1, 42, 99–101
Chechnya, 40t3.1, 42, 65, 138
child soldiers, 56–57, 113, 119
children, 40–42, 48–49, 50–51, 56–59, 71–72,
    76, 85–86, 113–14
China, 6t1.1, 28t2.1, 44–45, 96, 137
cities, 58, 89–90, 93, 109, 111, 136
civil society, 11, 34, 104, 105, 106, 117, 123
civil wars, 1, 10, 47, 49, 55, 58, 59, 74
civilians, 1, 54, 57, 60, 62–63, 72, 124–25

clean water, 112–13, 119, 122, 132
clusters, 82–83, 87–88, 95, 122
coalitions, 5, 9, 12, 23, 26, 42, 66, 75
collective action, 16, 101, 102, 103, 104, 105,
    106, 107, 108, 109, 110, 110t6.1, 112,
    113–14, 116–17, 118–20, 139
  contexts, 105–9
  and cultural/community context, 118–19
  definition and determinants, 102–5
  and duration context, 120–21
  and human security, 113–14
  informal, 112, 122
  and legal context, 114–18
  nature among dispaced persons, 109–12
  and NGO activity, 122
  political, 109–10, 114, 116
  problems, 102–3
collective mobilization, 107, 115
Colombia, 13–16, 29t2.1, 61–64, 89–92, 93,
    99, 111–13, 117–18
  ELN, 61–62
  FARC, 61–62, 117
  government, 62, 89, 94
  IDPs, 89–94, 109, 114
  kidnapping, 61–62
  Medellín cartel, 61
  NIAGs, 62–63
Committee for Coordination of Services to
    Displaced Persons in Thailand, *see*
    CCSDPT.
communication, 75, 104, 105, 108
communities, 20, 85, 90, 107, 109–10,
    116–17, 118, 119
  displaced, 36, 38, 62, 65, 105, 107, 138
  host, 2, 10, 34, 70, 72, 74, 78, 130–31
  local, 72, 95, 130
  vulnerable, 100, 140
community building, 13, 17, 101, 106, 107,
    121, 122
community context, 107–8, 109, 118
  and collective action, 118–19
community groups, building in displacement
    camps, 101–23
community mobilization, 121, 139
community-based organizations, *see* CBOs.
conditionality, 128
Congo, 6t1.1, 14t1.2, 28t2.1, 99, *see also*
    Democratic Republic of the Congo.
content analysis, 13, 18, 36, 39–40, 53, 138
context, 45–46, 67, 102, 104, 105–9,
    117, 120
control, 1, 13, 48, 71, 114, 116, 118

Index

Convention on the Status of Refugees, 2, 7–8, 82
cooperation, 47, 103–5, 108
coordination, 75, 88, 95, 105, 122
Core Countries, 52–53
Core Working Group, 51–52
corruption, 67, 77, 80, 88–89, 98, 126, 128, 138
costs, 16, 103–4
countries of origin, 6t1.1, 40t3.1, 126
country cases, 13–15, 110
coverage, *see* attention.
CRC (Croatian Red Cross), 68, 69, 84, 122
Croatia, 13–16, 35, 45–47, 67–69, 83, 109–10, 112–13, 121–22
    government, 68–69, 120
    IDPs, 16, 46, 68–69, 83–84, 112
crowd-funding, 2, 127, 129–30, 139
CRS (Catholic Relief Services), 8, 67
cultural context, 102, 105, 107–8, 109
    and collective action, 118–19

Dadaab refugee camp complex, 7, 9, 47–48, 53, 69–71, 72–73, 132–33
Danish Refugee Council (DRC), 8, 34, 67
Darfur, 18, 23, 44, 65, 124
data collection, 5, 18, 19, 21–23, 25–27, 109
databases, 13, 23, 25–26, 38, 110, 112
demobilization, 62, 118
Democratic Republic of the Congo (DRC), 6t1.1, 15t1.3, 29t2.1, 30–32, 40t3.1, 134, 137, 139
developed world, 11–12, 128, 130, 134
dignity, 10, 19, 20, 127, 129, 131, 135, 140
discrimination, 50, 63, 87, 114
disease, 42, 76, 106, 136
displaced entrepreneurs, 130–31, 134–35
displaced rights, 24, 93, 102, 105, 118, 123, 126, 128
displacement, 5–8, 35–36, 41f3.2, 57, 59f3.10, 63–65, 81–83, 89–91, 107–8
    camps, 22, 101, 139
    crises, 2, 4, 13, 15–16, 21–37, 38, 130
    forced, 2, 4, 5, 20, 23, 24, 45, 93
    internal, 18, 57, 63, 81–82, 87, 94, 99
    issues/situations, 4, 13, 21–23, 25–27, 32, 39f3.1, 102, 108–9
    protracted, 2, 4–5, 13, 24–25, 29, 31, 137–38
doctors, 44, 71, 86, 112, 125
DRC, *see* Democratic Republic of the Congo.

drug trafficking, 62, 105
durable solutions, 9–11, 19, 24, 51–53, 54, 65, 121
duration context, 102, 105, 108, 109, 120–21

economic leverage, 4, 67, 82, 125, 127, 135, 138
education, 85, 88, 105, 106, 109, 111, 114–16, 121–22
effective advocacy, 84–85, 87, 99, 126, 139
    barriers to, 74, 77, 78–80, 82, 87, 88, 95, 96
elections, 51, 55–56, 60, 62, 79–80, 88, 104, 111
End Warehousing campaign, 36
entrepreneurs
    displaced, 130–31, 134–35
    policy, 3, 11, 21, 24, 36
    refugee, 130, 133
entrepreneurship
    social, 2, 19, 129, 131–33
Eritrea, 6t1.1, 14t1.2, 28t2.1, 48
Ethiopia, 6t1.1, 10, 14t1.2, 27, 28t2.1, 48, 73
ethnic cleansing, 20, 42, 46, 81, 138
European Union, 21–22, 25, 33f2.6, 42–43, 60–61, 65, 79–80, 128
exploitation, 2, 68, 98, 107
extended families, 85, 109, 114, 118
extortion, 61–62, 78

failure, 2–3, 4–5, 8–9, 24, 36, 39, 64, 128
    as norm, 1–20
families, 63, 85–86, 90–91, 105–6, 115–16, 119, 132–33, 140
    extended, 85, 109, 114, 118
FARC, 61–62, 117
field interviews, 17, 109–10, 123
field outposts, 16
fieldwork, 2, 4, 13, 18–19, 46–47, 63, 84
fiscal austerity pressures, 127, 133
food, 34, 36, 68, 69–70, 106, 111, 112–13, 122
    aid, 69, 84
    distribution, 70, 111–12
    life-saving, 19, 67, 69, 74, 78, 94, 125
    rations, 7, 50, 75, 101, 122
forced displacement, 2, 4, 5, 20, 23, 24, 45, 93
forced recruitment, 63, 71
former Yugoslavia, 46, 47, 68, 83
freedom
    of movement, 36, 94–95, 96–97, 98–99, 114–15, 116–17, 126, 128
    to work, 36, 67–68, 69, 94, 95, 126, 128–29

frontline advocacy
  IDP rights, 81–100
  refugee rights, 66–80
frontline mobilization, 101–23
funding, 19, 52, 61, 69, 88, 132, 133
  external, 111

gender-based violence, 3, 11, 21, 24, 49, 74, 87–88, 99
genocide, 20, 32, 42–43, 46, 75, 81, 106
geopolitics, 5, 35, 38, 40, 64
Georgia, 6t1.1, 15t1.3, 29t2.1, 40t3.1, 42
Germany, 27–29
global activism, 11–12
global advocacy, 3–5, 12, 137
  campaigns, 11, 19, 128, 134, 139
  new data on, 13–18
global agenda, 21–23, 25, 29–31, 35, 39, 51, 56, 64–65
  setting, 23–24
global attention
  analysis, 27–37
  data collection, 25–27
  geopolitics vs. advocacy, 38–65
global citizens, 127, 129, 135, 139
Global North, 3, 4, 9, 11, 21–25, 36–38, 137–39
Global South, 24, 25, 37
Global War on Terror, 8, 35, 65, 137
governance, 2, 4–5, 12, 24, 80, 99, 117, 124
Guardian, 2, 25, 30–31
guerillas, 61, 63, 90, 93
Guiding Principles on Internal Displacement, 57, 81–82, 94, 99, 127
Guinea, 6t1.1, 14t1.2, 28t2.1
Gulu, 58, 86
Gulu Walk, 58–59

habitual residence, 7, 10, 72
Haiti, 6t1.1, 28t2.1, 135
health, 72, 78, 82, 86, 102, 106, 111, 114
  care, 34, 68, 85, 94, 109, 113, 122, 126
  workers, 8, 67, 111, 121
host communities, 2, 10, 34, 70, 72, 74, 78, 130–31
host governments, 18–19, 73, 74, 77–80, 125, 127, 128–30, 138–40
house arrest, 53, 55
human rights, 11, 20, 24, 44–45, 52, 54, 55, 125–26
human rights organizations/groups, 8, 23–24, 42, 44, 125–26, 134, 137, 138

Human Rights Watch, 3, 34, 44, 52, 71–72
human security, 102, 105, 106, 109, 113–14, 116, 118–19, 122–23
humanitarian aid, 5, 7, 8, 67–68, 88–89, 124, 125, 127
  organizations/groups, 66–67, 68, 72–73, 74–75, 78, 82, 84, 133
hunger, 49, 70, 106, 136, 140

IDPs (internally displaced persons), 8, 15–16, 46–47, 68–69, 81–83, 97–99, 112–17, 128–29
  camps, 5, 7, 10, 57, 96, 109, 121, 140
  Colombian, 89–94, 109, 114
  conflict-generated, 82
  Croatian, 16, 46, 68–69, 83–84, 112
  Sri Lankan, 94–99
  Tamil, 2, 10
  Ugandan, 10, 84–89
Implementing Partners (IPs), 16–17, 20, 67, 70, 77–78, 81, 84–85
incentives, 18–19, 78–79, 103, 105, 108–9, 112, 128–29, 130
income-generating activities, 20, 102, 105, 112, 115, 133
in-depth interviews, 2, 13, 16–17, 83
India, 6t1.1, 14t1.2, 28t2.1, 45, 73, 94, 96, 133
information, 16–17, 53, 86, 90, 91, 98, 108, 114
infrastructure, 10, 42, 72, 79, 102, 105, 118, 121
INGOs (international NGOs), 37–38, 74–75, 96, 97, 98, 113, 115, 122
innovation, 124, 129, 132–33, 134
integration, local, 9–10, 56, 73
internal displacement, *see* IDPs.
internally displaced persons, *see* IDPs.
international aid, workers, 71, 86, 96
international aid organizations, 50, 69, 72–73, 80, 88, 125, 126–27, 130
International Campaign for Tibet, 23, 44, 137
international community, 8, 10, 18, 19–20, 23–24, 36–39, 44–45, 52
International Crisis Group, 34, 44, 48, 61
international NGOs, *see* INGOs.
International Organization for Migration (IOM), 52, 74, 120–21
international organizations, 25–26, 74, 75, 87, 89, 125, 127, 128
International Rescue Committee (IRC), 8, 34, 44, 67, 70, 74, 76, 78

Index

internment camps, 61, 110, 115
interviewees, 17, 71, 76, 78, 92, 94, 96, 113
interviews, 16–17, 70–71, 75–77, 83–87, 88–92, 93–98, 113–14, 119–22
investments, 19, 36, 129, 136, 139–40
Invisible Children, 56, 59, 134
IOM (International Organization for Migration), 52, 74, 120–21
IPs, see Implementing Partners.
Iran, 6t1.1, 14t1.2, 28t2.1, 32
Iranian refugees, 26, 32
Iraq, 6t1.1, 9, 14t1.2, 29–32, 29t2.1, 40t3.1, 136, 138
IRC, see International Rescue Committee.
ISIS (Islamic State of Iraq and Syria), 1, 2, 139
Israel, 40–42

Jaffna, 97, 114, 115
Japan, 25, 83, 112
Jesuit Refugee Service (JRS), 8, 34, 67
jointness, 103
journalists, 1, 47, 53, 93, 134, 136
justice, 66, 118, 122
justice, social, 5, 11, 128
Justice and Equality Movement, 42–43

Karen, 39, 53, 65, 110, 111, 115, 134, 139
Karen, refugees, 65, 75, 101, 120
Karen Women's Organization (KWO), 101, 111
Karen Youth Organization (KYO), 111
Kenya, 9, 13–16, 48, 69, 72–73, 109–10, 114–15, 132–33
    authorities/government, 48, 69, 72–73, 77
    Dadaab refugee camp complex, 7, 9, 47–48, 53, 69–71, 72–73, 132–33
Kickstarter, 130
kidnapping, 61–62, see also abduction.
Kingdon, J.W., 3, 21, 23–24, 36
Kiva, 130, 135
Kony, Joseph, 56–59, 87, 129, 134, 137
Kosovo, 6t1.1, 46–47, 68, 84
Kyrgyzstan, 29–31, 34

lack of trust, 114, 119, 123
landmines, 90
latrines, 50, 73, 75–76, 86, 102
Le Monde, 25, 30–31
leadership, 102, 104, 105, 107–9, 118, 130
Lebanon, 1, 6, 15t1.3, 28t2.1, 40t3.1, 42, 65, 79
legal context, 102, 105, 106–7, 109, 114–18

lending circles, 131, 139
leverage, 52–53, 67, 74, 79–80, 96, 99–100, 125–26, 138
    economic, 4, 67, 82, 125, 127, 135, 138
    political, 19, 67, 80, 82, 125, 126, 138
Lhotshampas, 50, 65
life-saving food, 19, 67, 69, 74, 78, 94, 125
limbo, 2, 47, 68
loans, 129–32, 133, 134
lobbying, 26, 32, 66, 79, 81, 88, 93, 110
local authorities, 17, 72, 87–88, 96, 122
local communities, 72, 95, 130
local integration, 9–10, 56, 73
LRA (Lord's Resistance Army), 56–59, 85–86, 87, 88, 119, 129, 134, 137
LTTE (Liberation Tigers of Tamil Eelam), 59–60, 94, 96, 115, 117, 119

Mae La, 76–77, 111, 120, 122
Mae Sot, 75–76, 77, 110
Mala Gorica, 68–69, 112
malnutrition, 58, 69, 71, 76
marginalization, 48, 82, 125, 127, 128, 138
massive displacement, 23, 24, 27–31, 38, 39, 64, 137–38
media
    attention/coverage, see attention.
    social, 129, 134–35
medical services, 70, 84, 94
medicine, 19, 67, 71, 74, 75, 78, 84, 90
micro-finance, 2, 19, 131, 139
    person-to-person, 19, 127, 129–30
micro-grants, 130, 132
micro-loans, 130–31, 133
militias, 2, 48, 72, 105, 134, 139
minimum standards, 8, 70, 94
minorities, 29, 55, 73, 82, 96, 126, 127, 137
mobilization, 99–100, 106–7, 108–10, 111–12, 115–16, 117–19, 122–23, 125–27
    barriers to, 102, 106, 108, 118
    collective, 107, 115
    community, 121, 139
    frontline, 101–23
    political, 13, 19, 102, 111, 117
money, 63, 73–74, 78, 79, 86, 88, 93, 125
monsoons, 50, 73, 97
movement, freedom of, 36, 94–95, 96–97, 98–99, 115, 116–17, 126, 128
Myanmar, see Burma.

narco-terrorists, 113, 117
narco-traffickers, 62, 89

national advocacy
    IDP rights, 81–100
    refugee rights, 66–80
national authorities/governments, 8, 18, 67–68, 82–83, 89, 99, 125, 129, see also individual countries.
national NGOs, 68, 75, 79, 89, 97, 129
naturalization, 9, 11, 52, 68, 74
Nepal, 13–17, 50–52, 54, 65, 67, 73–74, 76, 109–10
New York Times, 25–26, 30–32, 38–39, 40, 45, 50, 61, 63–64
New Zealand, 22, 51–52
news stories, 30, 30f2.3, 40t3.1, 47, 49, 138, see also attention.
NFIs (Non-Food Items), 69, 71, 95, 112
NGOs (non-governmental organizations), 8, 16–17, 72–74, 96, 98, 105, 108–10, 121–22
    activity, 102, 108–9, 122
    activity and collective action, 122
    international, see INGOs.
    local, 8, 67, 76, 90, 118, 122
    national, 68, 75, 79, 89, 97, 129
    staff, 13, 16, 17, 110–11, 116, 119, 120–21
Nigeria, 6t1.1, 14t1.2, 28t2.1, 79
Non-Food Items (NFIs), 69, 71, 95, 112
non-governmental organizations, see NGOs.
non-priority citizens, 67, 72, 74, 82, 99, 125, 126, 138
norms, 1, 2–3, 4, 8, 20, 36, 39, 128
Norway, 39, 52, 65, 74
Norwegian Refugee Committee (NRC), 8, 34, 67, 70, 71, 121

observers, 7, 11, 43, 47, 57, 60
Operating Partners (OPs), 8, 67, 74
oppression, 42, 76, 78, 104, 107, 109, 115
Ostrom, Elinor, 102–4, 108

P2P micro-finance, 19, 127, 129–30
Pakistan, 6t1.1, 25, 29t2.1, 31, 40t3.1, 42, 134, 138
Palestinian camps, 40, 130, 134
Palestinian refugees, 6t1.1, 27, 29–34, 35, 40, 40t3.1
paramilitaries, 61–63, 89, 90, 92, 113, 117–18, 133
payoffs, 115, 126, 138
peace, 1, 9, 10, 45, 56, 58, 60, 68
    agreements, 43–44, 58, 114
    building, 9, 62

person-to-person micro-finance, 19, 127, 129–30
piracy, 48, 71
Plan Colombia, 62
Polak, Paul, 132, 133
police, 46, 68, 71, 113, 119
policy change, 3, 36, 39, 64, 69, 124, 126, 128
policy entrepreneurs, 3, 11, 21, 24, 36
policymakers, 3, 22–24, 34, 44, 74, 79, 123, 125–26
political leverage, 19, 67, 80, 82, 125, 126, 138
political mobilization, 13, 19, 102, 111, 117
politics, 4, 36, 60, 72, 88, 139
poverty, 93, 125, 132, 133
power, 3, 46, 55, 56, 88–89, 127, 128
    players, 3, 12, 36
    political, 125, 126–27
pressure, 10–11, 43–44, 52, 55, 72, 96, 97, 124–26
primary mission, 19, 67, 79, 80, 86, 125
privacy, 7, 50, 73, 75, 113
Pro Asyl, 34
profits, 62, 132
property, 46, 63
    rights, 52, 122
protected villages, 57, 58, 115
protection, 6–8, 20, 78–79, 81–82, 87, 89, 96, 98
    monitoring, 98, 113
protests, 1, 10, 45, 54, 66, 103, 115
protracted displacement, 2, 4–5, 13, 24–25, 29, 31, 137–38
psychological effects, 49, 87, 92, 94, 120
public agenda, see agenda.
public force, 89–90
public goods, 103
public policy, 34, 91, 92, 117

rape, 20, 49, 54, 63, 71, 81, 106, 109
real world solutions, 127–28
rebel groups, 1, 43, 56, 58–59, 82, 86, 124, 136
reciprocal altruism, 104, 108
reconciliation, 48, 55, 118
recruitment
    forced, 63, 71
    militia, 2, 139
refoulement, 20, 68
Refugee and Migrant Justice, 34
refugee camps, 13, 17, 49, 53, 59, 63, 106, 109

Bhutanese, 16–17, 19, 52, 67, 75–76
Dadaab, 7, 9, 47–48, 53, 69–71, 72–73, 132–33
Somali, 67, 69, 112
refugee entrepreneurs, 130, 133
registries, 23, 89–90
Registro Único de Población Desplazada (RUPD), 90, 91, 93, 99, 113
rehabilitation, 78, 85–86, 115
religion, 7, 96, 109, 119
repatriation, 9, 51–53, 109
resettled refugees, 22, 27, 129
resettlement, 9–10, 51–53, 55–56, 74, 82, 109–10, 120–21, 122
resources, 11–12, 67, 106–7, 108, 118, 125, 126–27, 138
responsibility, 8, 20, 72, 81–82, 92, 93, 118
return, 7, 9, 52, 56–57, 74, 82, 83, 120–21
returnees, 5, 26, 29t2.1, 68, 83, 121
rights, displaced, *see* displaced rights.
roads, 7, 86, 88, 103
Roma, 29
RUPD, *see* Registro Único de Población Desplazada.
Russia/Russian Federation, 6t1.1, 15t1.3, 28t2.1, 42, 136, 139
Rwanda, 6t1.1, 14t1.2, 20, 28t2.1, 79, 83, 84

safe return, *see* return.
safety, 2, 57, 71, 96–97, 106, 127
Saffron Rebellion, 38, 54
Samasource, 133
sanitation, 68, 70, 72, 76, 79, 85, 120, 122
Save Darfur Coalition, 23, 32, 43–44, 65, 137
schools, 71–72, 85, 88, 101, 106, 111, 116, 121
security, 34, 43, 71, 96, 98, 103, 105–6, 111
  forces, 29, 62, 68, 77
  human, *see* human security.
Security Council, 42–43, 55
self-interest, short-term, 102–3, 104
self-sufficiency, 34, 78
Serbia, 6t1.1, 15t1.3, 29t2.1, 46, 83, 112
sex slaves, 57, 86, 113
al-Shabaab, 48, 71–72, 73
shelter, 78–79, 84, 94–95, 99, 106, 113–14, 122, 125
skills, 93, 101, 106, 115, 116, 120, 134, 137
slacktivism, 135
slaves, sex, 57, 86, 113
slums, 4, 5, 63
small businesses, 19, 129–30, 132, 134, 135, 140

Soacha, 63
social capital, 101, 107
social entrepreneurship, 2, 19, 129, 131–34
social media, 129, 134–35
social movements, 11, 19, 104, 107, 128
Somali refugees/IDPs, 2, 9–10, 15–16, 67, 69–70, 71, 72–73, 132
Somalia, 9–10, 26, 29, 29t2.1, 35, 40t3.1, 47–49, 71–73
South Korea, 27
South Sudan, 6t1.1, 56, 57
sovereignty, 20, 81, 117, 127
Sphere standards, 70–71, 94, 113
Sri Lanka, 13–16, 59, 82–83, 97, 109–10, 113–17, 122, 125–26
  IDPs, 94–99
  Jaffna, 97, 114, 115
  LTTE, 59–60, 94, 96, 115, 117, 119
  Manik Farm, 94, 96–97, 113, 115–16, 119
  Sinhalese, 59–60, 96, 117, 119
  Tamils, 10, 60–61, 82, 87, 94, 95–96, 117, 119
  Vavuniya, 95, 97, 98, 114–16, 122
stabilization, 47–48, 137
stag hunt dilemma, 102–3
standards, 5, 86, 94
  minimum, 8, 70, 94
  Sphere, 70–71, 94, 113
stateless persons, 20, 26, 29t2.1
status quo, 4, 20, 123, 140
sub-optimal outcomes, 103–4
success, 3, 5, 10–12, 17, 62, 65, 133, 135
  rarity, 8–11
Sudan, 14t1.2, 29–32, 29t2.1, 40t3.1, 43f3.4, 57–58, 84–85, 125
  South, 6t1.1, 56, 57
Suddeutsche Zeitung, 25, 30–33
Syria, 1, 6t1.1, 28t2.1, 31, 124–25, 134, 136–37, 139
  Assad
    President Bashar, 1, 136, 139
  refugees/IDPs, 1, 81

Taliban, 42
Tamils, 10, 60–61, 82, 87, 94, 95–96, 117, 119
Tanzania, 10, 14t1.2, 28t2.1, 79
Tarrow, S., 3, 12, 104, 106
TBBC (Thai-Burma Border Consortium), 75, 110–11, 122
teachers, 71–72, 88, 101, 121
tents, 7, 48, 96, 119, 134, 136
terror, 8, 35, 40, 57, 58, 65, 92, 137

terrorists, 1–2, 8, 60, 105, 139
Thai-Burma Border Consortium, *see* TBBC.
Thailand, 13–16, 54, 56, 75–76, 77, 109–11, 114–15, 122
　government/authorities, 75–78
　Mae La, 76–77, 111, 120, 122
　Mae Sot, 75–76, 77, 110
　Tham Hin, 53, 101
Tibet, 23, 32, 38, 44f3.5, 124, 137
Tibetan refugees, 6t1.1, 26, 44–45, 74
transnational activism, 11–12
transnational advocacy, 3–4, 5, 11–12
transnational coalitions, 12
trust, 101, 104, 107, 109, 114, 117, 118–19, 123
Turkey, 1, 6t1.1, 28t2.1, 81, 136

UDHR (Universal Declaration of Human Rights), 7, 20, 72
Uganda, 13–17, 56–59, 82–83, 84–86, 87–88, 109–10, 112–13, 114–15
　government, 56–57, 87, 88, 115
　Gulu, 58, 86
　IDPs, 10, 84–89
　LRA (Lord's Resistance Army) and Jospeh Kony, 56–59, 85–86, 87, 88, 119, 129, 134, 137
unemployment, 10, 90, 93, 128
UNHCR (United Nations High Commissioner for Refugees), 7–9, 13–17, 26–27, 67–70, 74–76, 77, 81–83, 84–85
UNICEF (United Nations Children's Fund), 5, 72, 74, 82, 87, 111
United Nations Guiding Principles on Internal Displacement, 57, 81–82, 94, 99, 127
United Nations High Commissioner for Refugees, *see* UNHCR.
United Nations Mission in Sudan (UNMIS), 43

United Nations Relief and Works Agency for Palestine Refugees, *see* UNRWA.
United States, 8–11, 21–23, 25–26, 30–32, 43, 50–52, 53–54, 65–66
　role in displacement aid, 22f2.1
Universal Declaration of Human Rights (UDHR), 7, 20, 72
UNMIS (United Nations Mission in Sudan), 43
UNRWA (United Nations Relief and Works Agency for Palestine Refugees), 6, 27, 29
US Committee for Refugees and Immigrants, 2, 34

Vavuniya, 95, 97, 98, 114–16, 122
Viet Nam, 6t1.1, 29t2.1, 75
villages, 43f3.4, 48–49, 57, 93, 102–3, 118
　protected, 57, 58, 115
violence, 5, 35–43, 48–49, 55–56, 59–61, 62–65, 71–72, 89–90
　and attention, 64
　gender-based, 3, 11, 21, 24, 49, 74, 87–88, 99
voice, 36, 44, 68, 97, 99–101, 117, 126, 137
votes, 74, 79, 88, 96, 125, 127

warehousing, 2, 36, 124
Washington Post, 25, 32f2.5, 64
water, 70–71, 76, 78–79, 83, 97, 105–6, 112–13, 122
women, 21, 49, 55, 68, 111, 115, 117, 122
work, 10–12, 66–70, 77, 86–88, 91–92, 95, 116–17, 125–30

Yemen, 6t1.1, 14t1.2, 29t2.1
Yugoslavia, former, 46, 47, 68, 83
Yunus, Mohammad, 131–32

CPSIA information can be obtained
at www.ICGtesting.com
Printed in the USA
LVHW03s2304300718
585453LV00023B/506/P